Unite the Union honour the Ascott Martyrs and all women throughout history who have fought for the rights of women workers within the agricultural sector.

– Bev Clarkson, Unite National Officer for Food, Drink and Agriculture

April/May 1873 – August 2023

THE ASCOTT MARTYRS

Why did the rural establishment imprison sixteen women and two babies in 1873?

Edited by
KEITH LAYBOURN

The Ascott Martyrs were 16 poor women, some with babies in arms, who were imprisoned in 1873 for supporting striking farm workers in the Oxfordshire village of Ascott-under-Wychwood. The traumatic event led to a major riot in Chipping Norton, a national furore, several letters to *The Times*, protest demonstrations in London's Hyde Park and a hard labour reprieve from Queen Victoria. The legacy of the Ascott Martyrs case called into question the right to picket, raised the question of the use of the clerical magistracy and above all drew attention to the inequalities in the rights of men and women alike in Victorian society. This book restores the Ascott Martyrs, who became 'secular martyrs', to their rightful place in the battle against injustice and for the democratic rights and liberty of women.

ISBN 978-1-7393278-0-4 (paperback)
ISBN 978-1-7393278-1-1 (ebook)

Typeset in Calluna by preparetopublish.com.

Contents

Dedicated to the Ascott Martyrs, the 16 women who were imprisoned in 1873 for protesting at the injustices of living in rural Victorian society, where poverty was rife, work badly paid, educational opportunities restricted, and democracy denied by an established oligarchy. Accidental secular martyrs, their story has unjustly been ignored by the male-dominated society of the past and the present.

Preface

PAUL JACKSON

In 2011 I moved to the small village of Ascott-under-Wychwood (15 miles north-west of Oxford in the beautiful Cotswolds, and often known just as Ascott) and soon came across some splendid seats on the village green. There were several women's names displayed and a simple 'Imprisoned 1873' plaque. It raised my interest and I asked what this was all about.

I soon established that the seats were in memory of the Ascott Martyrs. Checking Google, I found that there was nothing recorded on the events under 'Ascott Martyrs'. I then researched and found in the village magazine archives a story of 16 women sent to prison in 1873, but no more information seemed available. Eventually I was told to Google the 'Chipping Norton Incident' and, bingo, there was the story largely lost to history, although I now know that Keith Laybourn did make a brief reference to them in his *A History of British Trade Unionism c.1770-1990* (1992), though the real academic pioneer is Karen Sayers, who published an article in *Women's History Review* (1993) and included a section in her 1993 book – both are referred in essay 3 by Nicola Verdon.

There were two other 'missionaries' like me. The first was Doris Warner, a village resident who brought the Martyrs to life as well as being responsible for the planting of the Martyrs Tree on the village green 50 years ago; the second was descendant Beverley McCombs, living in New Zealand, who published the first book on the subject a few years ago – we must be grateful for their dedication and persistence.

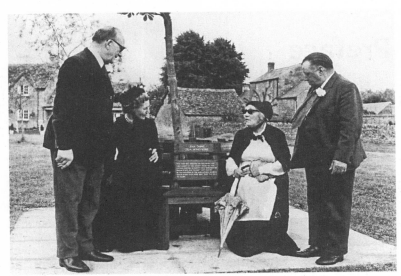

The original commemorative seat and its replacement.

The more I researched parliamentary records and newspapers of the time, the more I realised the story had to be fully told. Approaching the parish council, I soon realised that this essentially conservative village had 'lost' the story over the years and didn't want Ascott to become another Tolpuddle in Dorset (home to the 'Tolpuddle Martyrs') and thus a potential attraction for many of the 12 million annual visitors to the Cotswolds.

The answer was to set up the Ascott Martyrs Educational Trust and build relationships and a research centre. Although I found there was some anti-union feeling in the village, the first call for support was naturally to Unite, the union that was now concerned with the agricultural sector. It had never heard of the Ascott Martyrs! It did, however, provide some initial funds enabling the funding of a commemorative hanging textile (a photo is on page 12) made by descendants and other villagers with the support of the Workers' Educational Association (WEA). I then had a lengthy debate with the parish council over providing more information on the seats (with grants from Midlands Co-op and West Oxfordshire District Council); this was finally achieved in October 2019, the plaques containing the extra information unveiled by Ivor Townsend, a grandson of martyr Fanny Rathband, née Honeybone.

The two photographs that appear with this preface are those of the original seat with full recognition to the role of the union and then the replacement seat in 2000 with the minimum information, reflecting village society's changes over the 50 years.

As the Trust was getting under way, out of the blue came the publication by Beverley McCombs, a descendent in New Zealand, of her book on the Ascott Martyrs, which gave our mission a big boost. Several hundred copies of this book have now been sold by the Trust, helping to raise awareness of the Ascott Martyrs and their story. For a detailed study of the 16 women themselves it is highly recommended and copies are also available from Chipping Norton Museum or the Ascott village shop.

As I moved on to the nearby town of Charlbury I retired as a trustee, but I still felt that as June 2023 would be the 150th anniversary of the unfortunate, unfair and unacceptable incident, the wider story still needed to be told. I am incredibly grateful for the many who have supported me especially editor Keith Laybourn, ensuring that the story of the Ascott Martyrs is kept alive and not lost in history. This book is the outcome of their efforts. I do encourage you to read Appendix A referred to in the first essay; it includes many contemporary letters to *The Times* so sets the scene admirably, as would a look at the short film on YouTube.

All profits from the book will go towards maintaining the legacy of the Ascott Martyrs. The story should not be forgotten again.

Paul Jackson
Publisher and founder of the Ascott Martyrs Educational Trust
Charlbury, August 2023

Introduction

KEITH LAYBOURN

They have given the Union which I have advocated an impetus that it had never received before. It has done a world of good to that Union and has been the means of bringing more men into it and showing them what can be done by such a combination.

> Gabriel Banbury at a meeting of the National Agricultural Labourers' Union, quoted in the *Oxford Chronicle and Berks & Bucks Gazette*, 7 June 1873

It is refreshing to turn from the comments of the London liberal press on the Chipping Norton rebellion to your sensible and appropriate remarks – that the law was broken –justice administered – the farmer protected- the farm labourer rebuked... The sympathy of the Liberal Press is with the Ascott women who unsexed themselves, the mob who broke the peace and the committee of the Labourers' Union who is fanning the embers of discontent into an open blaze from John O'Groats to Land's End.

> Chipping Norton landlord, *Jackson's Oxford Journal*, 14 June 1873

These contrasting newspaper reports relate to the Ascott Martyrs, a group of 16 Oxfordshire women arrested and imprisoned in May and June 1873 because of their action in attempting to stop two farm labourers going to work. Their action was in support of Joseph Arch's National Agricultural Labourers' Union (NALU), formed in February 1872, which demanded wage increases for agricultural labourers and challenged the exploitation of farm workers by the farmers, the landowners and the social and economic system. Despite their sacrifices, their story has all but been expunged from history. In the realms of secular, non-religious martyrdom, they have been ignored in favour of their much more lauded male counterparts. Indeed, in 1834 the government made an example of the 'Dorchester Labourers', six agricultural labourers who were deported to Van Diemen's land (Tasmania) for taking secret oaths. They were, in a sense, judicial martyrs who threatened the existing social controls in rural society but were eventually pardoned and allowed to return to Britain because of the public outrage against their trial and imprisonment.

In contrast to their story, the gendered neglect of the story of the Ascott Martyrs reflects the fact that in 19th and, indeed, 20th century society, Britain was a male-dominated, misogynist society, in which even trade unionists wished that women would keep to the home. Even more specifically, the Trades Union Congress, a male-dominated institution, turned the 'Dorchester Labourers,' as they were initially known as, into the 'Tolpuddle Martyrs' in 1934, on the centenary of their arrest, imprisonment and deportation.

That is not to say that female martyrs have not emerged. Famously, in 1819, men, women and children were killed by the actions of the magistracy at Peterloo in Manchester, and in 1913 Emily Wilding Davison gave her life for the cause of the women's parliamentary vote when she fell in front of the King's horse in the Epsom Derby. On the whole, however, it has been men who have been seen to die or suffer for 'the cause' and 'justice' in the face of the establishment in the United Kingdom, and men who have been the called martyrs. Indeed, secular British female martyrs are rare, and then often neglected even when involved in broader examples of secular martyrdom. This is a great omission in a world where women form half the population and where their rights are increasingly asserted. This collection of essays seeks to correct this neglect by exploring the events that led to one group of women whose story, after an initial bout of interest in the 1870s, had all but disappeared from history.

The Ascott Martyrs lived in Ascott-under-Wychwood in Oxfordshire – a small village of about 90 houses and 462 people in 1873. Ten of the martyrs (if one includes Levia Dring, whose maiden surname was Moss) had the surname Moss, three Pratley, two Smith, and one was a Honeybone. Seven of them worked in the fields, eight worked in the sweated home trade of glove-making, and one was a servant in this small close community. They were charged with attempting to prevent two young agricultural labourers going to work for Robert Hambidge, a tenant farmer, in breach of the Criminal Law Amendment Act of 1871 which did not allow threatening picketing. This led to their arrest and trial at Chadlington petty sessions, held at Chipping Norton police station, and their brief imprisonment, with hard labour, by the local rural clerical magistracy (Rev. Thomas Harris and Rev. William Edward Dickson Carter). This led to riots and protests in their support, which may have led to their imprisonment in Oxford County Gaol becoming briefer or less onerous via a document signed by Queen Victoria, although this was a reduction of part of the sentence than a pardon and may not have been indicative of the oft-stated deep interest and concern that Queen Victoria showed to their case. The event led to a fleeting period of attention and notoriety, which soon faded. The experiences of these women occurred in a society of immense social inequality where most men, and all women, did not have a municipal or rural vote, never mind a parliamentary one. More to the point, these women lived in the rural society of Oxfordshire in which there was great social inequality arising from the lack of democratic political power, and where the landowners, the farmers, the law, the magistracy and the education system operated against the rights of workers to ensure their economic, social and political servility in what was a denial of citizenship.

Urban areas had begun to see changes, and modernisation in policing, from 1829, but rural areas were slower to change – modern county police forces often not emerging until the 1850s (after the 1856 County and Borough Police Act) and then being operated through the county magistrates, the Lord Lieutenant and the quarter sessions – dominated by the landowners and farmers. In other words, rural life remained powerfully dominated by the elitist landowners, who imposed the law, and those who wanted change faced an oppressive system with direct links to government and the law lords.

The story of these 16 women clearly relates to the society in which they operated and were protesting against as outsiders challenging the system. The fact that they were women meant that they had few rights. Their husbands were mostly poorly paid agricultural workers, and whether they worked in agriculture or in the sweated trade of glove-making they were barely able to survive on the low wages they earned. The system of rural control, through the farmers, landowners, established Church, the law, the magistracy and educational institutions ensured that their social position gave them no voice. Fundamentally, for instance, they were deprived of an elementary education, although there was a Church of England National School which they could attend if their parents wished. However, education in a rural environment was often determined by the weather, sowing and harvesting. It is certain that these women would have had a basic education, would have learned the scope of their actions through the community and would be unaware of the finer points of the law that related to their actions. Their protest occurred at a time when arable agriculture in Britain was being seriously threatened by the influx of cheap American wheat and the declining demand for British agricultural products. This certainly accounts for the subsequent departure of some of these women to New Zealand, along with a large number of other inhabitants of Ascott-under-Wychwood, to seek a better life abroad.

The cajoling of two farm workers by the 16 women was clearly seen as a challenge to the establishment of rural Ascott-under-Wychwood and wider Oxfordshire, as indicated by the Chipping Norton landlord in the opening quote. The actions and the events that surround their brief imprisonment are, therefore, seminal moments, if not a catalyst in the emergence of a movement to bring about change.

Until recently, the Ascott women enjoyed only a brief moment of fame in the 1870s. However, in 1973 a memorial seat in their honour was set up under a tree on the green at Ascott-under-Wychwood and other symbols of local recognition emerged. Eventually in the 1990s Karen Sayers published work on these women, as referred to in the preface and in Nicola Verdon's essay, and, in 2016, a book entitled *The Ascott Martyrs,* by Beverley McCombs, a descendant of one of the Ascott martyrs, was published in New Zealand after a personal odyssey by the author.[1] There is also an impressive academic article by Mark Curthoys which appeared in *Oxoniensa* in 2021.[2]

Significant as these publications are, this collection of essays intends to be broader. This book aims to adopt a comprehensive approach by examining the cultural context in which the events occurred. It raises several questions. What was the nature of the society of Ascott-under-Wychwood in which the Martyrs lived? What was the life of the poor like in that community? How did social control operate, both formally and informally? Why were there attempts to form an effective agricultural union? How did the farmers, the magistracy and law operate against them to maintain their social control? How did religion respond to the events? How did the limited educational provision endorse the existing inequalities?

Indeed, the essays in this collection attempt to provide the context in which these women operated. There are ten essays, although more than a dozen people have contributed to this volume in their memory. Carol

Anderson, in her narrative account of events, suggests that Ascott was far from the peaceful village depicted by the tenant farmers who blamed the agricultural union, the NALU, for the disturbances and conflict that occurred in 1873. Indeed, she examines the tensions in the village and the Oxfordshire countryside which saw the vested interests of landed paternalism pitted against the less deferential agricultural labourers and their supporters, which in turn led to the magistrates at Chipping Norton imprisoning the Ascott Martyrs.

Les Kennedy reveals that the agitation and subsequent harsh treatment of rural workers was nothing new and had been emphatically established in the public mind by the case of the six Tolpuddle Martyrs who were transported in the 1830s, before they were released after considerable public protest in Britain. In contrast, however, in the case of the Ascott Martyrs, it was women who were imprisoned and Nicola Verdon vividly examines the exploited and oppressed nature of women and their work in the rural environment of Oxfordshire, which throws a light on their actions.

Nevertheless, it was not only the rural poor who were exploited, and John Martin examines the extent to which the tenant farmers, who took action against the 16 women, were themselves victims of oppression as they were pressured by their landlords to maintain a high level of rent in the vertical hierarchy of paternalism in the countryside. Mr Hambidge and the supporting tenant farmers were clearly being pressured to produce high returns on the land that they farmed and to defeat Joseph Arch and his trade union, and were victims in their own right of the established rural system.

Indeed, as Brian Cox reveals, Oxfordshire was an immensely unjust and unequal society in which poverty, ignorance and inequality prevailed and was somewhat endorsed by the Church of England, if not necessarily by the Nonconformist churches which gathered support in the countryside, as John Bennett endorses in his contextual study of religion in the Wychwoods. And, as Keith Ewing reveals, the legal system was on the side of the establishment and the farmer in the 1870s.

Trade unions were restricted under the Criminal Law Amendment Act of 1871 which, while not including the offence of 'obstruction and molestation', though it was part of the 1825 Combination Act, was the charge that led to imprisonment of the Ascott Martyrs by the clerical magistrates at Chipping Norton. The grounds for their imprisonment were, therefore, potentially dubious and confused, and may well have contributed to the withdrawal or replacement of parts of the 1871 Act by the introduction of the Criminal Law Amendment Act of 1875. However, there is little evidence of a direct link between the case of the Ascott Martyrs and the 1875 Act, and the women, had they faced the same charges under the latter Act, may not have fared any better. In a more specific study of the application of the law, Christine Gowing examines how these clerical magistrates who presided over the case were restricted as to what they could do by the law and debunks the suggestion that the Ascott Martyrs' case led to the demise of the clerical magistrate, for the clerical magistracy was declining rapidly well before 1873 but lingered on.

Legal oppression in a paternalistic and oligarchic society in which poverty was rife raised its own problems and Martin Greenwood explains how the NALU, the trade union, encouraged many from the rural counties, including Oxfordshire and Ascott-under-Wychwood, to emigrate to New Zealand, Australia and Canada. This meant, as Nick Mansfield reveals, that rural Oxfordshire, and Ascott-under-Wychwood, remained in the hands of the Conservative landed patriarchy (other than a brief period of Liberal representation) rather than shifting to the Labour Party (founded in 1900) and more radical forces until well into the 20th century.

The case of the Ascott Martyrs is a reflection of the state of injustice that operated in English rural society in late 19th century Victorian England. The essays in this book offer the story of what occurred, why it occurred, how oppressive rural society in Oxfordshire was in the 1870s, and also the impact of the case on emigration and rural politics. Above all, it restores the Ascott Martyrs, the 16 women who were accidental secular martyrs, to their rightful place in the battle against injustice.

A note on relative values

It is almost impossible to represent monetary values of the past in today's values – there are many different ways to estimate relative purchasing power.[3] To set the wage figures given in this book in context, this table provides a simple guide for a family of two adults and three children:

Weekly income	Status
10 shillings (plus rent income)	Poverty
£1 (plus rent income)	Modest means
£2 (plus rent income)	Well off

Even then, a big issue is broken time. The fact that one might only be employed for 40 weeks in the year might well put a family on £1 per week on the edge of poverty. This was a frequent problem in the textile trade and mining, and likely to be similar in farming, glove-making and other rural activities.

Christopher Holloway was born in Wootton, Oxfordshire in 1828 and by 1851 was a farm labourer. He became a Methodist lay preacher and was active in the local circuit. In May 1872 he became the chair of the Wootton branch of the National Agricultural Labourers' Union. He became district chairman of the NALU in October 1872. In 1873 he became interested in emigration to New Zealand and became an emigration agent, relinquishing some of his union responsibilities. By 1880 he had become a shopkeeper and he remained as such until his death in 1895. By writing to *The Times* (see appendix A), he made the nation aware of the injustice of the imprisonment of the women.

Textile hanging in Holy Trinity Church, Ascott-under-Wychwood, commemorating the Ascott Martyrs.

I

How 'just a bit of fun' led to the imprisonment of 16 women and raised a national furore

CAROL ANDERSON

T here was little upon which the opposing parties in the fierce debates that followed the 'Chipping Norton Incident' could agree, except that the area around Ascott-under-Wychwood, on the surface at least, appeared to be a quiet and pleasant place.

> The Great Western Railway runs through the valley, and from its gentle undulations the land rises until it merges into the Cotswold hills. At this season of the year the eye delights to feast upon these verdant spaces and bright woodlands.
>
> *Oxford Chronicle and Berks & Bucks Gazette,*
> 31 May 1873

According to seven of its tenant farmers in a letter to *The Times* published on 2 June 1873 (see appendix A), Ascott was a peaceful place. A small village with a population of approximately 460, two thirds of whom were agricultural labourers. Indeed, 'There is not one distressed family in the village, with two exceptions, the cottages and the gardens are good, the rents low, and the allotments close to the village, and the general condition of the labouring poor above the average of that class.'[1]

Nevertheless, this description of a rural idyll did not reflect the reality of life in Ascott-under-Wychwood in 1873. Rural poverty was widespread and even 12s (approximately equivalent to a wage of £360 today) a week was not enough to feed and clothe a family. In subsequent commentaries that appeared in both local and national press we learn that while living conditions for some were comfortable, for others they were 'very bad indeed', being described as little more than 'poverty-stricken holes' and a 'disgrace to a Christian country.'[2] Cottage gardens and allotments

Crown Farm, Ascott-under-Wychwood, leased from the Crown Estates by Robert Hambidge. His workers were the first to strike, withdrawing their labour on 21 April 1873.

provided a steady supply of fruit and vegetables for much of the year, but the wives of agricultural labourers still needed to work to supplement the meagre wage of their husbands. For the majority this involved casual work on the land for less than 1s (£30 today) a day, but for some there was piecework at home hand stitching gloves for the local manufacturers, work that was more attractive to many, potentially better paid than fieldwork, and more easily fitted around the demands of home and family.

We are told that it was against this background that 'the Agricultural Labourers Society (National Agricultural Labourers' Union) came to this village last year, since which time the quiet and well-being of this hitherto peaceful and orderly place have been disturbed by the disrespectful, vexatious and riotous conduct of the employed to their employer.'[3]

The men strike and the women protest

The National Agricultural Labourers' Union (NALU) aimed to raise the standard weekly wage from 10s to 12s, and from there to 14s, to meet the growing economic pressures on the labourer and his family. With strong support for the NALU having developed in the Wychwood villages, in the spring of 1873 the Union urged its members to ask for a 2s a week increase in wages. As the tenant of what, at almost 400 acres, was by far the largest farm in the parish, Robert Hambidge of Crown Farm was the prime target for these demands.

On Saturday 12 April 1873 he paid his workers as normal but, subsequent to their attending a Union meeting, they arrived for work the following Monday and informed Hambidge that unless he increased their wages by 2s a week to 14s they would leave. Subsequently all the farmers in the village, the majority of whom were tenants, met and agreed to act in unison with those in neighbouring parishes, where the landowners had met their tenants and agreed that 12s a week for day labourers was a fair price.

This being a crucial time of year for the farm, Hambidge agreed to the increase for the most efficient workers, but not those whose capacity he regarded as limited by age or infirmity, and gave assurances that there would be plenty of piecework for them. His offer was refused and the men were unanimous that unless they all received the additional 2s a week rise they would withdraw their labour. Hambidge advised them to consider where their best interests lay and, although work on the farm would stop without them, he determined he would not be dictated to.

Having given the required week's notice, on Monday 21 April all the labourers belonging to the Union left the farms in the village, refusing to do any more work for their employers. They were paid 9s a week by the Union to be, in the opinion of the farmers, 'idle and offensive'. After a fortnight work was found for upwards of 20 men felling and barking timber five miles away, for 2s 6d a day. The farmers later pointed out, with a degree of satisfaction, that striking labourers could have earned twice as much hoeing close to their homes on piecework.

To judge from the account given by the tenant farmers in their letter to *The Times*, unrest continued in the village with verbal abuse being directed against those who did not support the Union, cries of 'Baa, Baa Blacklegs' and the like being heard. There was also a hint of intimidation, with the farmers inferring that some men wanted to return to work but feared for the consequences if they did.

In the absence of their Union labourers, the farmers sought to employ non-Union labour. Feelings were clearly running high when on 12 May Robert Hambidge sent two young men, John Hodgkins and John Millin from Ramsden, some five miles away, to hoe a bean field while he joined his fellow farmers at Stow Fair.[4] He had recently engaged their services at the (possibly to them fabulous) sum of 7s 6d a day each.

Accounts of what happened next vary considerably, depending on the source from which they come. But all agree that early on the morning of Monday 12 May a group of women from the village, numbering between 20 and 30 at various times, being the wives, daughters and relatives of the striking labourers, attempted to persuade the two non-Union men not to go to work and ideally to join the Union. The precise order of events becomes confused in the telling, as did the numbers involved and the extent to which these 'Amazons' carried sticks or posed a real threat to the men. Undoubtedly rough words were exchanged between the young men and some of the women, and it's unlikely that in such circumstances all behaved with restraint. In an article that appeared in *The Times* on 26 May, its correspondent described the women's actions as a 'physical force demonstration in favour of Union principles' and gave it as his opinion that threatening and abusive language was used (in the best traditions of 'rough music'), but that as the men were eventually able to return to work there the matter should have been left to rest.

Another element in the mix of events that took place was undoubtedly the frisson of several young unmarried girls encountering two young men new to the village. Popular memory in the village suggests that the most serious danger faced by the young men was a threat to 'remove their trousers'. Whatever the truth of the matter the young men abandoned their attempt to work and returned to the farmhouse where Hambidge's wife summoned the constable. The women were eventually persuaded to disperse, reluctantly, and the young men returned to their work in the field under the watchful eye of the law. The women maintained that they had not intended any harm to the young men and had in fact offered them refreshment in the village if they abandoned their work. *The Daily News* suggested that 'not a blow was struck; on the appearance of one policeman the gang of agricultural Amazons made good their retreat'.[5] Looking back on the events of that May morning in an interview for the *Landworker,* published in 1929, Fanny Rathband (née Honeybone), the youngest of the women who was identified as one of the ringleaders, maintained that they had meant no harm and that it was all just a bit of fun really, a view not shared by everyone.

To the tenant farmers and their supporters this behaviour was regarded as 'unseemly and outrageous'. The day following the incident being rent day, Abram Rawlinson, the clerk to the Chipping Norton justices, acting in his capacity as an agent, visited the Swan Inn in Ascott to receive rents. This provided an immediate and ideal opportunity for Hambidge to consult with other farmers in the parish, and perhaps take some legal advice from the clerk. The result being that he decided to bring a private prosecution against the women under the provisions of the Criminal Law Amendment Act. Proceedings against the women were formally initiated at Sarsden Rectory on 19 May by Rev. Carter, as magistrate sitting on the Chadlington Bench. Seventeen women of the allegedly 20 or 30 who played some part in the events were duly summoned to appear before the magistrates in Chipping Norton on 21 May.

This was exactly the sort of situation that the Criminal Law Amendment Act was intended to deal with. Act 34 and 35 Victoria, cap 32, was 'an Act to amend Violence, Threats and Molestation' and under its first section it was an offence to 'threaten or intimidate any person in such a manner as would justify a Justice of the Peace to bind over the person threatening or intimidating to keep the peace'.

Summoned before the magistrates

The 17 women were summoned to appear before the magistrates to answer charges of preventing, by molestation and intimidation, John Hodgkins and John Millin from going about their lawful business.

The 17 women identified as having been involved in the incident were summoned to appear before the Chadlington bench sitting in the court in Chipping Norton Police Station. The bench comprised two local clergymen, Rev. T. Harris (chair) and Rev. W.E.D. Carter, with Abram Rawlinson as clerk to the court and Henry Wilkins, a local attorney, appearing for the complainant. Also present were Christopher Holloway, who, as the local Union representative, observed the proceedings, as did Robert Hambidge. As this was a private prosecution no formal record of proceedings was maintained. The *Oxfordshire Weekly News* for 28 May provides an account of the trial,

Chipping Norton police station.

naming the women and detailing the evidence provided against them by Hodgkins and Millin. The women had no legal representation. They had left Ascott expecting that if found guilty they would be fined, and never dreamt that they might be sent straight to prison. Witness accounts suggest that the women called one witness, Emma Wright, the wife of an agricultural labourer, who declared that, contrary to what the young men alleged, none of the women had sticks or whips, and did not molest or obstruct them. In turn each women protested her innocence, but to no avail.

Although the charge against Jane Pratley was dismissed as Hodgkins and Millin were unable to identify her as having taken part in the incident, the remaining 16 were judged to be guilty of assault and intimidation. Harris is reported as having remained firm in the course of action to be taken. The Rev. Carter was, however, less sure and asked Hambidge whether he really wanted to press his case, given the likely outcome. Hambidge responded by asking what else could he do if he could not get anyone to work for him, presumably because of the intimidation that we later learn was taking place in the village. Rev. Carter therefore suggested that the trial itself might suffice to serve as a warning without the need for further action. He was very reluctant to send the women to prison, especially as two of them were nursing babies. Subsequently the 'special correspondent' of *The Daily News* reported that 'several labouring men expressed sympathy with him as they felt he had been led astray in his decision by the more experienced magistrate.'[6]

The magistrates felt they had no option but to impose a custodial sentence, the Act not making provision for a fine to be imposed. Mr Banbury, from the Oxfordshire branch of the NALU, also later gave it as his opinion that some of the blame for the harshness of the sentence lay with Rawlinson: as clerk to the court he had evidently failed to advise the magistrates of the range of options open to them under the terms of the Act. The magistrates therefore ordered seven of the women, judged to be the ringleaders, to be imprisoned for ten days and the remaining nine for seven days, with the addition of hard labour in every case.

Jackson's Oxford Journal, published on 24 May, reported on the conviction of the 16 women, naming them and giving their marital status and the term of their imprisonment. The surviving committal documents provide further information including details of their age, occupation, where they were born, and their religion. They were listed as follows:

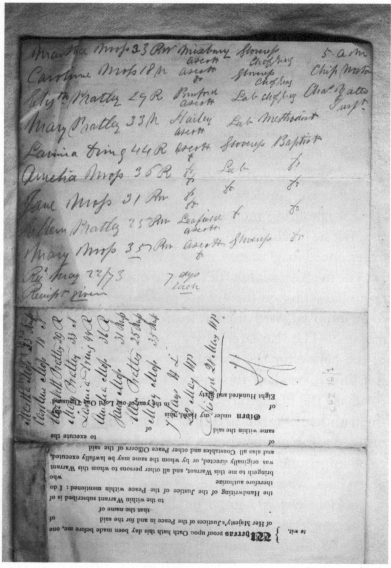

Reverse of the Warrant of Commitment for the women sentenced to ten days in prison, giving their personal details and including a note of the time of handover by Superintendent Yates.

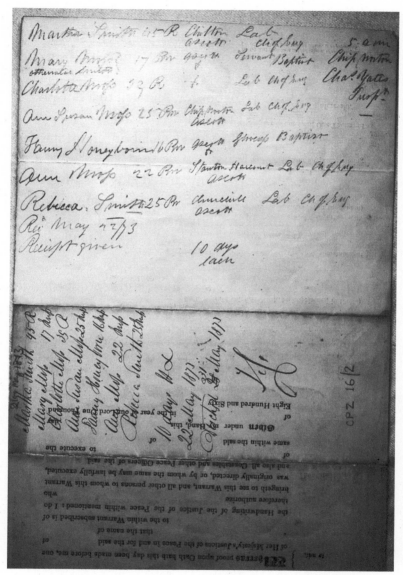

Reverse of the Warrant of Commitment for the
seven-day women, giving their personal details.

- Martha Smith (45), labourer married to an agricultural labourer. Church of England.
- Mary Moss (otherwise Smith) (17), unmarried servant. Baptist.
- Charlotte Moss (41), labourer, married to a railway servant. Church of England.
- Ann Susan (Susannah) Moss (25), labourer, unmarried. Church of England.
- Fanny Honeybone (16), unmarried gloveress. Baptist.
- Rebecca Smith (27) labourer, married to an agricultural labourer. Church of England.
- Ann Moss (22) labourer, married to an agricultural labourer. Church of England.

They were seen as the ringleaders and sentenced to ten days' hard labour. Those listed below received the lesser sentence of seven days' hard labour.

- Lavinia (Levia) Dring (44) gloveress, married to an agricultural labourer. Baptist.
- Amelia Moss (36), labourer, married to an agricultural labourer. Baptist.
- Caroline Moss (18), unmarried gloveress. Church of England.
- Jane Moss (31), gloveress, married to a shepherd. Baptist.
- Martha Moss (33 – she was actually 36), gloveress, married to a sawyer. Church of England.
- Mary Moss (35), gloveress, married to a carpenter. Baptist.
- Ellen Pratley (25), gloveress, married to an agricultural labourer. Baptist.
- Elizabeth Pratley (29, with child Eli 9m), labourer,

Fanny Rathband (née Honeybone). The youngest of the Martyrs, Fanny was identified as one of the ringleaders and sentenced to ten days' imprisonment with hard labour.

married to an agricultural labourer. Church of England.

- Mary Pratley (33, with child Thomas 2m), labourer, married to an agricultural labourer. Methodist.

Imprisonment and riot

The Act may not have allowed the magistrates the option of imposing a fine, but it did give them discretion as to whether or not to impose hard labour. They seem not to have been aware that they had the option of allowing the women to stand on their own recognisances (bonds), binding them to keep the peace. In August of the previous year men summoned before the Woodstock bench under the same act, who had caused some limited actual bodily harm, were bound over. This course of action had clearly provided a sufficient deterrent as there had been no further incidents in the area.

As the *Daily News* reported, the general feeling was that the women were victims of perjured justice.[7]

The statements on which they were convicted they unanimously denied, and there was general disbelief that the testimony of 16 respectable women could be overborne by the assertions of two 'raw youths'. For some time there persisted a belief in Ascott that once the Home Secretary was in full possession of the facts, the women would all be released.

Once in prison the women would have had no contact with their families until their release. Therefore, following their sentence and removal from court a request was made that before the women were taken to Oxford Gaol they should be allowed to speak to their husbands. This was agreed to on condition the men left the town in an orderly fashion, but instead we are told that they returned to Ascott in an excited state. Reinforced by a complement of Union men they returned to Chipping Norton about 7 pm and marched, with blue ribbons floating in their hats, to the police station, apparently with the intention of rescuing the women from police custody, should an attempt be made to take them to Oxford by train. Superintendent Lakin telegraphed to Oxford to request reinforcements and a vehicle to take the women to Oxford, rather than wait and attempt to put them on the train the following morning. As it got dark the crowd outside the police station grew, until it was estimated that there were some 2,000 people present. Cheers for 'the Union' and 'the Women' followed in quick succession accompanied by threats to raze the police station if the women were not released. Stones were hurled at the windows, breaking tiles on the roof and damaging a door, and street lights were smashed. Inside the police station the women had been secured in the cells, where they took it in turns to stand or sit in the cramped conditions, while keeping up their spirits by singing.

At about 10 pm the mayor of Chipping Norton and other notables arrived and urged the crowd to disperse quietly, but their words had little impact and the riotous behaviour continued until at about 11 pm when the Riot Act was read and things gradually calmed down. By midnight the crowd had finally dispersed ahead of the arrival of police reinforcements from Oxford.[8] Of those who subsequently appeared before the bench to answer for their part in the riot, few, if any, were agricultural labourers. This confirmed Holloway's belief that his advice to them, following the passing of the sentence, to behave with restraint had been heeded.

In the early hours of the damp, dark morning of 22 May, the 16 women and two babies were put into the wagon that had been brought up from Oxford to begin the 19-mile journey back to the County Gaol. The horses were fed and watered at Enstone, where the women were provided with bread and beer, for which Superintendent Larkin paid 6s. According to his account the women protected themselves against the damp with their umbrellas, sang songs on the journey, were generally light hearted and made no complaints about their treatment.

They passed through the gates of the prison shortly after 5 am and nothing further would be heard from the women until after their release.[9] They were housed in the female wing of the prison and, with the exception of the two women nursing infants, were required to undertake their hard labour by working in the prison laundry.

A national scandal?

While the women languished in prison with their children left behind in Ascott being fed by the Union,[10] arguments about the rightness of the decisions taken by the Chipping Norton magistrates began to be writ ever larger across the pages of both the national and local press. In a subsequent response through a letter in *The Times* of 12 June, in answer to questions about why the women had not lodged an appeal against their sentence, Holloway argued that experience showed that appeals to the government met with no response, so the Union had decided to appeal to the 'people of England' through the press. This tactic worked supremely well, giving the Union the oxygen of publicity to maximum effect, especially when at its heart was a case that involved 'decent women' and babies.

Holloway's letter published in *The Times* on 23 May

A fieldworker married to an agricultural labourer and mother of three young children, Rebecca Smith was released on 31 May after serving ten days with hard labour.

1873 (see appendix A) had already brought the case to the attention of the nation. Under the banner 'IMPOSSIBLE!', Holloway, who had attended the trial, gave a brief account of the events that led to 16 'very respectable women in the class to which they belong' being 'dragged off to prison and some of them with infants at their breast' for an offence they were unaware existed and all stoutly denied. The riot in Chipping Norton that followed the passing of sentence upon the women immediately drew the interest of the local weekly press. The first detailed account of the trial, committal of the 16 women and subsequent riot appeared in the *Oxfordshire Weekly News* of 28 May.

Perhaps alerted by Holloway's letter, *The Times* and *The Daily News* sent their correspondents to the area to investigate and it is from their reports that we learn much of the details of living conditions in the village, the incident and the events surrounding it. Although Archibald Forbes of *The Daily News* was a well-respected war correspondent, he was also already well acquainted with Joseph Arch and the issues facing the agricultural labourer.

In the days that followed the riot the area remained volatile and labourers at work in the fields could be seen proudly displaying blue ribbons in their hats. A renewal of the rioting was anticipated on the evening of Saturday 24 May and telegrams were sent to the various divisions in the county for police reinforcements, including several plain clothes officers, to be sent to Chipping Norton, under the command of the chief constable. Although feelings were still running high and the police were jeered as they patrolled the town, the evening passed without incident. A body of police were also sent to Ascott, but all remained quiet.

Questions in Parliament

Thanks no doubt to the Union, news of what had happened in Chipping Norton quickly reached the ears of MPs. On Monday 26 May Mr Bowring (Liberal MP for Exeter) gave notice in the House of Commons that he would ask the Secretary of State for the Home Department whether he would be willing to institute an immediate enquiry into the circumstances connected with the severe sentence passed by the Chipping Norton bench. Mr Mundella (Liberal MP for Sheffield and a reformer) enquired as to whether there was any truth in reports of the Chipping Norton case and its outcome and if so did it, in the Home Secretary's opinion, warrant his interference in favour of the prisoners. Home Secretary Henry Bruce responded to the effect that he had received no communication on the matter, but had that day written to the magistrates. He received a reply three days later, to the effect that the sentence which they passed was one which they considered to be required under all the circumstances of the case, since when they had seen no reason for altering their opinion.[11] This response was undoubtedly what caused Bruce to send a telegram to the governor of the County Prison at 1.39 pm on 29 May stating that having received further information from the magistrates, the women were 'not to be kept any longer at hard labour'.[12]

In the same edition that reported on the questions asked in the House, *The Times* attacked the actions of the magistrates as 'deplorable' and was of the opinion that their decision had set ablaze those who opposed the Criminal Law Amendment Act and clerical magistrates. The Lord Chancellor, Lord Selborne, was called upon to review the case and ask the magistrates to explain why they should be deemed competent to remain in office. They thought Harris should resign, having shown such a lack of judgement. Subsequently *The Times* argued that even if the magistrates felt they had no option but to enforce a custodial sentence, it could have been for a nominal period and without hard labour.[13] The same day *The Daily News* published an article by its correspondent Archibald Forbes criticising the system of unpaid clerical magistrates and suggesting that the women might 'console themselves with the reflection that the magistrates had made them martyrs'.

Shortly after 10 am on 28 May the nine 'seven-day women' walked out of Oxford Gaol to be met by two of their husbands and Christopher Holloway. They breakfasted at Union district secretary Mr Leggatt's house in Botley Road and, at noon, their tickets paid for by the Union, they caught the express train to Chipping Norton Junction. As the train passed through Ascott the 'window of one carriage was blocked up with hands waving handkerchiefs, and a number of little chubby children looking over the blossoming hedges in the village cried with delight as they recognised their mothers'. An hour later, having had to wait for the stopping train to come back down the line to Ascott, the women were reunited with their waiting families and friends. There was certainly no need of the significant police presence provided in case of disorder as the village remained quiet.

Magistrates' decision challenged

On the same day the Union held its first annual conference in Leamington. Following introductory remarks by the chair, Birmingham MP George Dixon, ordinary business was suspended to enable Joseph Arch to move a resolution signifying the conference's 'deep abhorrence of the conduct of the Chipping Norton magistrates in straining the law to commit 16 women with hard labour to Oxford Gaol for an act they were not aware was illegal'. The conference called for the repeal of the Criminal Law Amendment Act and declared that the case afforded further proof of the need to appoint stipendiary magistrates without which the agricultural labourers were convinced they could not obtain justice. In seconding the motion, Gabriel Banbury from Woodstock gave his account of the differences between Hambidge and his men that had led to the conviction of the women in question. These proceedings were widely reported and triggered a response from Hambidge who, in a letter published in *The Times*, took Banbury to task over the accuracy of many of the statements he was reported to have made at the NALU conference, including an assertion that the men had been 'locked out'.[14]

The magistrates were confident in the support they had locally as both local press and the 'occupiers of land' sprang to their defence. An article published in the weekly *Jackson's Oxford Journal* on 31 May, the day the 'ten-day women' were released from prison, gave its opinion that 'a great deal of nonsense has been written on the subject. There is no doubt that Mr Hambidge did quite right in prosecuting these women, who are not such innocents, at least some of them, as the London papers would have us believe, and there is no doubt also that the Magistrates... acted strictly in accordance with the law in committing them to prison.' Before the start of public business at the petty sessions in Chipping Norton held on 18 June, a deputation composed of representatives of the principal occupiers of land and inhabitants of the 31 parishes in the Chadlington division and some beyond, presented an address to the presiding magistrates, Rev. Harris and Rev. Carter. Above 298 signatures it expressed their support for the decisions they had taken in respect of the 'case of intimidation at Ascott'. They expressed the hope that the sentence passed would check any further attempts to interfere with the freedom of labour.[15]

In the same column *Jackson's Oxford Journal* printed a letter sent to the Rev. Carter by his parishioners in Sarsden-cum-Churchill supporting him personally and giving it as their opinion that a 'more just, fair, upright and honourable gentleman' had never filled the office of county magistrate and that 'in as far as was compatible with the just performance of the onerous duties of that responsible position, he had always leaned to the side of mercy'.

On 4 June Lord Selborne wrote to the Duke of Marlborough who, as Lord Lieutenant of Oxfordshire, was responsible for the magistracy. He considered that while punishment might have been necessary, the severe and indiscriminate punishment of such a large number, many of whom might have been led astray, created sympathy for the lawbreakers and weakened the law.[16] The Duke of Marlborough, no friend of the Union as his actions on his Oxfordshire estate had shown when in the previous summer the army had brought in the harvest, in place of striking agricultural labourers, was of the opinion that the magistrates had acted 'not unwisely' and the fact that the assailants were women did not exempt them from the law. He might not like clerical magistrates but argued that laymen would have done just the same. Selborne responded to the effect that in his opinion the magistrates had made a mistake, and requested the Duke to communicate his views to them. He further trusted that the views he had expressed would on another occasion receive more consideration than they appeared to have done on this. Having reported on this exchange, *The Spectator* for 8 August (see appendix B) gave its considered opinion that with the Duke supporting them, the magistrates were unlikely to heed the words of the Lord Chancellor, which was perhaps not surprising given the strength of support locally from the 'occupiers of land'.

Having had no option but to remain silent during their imprisonment, when the 'seven-day women' returned to Ascott, Archibald Forbes of *The Daily News* arranged an interview with some of them. They gave their account of the events of 12 May. One of the women he described as being a decent artisan's wife 'in appearance and behaviour, to be taken as a good specimen of a lower middle-class Englishwoman' who had told her story with various corroborating evidence and added with a sigh, 'I little thought I should ever see the inside of a prison; but if it does... good for others I shan't trouble.' This testimony only served to add weight to the view that the women were martyrs to a good cause and not Amazons, but rather 'heroines of the wash-tub'.[17]

The tenant farmers have their say

It was now the turn of the 'parochial officers' and tenant farmers of the parish to give their views. In a letter dated 30 May and published in *The Times* on 2 June (see appendix A) and subsequently in the local press, they

An 1868 cartoon of farmer 'John Bull' in his fields.

gave their version of the incident and argued the need to appeal to the law for public and private protection against any repetition of the 'unseemly and outrageous' conduct of the women. They firmly believed that the magistrates had shown compassion in not imposing a three-month sentence on the women and stressed that prior to the men withdrawing their labour, they had enjoyed good relations with Hambidge.

Christopher Holloway penned a detailed reply to the letter from 'the parochial officers', explaining that he and another member of the Union committee had visited the village and carried out their own detailed investigation.

In response to the accusations levied against the women by the feoffees (a medieval term for trustees who had a 'fief' or 'fee', that is a piece of land for a beneficial owner), he reminds the reader that he had attended the trial and heard the evidence of the two young men. Their contradictory replies required all the skill and abilities of a practised advocate to enable the magistrates to convict. The evidence of the woman who spoke in defence of the 16 women to the effect that 'no sticks were used, no violence offered, no attempt made to stop the men from going into the field'. was ignored by the magistrates, although corroborated by many people in the village. He had spoken to all but one of the women involved, who confirmed this version of events. He also noted with interest that since the trial, the young men involved seemed to have left the district.[18]

The exchanges continued. In a letter written on 13 June in response to Holloway's letter (see appendix A), the feoffees explained that the building inhabited by the two Pratley women and their families and described as 'horrible and a disgrace to a Christian country' was in fact the old workhouse, which had become a last resort lodging house for those who could not pay more than between 6d and 1s per week for rent or those who had been turned out by their previous landlords.

The release of the 'ten-day women'

Shortly after 10 am on Saturday 31 May, the seven women who had been committed for ten days were released to be met by a crowd of some 150 people, together with Holloway and Mr Taylor, the general secretary of the NALU. A few cries of 'shame' and sounds of disapproval were heard, but one man loudly remarked that 'they be martyrs to a good cause', a sentiment that seemed to meet with popular approval.[19] 'Having breakfasted at Mr Leggatt's House on the Botley Road, they started in a 'drag and four' for Ascott, and were cheered along the route in a manner that showed they were not seen as criminals, but rather victims of oppression and martyrs to a good cause.

At 7 pm that evening an open-air meeting was held in Chipping Norton marketplace which attracted a crowd of some 2,000–3,000, consisting of agricultural labourers from the surrounding district, many accompanied by their wives. Using a waggon as their platform, Arch, Holloway and others addressed the meeting speaking against the Criminal Law Amendment Act, criticising the clerical magistrates for their unchristian actions in enforcing it and calling for the appointment of stipendiary magistrates. Banbury's speech praised the women and the contribution they had made to the growth of the Union. 'They have given the Union... an impetus that it had never received before. It has done a world of good to that Union and has been the means of bringing more men to it, and showing them what can be done by combination.'[20]

Reflecting on what had happened in the preceding week, Archibald Forbes observed that 'the roots struck by Mr Arch's movement into these purely agricultural districts would not have been so deep had not the wives of the labourers espoused the cause with unflagging earnestness... The poor souls who have to solve the problem of bringing up a family of strong hungry children at a few pence per head per week may be... intimately acquainted with the pinch of low wages.'[21]

On the Monday following, Whit Monday 2 June, a large trade union rally was held in Hyde Park and the Chipping Norton case was a major topic on the hustings (see appendix B). *The Times* commented that in its opinion Rev. Harris and Rev. Carter deserved a vote of thanks from the promoters of the demonstration for providing them with such a 'palpable grievance'. Mr Banbury of Woodstock, speaking on behalf of the Oxfordshire branch of the NALU against the Criminal Law Amendment Act, again expressed the view that the imprisonment of the women, whom he described as 'martyrs to a good cause', would do more to procure the repeal of the Act than 'all the talking in the world'.[22]

'My child coughed so much I thought it would die'

Other interviews were also taking place in homes throughout Ascott and on 2 June the barrister and supporter of the NALU William Mackenzie wrote to *The Times*, in a letter published the following day, about statements made to him the previous day by Mary and Elizabeth Pratley regarding the treatment they and their infants had received while in prison. Mackenzie gave it as his opinion that the Home Secretary should institute an enquiry into the charges made by the women, who 'though very poor, and living in miserable habitations had every appearance of being respectable and trustworthy persons'.

Mary Pratley complained that she had been breastfeeding her baby without any problem until she went into prison, when her milk all but dried up, allegedly because she was not properly fed, receiving nothing but 'bread and skilly' (oatmeal broth) and feeling 'the want of a little tea very much'. She complained that she had rheumatism in her shoulders and limbs very badly as a result of the cold, wet drive through the night from Chipping Norton to Oxford. She also claimed that she wasn't given time to dress her baby properly against the weather before the long journey south in the early hours of the morning, as Superintendent Lakin had insisted, they 'come at once, as there is no time to lose'. As a result of this exposure to the elements, the child developed a severe cough (see appendix A). Although the doctor visited each morning and had looked at her hands on the first day, he had made no enquiry as to her health or that of her child.

Mary's sister-in-law, Elizabeth Pratley, also complained of the diet and treatment she and her young son had received in prison. The quantity of milk she received for the child was inadequate and nothing was provided for a night feed. The child suffered from want of nourishment and the lack of a fire in the cell, and slept badly. Although the doctor saw her twice, he made no inquiry about the baby nor ever looked at it. The child caught cold and coughed so much that on the night before their release she thought it would die. She too had suffered from travelling by night, the cold and the damp of the prison cell, and the lack of proper nourishment – 'no milk, beer, meat or broth'. She stated, 'I could hardly speak the day after I came home, my throat and chest were so bad and my limbs ached so. I am still not well by a long way.'

The day following publication of the women's complaints, the Secretary of State wrote to the visiting justices for Oxford Gaol enclosing the letter from Mackenzie, together with the statements from the women, and requesting that they provide him with a report. All concerned were interviewed and statements taken, including from Superintendent Lakin regarding the journey from Chipping Norton.[23] A report was sent to the Secretary of State, who was able to report accordingly to the House of Commons on the following Monday evening, 9 June. The detailed account provided by all involved effectively dismissed the women's complaints as being groundless and asserted that their diet, and that of their children, while they were in prison was in accordance with prison regulations. Furthermore, they had regularly been asked if they had any complaints and had said not. So, it was the word of the two women against those of the police and prison authorities and no further action was taken.

In its edition of 5 July, in addition to the visiting justices' report, *Jackson's Oxford Journal* published details of the prison's dietary table as set down in the prison rules to show that the women had been fed as required. It added that the two women nursing infants were assigned only light work such as sewing during their imprisonment and were engaged in washing clothes for only half a day, in addition to keeping their own cells clean. They were also allowed to walk at intervals in the courtyard with their babies.

In a subsequent letter to *The Times* (see appendix A), Mackenzie expressed his opinion that the women's experiences in gaol may have been in accordance with prison rules, but he disputed that such treatment was 'in accordance with the dictates of humanity' and urged that what had transpired should lead to an alteration in the diet allowed to women for nursing children.

Blue dresses and matching 'headgear'

On Friday 20 June Joseph Arch and the Rev. E. S. Attenborough of Leamington and others arrived at Ascott station by the 5 o'clock train, and were met by Holloway, several other Unionists and the 16 women all attired in Union blue dresses, with 'head gear' to match. Arch was loudly cheered as he left the platform and, accompanied by the 16 women and the delegates, proceeded to the Swan Inn, where tea was provided. Shortly after 6 pm a public meeting was held on the village green, which 'presented quite a lively appearance, stalls, swings etc having been set up there'. A waggon served as a platform for the speakers who included Mr Arch, Rev. Attenborough, Mr Banbury, Mr Holloway and Mr Leggatt. The weather was fine and a large crowd drawn from Ascott and the surrounding villages had assembled to watch the proceedings, including, for a time at least, Robert Hambidge.

In a letter to *The Daily News* published on 29 May, Joseph Arch, writing on behalf of the NALU, had appealed for public subscriptions to 'show these poor women upon their release, that they are not regarded by all as being criminals and outcasts'. He explained that the aim was to raise funds to enable them to give each woman £5. Anything collected in excess of the sum needed would be 'devoted to the funds of the Union'. The same appeal had been made through the *Birmingham Daily Post*. Reporting to the crowd gathered to hear him speak in Chipping Norton on 31 May, Arch praised the response he had received to the appeal and announced that they had already raised £30 and he was confident that this would be further swelled by donations awaiting him on his return to Leamington.

Clearly the Union met its target as the Rev. Attenborough explained that donations had come in from across the country, also from Wales and France, from people of all ages, classes and both sexes in amounts ranging from 2½d to £10. He expressed his hope that the money would be made good use of and that it should not find its way to the alehouse. The money was then distributed; each woman on stepping up to the waggon was loudly cheered. In the speeches that followed, yet again Arch denounced the Criminal Law Amendment Act as unjust and oppressive, and advocated the extension of the franchise to labourers.[24]

Three days earlier than this at an open-air meeting at Ham Hill near Yeovil (attended by over 5,000 labourers and their wives) Arch had made clear his disgust at the action of the Chipping Norton magistrates and his disappointment that the Home Secretary, Bruce, had not taken more action in the matter. 'I should like to know whether if one of these females had been a clergyman's wife whether Mr Bruce would have shelved it,' he asked the crowd, who responded with loud applause.[25]

Discontent rumbled on not only in the pages of the press, but in Ascott itself, where on 24 July William Pratley of Ascott was summoned to appear before the magistrates to answer a charge of assault on PC Yeats at Ascott during the course of a NALU meeting on the village green.

Life after imprisonment

We do not know the final fate of the men who withdrew their labour but some, with the help of the Union, may have taken the opportunity to obtain work out of the area, in particular in the northern industrial towns where there was a demand for labour. Of the women, we know that

Elizabeth Pratley with baby Eli and the rest of the family emigrated to Canada leaving Plymouth on the SS *Nyanza* on 14 July. The Pratleys were not the only ones to leave Ascott, as the school log book reports that in the week beginning 21 September the school lost about 11 of its scholars through families emigrating to New Zealand. The following year Mary Pratley and Amelia Moss and their families left for New Zealand. By 1880 Ann Moss, the last of the women to emigrate, was living with her husband in Mississippi.[26] In addition to those who emigrated, within a decade six of the women were dead and others had left Ascott taking their story with them into obscurity.[27]

Conclusion

The events leading to the arrest, imprisonment and release of the Ascott Martyrs are a reflection of the injustices of life for the rural poor in mid-Victorian society. Struggling to survive poverty, poorly educated, with few social and economic rights, and with the Anglican Church and the landed establishment against them, and working through repressive laws and in a hostile policing environment, it is no surprise that the 16 Ascott women would, because of their actions, become unwitting secular martyrs. The injustice of the economic, social and political environment in which they operated is examined in the essays that follow. It is sufficient here to reflect upon their lack of rights and lack of citizenship in English rural society in the 19th century. Their demands for liberty and rights might have seemed 'unseemly and outrageous' to the farmers and the establishment, but were fundamental to the emergence of full citizenship, for both men and women, for the mass of the population of England.

2

From Tolpuddle to Ascott

LES KENNEDY

For years past our aristocracy, members of Parliament, preachers in the pulpit and speakers on public platforms had deplored the position of the agricultural labourer and had said they hoped to see him in a better position. But, with all their sympathy, they had never taken one step to aid him in securing any improvements in his condition... And as the agricultural labourers had trusted to the farmers, to an aristocratic House of Lords and Commons, to help them quiet long enough, without receiving any aid from them, they at last determined to help themselves and if they were united and determined they would succeed.

> Mr Geo. Odger, president of the London Trades Council speaking at a meeting held at the Boston at the Boston Corn Exchange on 15 November 1873 (extract from *The Boston Guardian* 29 November 1873)

In the TUC's book *The Martyrs of Tolpuddle 1834–1934*, George Bernard Shaw makes the point that 'Martyrs are a nuisance in Labour movements. The business of the Labour man is not to suffer but to make other people suffer until they make him reasonably comfortable.'[1] His idea that martyrs are a nuisance is an interesting one and applies to both the Dorset labourers and the women of Ascott. The case of the Tolpuddle Martyrs aroused huge public interest at the time and they were then largely forgotten, but a hundred years later they went on to become part of trade union history. On the other hand, the Ascott Martyrs were quickly forgotten partly because of the misogynistic nature of 19th century British society, which was also reflected in trade unions at the time.

The arrest and sentencing of the six Tolpuddle men in 1834 followed a decade of recession, which included mass migration from the countryside to the growing towns and cities and a fear in the establishment that Britain would undergo a revolution similar to the French Revolution, still strong in popular memory. In these conditions early trade unions were formed to defend the rights of workers. They were faced with repression from the government in the form of the Combination Acts of 1800 and 1801 which effectively were a universal ban on trade unionism, replacing the ban on combinations of workers in specific industries of the 18th century. When the Combination Acts were repealed in 1824 and 1825 the result was a huge surge in trade union activity and industrial unrest.

In rural areas the formation of trade unions, or combinations, was difficult. One response to the new machinery introduced by landowners was the 'Swing Riots', which led to the destruction of the new threshing machines across southern England from 1830. Swing mainly affected Kent but there were incidents around Tolpuddle which its Martyrs would have been aware of. In addition to the growth of unrest in agricultural areas there was also the growth of Methodism and Nonconformity, which was spreading across the country from the 18th century and was particularly strong in inner cities and remote rural areas. The men in Tolpuddle were already marked out as troublemakers for the establishment of a small Methodist Chapel in 1819. Aware of government spies and repression from the landowners, the agricultural workers took to meeting in the open. This nascent trade union, contrary to public belief, was not a totally 'underground' nor secret affair. In 1832 George Loveless led a deputation asking the masters/employers for a wage increase to 10 shillings per week; the farmers agreed and the vicar of Tolpuddle, Dr Thomas Warren, stood as witness to the deal.[2]

The masters reneged and Warren denied that he had made a promise of support. The result was that the masters reduced the wages to 7 shillings per week, and shortly afterwards tried to reduce wages to 6s shillings a week.[3] Even with relief from the Poor Law this was scarcely enough to live on.

George Loveless, a Methodist lay preacher, was in contact with activists from Robert Owen's Grand National Consolidated Trades Union (GNCTU) and as a result a branch was formed in Tolpuddle – such was the need for secrecy that all new members were required to take an oath. We know that two delegates from the GNCTU came to Tolpuddle in October 1833 and addressed a meeting.[4] Squire Frampton was desperate and wrote to the Home Secretary, Lord Melbourne, warning him of the spread of trade unionism and complained that meetings were difficult for him to spy on. Melbourne was under pressure

Tolpuddle poster 'Guilty of Felony...
liable to be transported...'

to reintroduce the Combination Acts and suggested that Frampton, also a magistrate, use a law (introduced to prevent naval mutinies) that forbade the taking of secret oaths.[5] Frampton had established a network of informers, two of whom, Edward Legg and John Lock, were initiated into the Tolpuddle Friendly Society on 9 December 1833.[6]

On 21 February 1834 Frampton set up placards threatening to punish any man who should join the union with seven years' transportation. As a result, on 24 February George Loveless, James Loveless, James Brine, Thomas Standfield, John Standfield and James Hammett were arrested by the parish constable and marched to Dorchester.[7]

Edward Legg gave evidence against them and made clear that in almost masonic circumstances he and John Lock had taken an oath binding them to the Friendly Society and that they had sworn to keep this oath secret. There is little doubt that the trial in Dorchester was rigged and the outcome predetermined as an example of what the state would do, and all six men were sentenced to seven years' transportation on 19 March 1834.

The tale of the Tolpuddle Martyrs is known by most trade unionists, who believe they understand it but hold many misconceptions. The truth is that the Tolpuddle Martyrs were not charged with creating an illegal trade union, the Friendly Society of Agricultural Labourers. Trade unions had been legal since the repeal of the Combination Acts in 1824 and 1825, but they were charged with taking an illegal oath under conspiracy. Under the 1799 Seditious Societies Act the maximum sentence would have been three months. However, the Mutiny Act of

1797, formed to prevent mutinies in the Navy, was invoked and its punishments were much harsher, resulting in transportation.

The significance of this story is not in the arrest and transportation of the Dorset men but in the huge public outcry the sentences engendered. The British public demanded a repeal of the sentences and backed their demands with large public protests and petitions. As news of the verdict spread, the GNCTU organised a march on Easter Monday, 21 April 1834, from Copenhagen Fields to Kennington in London.[8] The authorities tried to prevent people assembling but the land at Copenhagen Fields was outside the jurisdiction of the London magistrates. This was another sign of a government living in fear of a workers' revolution. Public concern resulted eventually in the men being returned from Australia.

It is almost heretical to ask what these six labourers had to do with trade unionism since they refused opportunities to join unions, and after farming in Essex for several years, a county which hardly welcomed them, they emigrated to Canada vowing never to speak of their experiences. They were never on a picket line, never organised a strike and in general were not committed to the trade union movement.

When the Trades Union Congress were looking for a group of workers to celebrate in the 1930s they could not have chosen a better group than the Tolpuddle men who were both non-violent and law abiding. They had no atrocities marked against their names and in all respects were involuntary martyrs. As Keith Laybourn has said, they were originally referred to as the six 'Dorchester Labourers' and it was only after 1934 in the labour movement that they were known as martyrs. However, the Methodists had erected an arch outside the new Methodist chapel in Tolpuddle in 1912 dedicated to the 'Tolpuddle Martyrs'.

The economic depression which had followed 1825 made life difficult for trade unions in the 1830s as the government looked at reintroducing anti-trade union legislation, after they had repealed the Combination Acts. They decided against such a step but unions were still under attack from both employers and politicians. It wasn't until the 1840s that unions began to realise they had to seek a political solution, which was to become involved in the fight to make sure all working men had the right to vote. The unions began to echo the demands of the Chartists.

It should be remembered that agricultural labourers in this period lived on the verge of poverty, often claiming outdoor relief from the parish Poor Law and living in tied houses. Tied houses had no security of tenure apart from the job they were tied to and any transgression against the employer could result in homelessness. The New Poor Law Act, introduced in 1834, made the provision of poor relief more onerous by attempting to ensure that it was indoor relief, requiring the destitute to live in the workhouse. This was applied more readily in rural areas than industrial ones such as Huddersfield and the textile district of the West Riding of Yorkshire, where there was staunch resistance to the New Poor Law which delayed its effective imposition until the mid/late 19th century.

Trade unions of the 1840s and 1850s were often bodies representing skilled workers, ignoring many of the unskilled and semi-skilled. They were often reluctant to strike and concerned to extend their right to represent their members. The problem was that the legal position of the unions was still insecure in the 1850s, since they were not recognised as legal bodies unless their activities of providing benefits to their members fell under the Friendly Society Acts of the day. In this situation there were strikes and violence, most notably among the metalworkers and cutlery workers in Sheffield in 1866/1867. This led the government to set up a Royal Commission on Trade Unions.

At the same time there was the *Hornby v Close* affair, in which a union treasurer was charged, by his union, with embezzling union funds. The charge was dismissed since the trade union was not a legal body, unlike friendly societies protected by a Friendly Society Act because they were providing benefits to their members. The legislation did not cover trade unions primarily formed to threaten strike action in the case of a dispute. The judge in this case noted that trade unions were illegal bodies as they were a restraint of trade.[9]

This led the unions to redouble their efforts to secure both legal rights and the vote for the working man. The Royal Commission made recommendations to grant legal recognition to trade unions, which meant that they could protect their funds in court. In 1871 the government accepted this recommendation in the Trade Union Act of 1871, as long as trade unions registered as such, but the government also passed the Criminal Law Amendment Act which kept the law as it was from 1825: coercion in picketing remained a criminal offence, separate from the criminal law of the land.

After the 1850s highly organised unions for skilled workers appeared on the national scene but these new London-based

Joseph Arch (1826–1919).

national craft unions were accompanied by the formation of smaller regional or local unions. The Agricultural Labourers' Union led by Joseph Arch was an example of a regional union which faced opposition from smaller agricultural labourers' unions in various parts of the country, though it soon expanded to become a national organisation, the National Agricultural Labourers' Union (NALU).

Arch, who led the NALU, was born in November

Farm labourers' strike meeting.

1826 and started work on the land aged nine.[10] On the 13 February 1872 he gave his first speech at an open-air meeting of agricultural labourers. He was a Methodist lay preacher and was used to addressing meetings. On the 29 March the inaugural meeting of the Warwickshire Agricultural labourers was held at Leamington and by the 29 May workers from 26 counties met in Leamington in a conference where the Warwickshire Agricultural Labourers' union was merged into a National Agricultural Labourers' Union, with Arch as its Chairman.

The growth of this union was dramatic and by the first week of September 1872 subscriptions in aid of the union had reached £1,000. The spread of the union was helped by improvements in communication and often by Methodist lay preachers, many of whom were themselves labourers. Interestingly, reflecting the misogynistic nature of the time, the union demanded that women should not be employed upon work that was only suited for men and that as a rule women should not be employed to work in the fields.[11] By the end of 1873 the union had 700,000 members according to its general secretary, Mr H. Taylor. In fact, this was an enormous exaggeration, the union peaking at 86,214 members in 1874 as registered under the Trade Union Act of 1871, its membership declining to fewer than 1,000 members by the time it dissolved in 1896.

The central issue that the union faced was the low pay of agricultural workers. The union's paper, the *Labourers' Union Chronicle*, called for a rise in wages to 16s shillings a week, and £1 for shepherds and waggoners (roughly equivalent to wages of £480 and £600 per week in today's values). This was coupled with a call for the electoral franchise for agricultural labourers (at this point only male landowners of property worth £10 pa, or tenants occupying property worth £50 pa, had the vote). Agricultural labourers were more than willing to strike if their demands for an increase in wages were denied by their employers and it was this willingness to engage in trade unionism that led to the events in Ascott. Given that Joseph Arch was also an ardent Methodist and teetotaller who often talked about the value of sobriety, and emphasised that 'courtesy, fairness and firmness characterise all of our demands', it is not surprising that Nonconformity and teetotalism, and the enfranchisement of the working man, were part of the appeal and approach of the NALU.[12]

In November 1872 the NALU was discussing the enfranchisement of agricultural labourers in St. James Hall, London[13] and in December a resolution was passed at a meeting in Exeter Hall, with Arch and Sir Charles Dilke (a leading radical MP) present, which declared 'the present condition of agricultural labourers is a national disgrace'.[14] The union also called for a plan akin to the nationalisation of land in its paper the *Labourers' Union Chronicle*, which had been established in 1872.[15] Arch certainly developed the idea that not only should agricultural labourers be better paid but that they should also be better men, to have not only enough to eat and drink but also to be better educated, clothed and have better housing.[16]

As agricultural labourers began to demand higher wages, farmers resorted to lockouts often acting in combinations called Local Defence Associations. As union strikes and the employers' lockouts spread in 1872, the NALU helped men and their families to move north where there was employment. Battle lines were being clearly drawn, agricultural labourers had few savings to fall back on and as lockouts continued throughout the harvest season, which was often the time of most work, they began to suffer and as a result union membership began to fall (see graph).

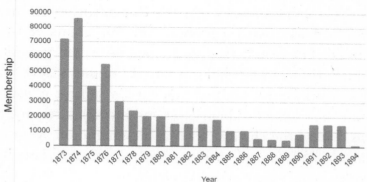

Decline of the National Agricultural Labourers' Union 1873-1894

At the second annual conference of the NALU in May 1873 it was reported that the membership was 71,835 spreading across 23 district unions and 982 branches.[17], However, by this time the union was facing financial difficulties as strike pay exhausted the union funds. Slowly, the farmers also began to break the strike and the union was forced to consider both migration in England and emigration to the colonies 'to seek in a foreign land the bread that is denied then in their own'.[18] It was at this point that the Ascott Martyrs affair, often reported under the title of 'Rioting in Chipping Norton', occurred in May 1873, which, as we have seen in the previous essay, led to 16 women from Ascott-under-Wychwood being imprisoned for threatening or intimidating two young men who were on their way to work at Mr Hambidge's Crown Farm.

Arch and other union leaders were now faced with the fact that workers were leaving the union because they needed to work to avoid being driven to the workhouse. Originally Arch had been opposed to the idea of emigration but in 1873 accepted an invitation from the Canadian government for an all-expenses-paid visit to Canada. During the seven-week visit the Canadian government discussed with Arch a proposal for free grants of land, a rough house and free seed alongside some provision to help those who could not afford the move. Arch was significantly impressed and thought that at least 'emigrees would be toiling for themselves and their children'.[19] Arch was offered the chance to act as an emigration agent for Canada and was allowed to sign recommendations for workers who were seeking to emigrate.

By 1874 the farmers were organised and there were lockouts in all the main rural areas. Although there was a great deal of public and union support for the agricultural labourers it was not enough, and many workers were forced to return to work. Unfortunately, in many cases a return to work also meant that a worker was forced to renounce the union. The union had hoped the dispute would be resolved before the harvest of 1874, but farmers resorted to using non-union labour including women and children alongside new machinery to ensure the harvest was completed.

By 3 August 1874 the Union had decided the strike must end and that the following week would be the last in which they would pay strike pay.[20] As a result, labourers lost confidence in the union and Arch was undermined as a leader. In June 1874 the union claimed 84,000 members but by the end of 1875 this was down to 40,000.[21] Another factor which caused the union financial problems was the establishment of a benevolent scheme which paid out to labourers if they were ill and unable to work. Unfortunately, there were no checks on admittance and in a short time more was being paid out than was being collected. In addition, the union's administrators failed to create the scheme as a separate entity and it created a serious drain on union resources. By 1879 union membership was down to 20,000 and by 1885 10,700 (see graph above).[22] Although there was a slight revival in membership in the 1880s, the NALU was a spent force.

Nevertheless, the Union and its officials exerted a major influence on Oxfordshire and Ascott. One of the NALU officials who became particularly important in the Ascott case was Christopher Holloway. His background was that of an agricultural labourer who had suffered a number of personal tragedies in the 1850s and 1860s. He had lost two sons, one in 1859 and another in 1861. Both his parents died within months of each other in 1861 and his wife died a few months later. Like Arch, Holloway was a committed Methodist, and he was made a trustee of Wootton Chapel in February 1864.[23] Oxfordshire followed the example of South Warwickshire and set up a local union in Milton-under-Wychwood in April 1872.

Holloway was elected as chairman of the branch of 185 members and they began to press local employers for a rise. The farmers set up a local defence association and refused to pay. The dispute lasted for two months and the farmers resorted to bringing in soldiers from Aldershot to bring in the harvest. Incidentally the fuss this caused led to change in the Queen's regulations to forbid soldiers doing such work. When the Duke of Marlborough offered farmers the cottages he owned, to improve their bargaining position, Holloway reacted strongly: 'Let them... have a revolution rather than go back to the dark ages and be serfs and slaves of the owners.'[24]

As the conflict continued, Holloway asked to be relieved from some of his preaching duties which did not go down well with other preachers on the circuit who tried to censure him 'on account of his taking a prominent part in the labour agitation'.[25] Holloway witnessed several labourers emigrating to Sheffield to work in the steel industry in July 1872 and the strike collapsed at the end of August with some labourers achieving small increases in their wages. Holloway was clearly held in high regard by his members and he was elected as district chairman, which allowed him to attend the NALU Executive Committee meetings in Leamington.[26]

Following Arch's visit to Canada in 1873 the idea of emigration was discussed in these meetings and the Union's rule book was amended to make emigration an aim of the union.[27] Holloway became attracted to the idea of emigration to New Zealand and after a successful meeting in Milton-under-Wychwood in November 1873 he offered to lead a party of several hundred labourers and their families to the colony. The New Zealand government were keen to encourage emigration and offered Holloway an attractive proposal which included a free return passage, subsistence payments for his family of 25 shillings a week and £1 a day for travel expenses. Holloway leapt at the chance, relinquished his union responsibilities and in

December 1873 set sail from Plymouth, leading a party of 500 labourers and their families.[28]

Part of Holloway's position was to ensure that his charges were settled and he used his time in New Zealand to explore the possibility of further emigration, writing several letters to the *Union Labourer's Chronicle* praising life in the colony. It is important to remember that Holloway was benefitting financially from his new role. He stayed in New Zealand until November 1874, when he returned to England as a special travelling agent of the New Zealand government. He remained in this post until 1900 when New Zealand faced an economic recession and dispensed with his services. He continued his close links to the union and was presented with a timepiece at the annual celebration of the Wootton branch in October 1876.[29]

Conclusion

The Ascott Martyrs were merely one point in the history of agricultural trade unionism in the 1870s, and gathered little attention for more than a month. The Tolpuddle Martyrs drew attention for longer, but had faded into obscurity by the end of the 19th century. If George Bernard Shaw was right when he declared, tongue in cheek, that martyrs were a nuisance, both the Tolpuddle men and the Ascott women fitted the bill. There are clear similarities between the two groups. Both events involved agricultural workers who were loosely connected to trade unions and agricultural unrest. Both groups had dubious trials and both were given harsh sentences which led to public protests. Both groups were given the title 'martyrs' some considerable time after their respective events had taken place. Both events had strong links to Methodism.

However, while we have some idea of what the Tolpuddle Martyrs looked like and George Loveless wrote a couple of pamphlets outlining his views, the Ascott women were forgotten very quickly. Indeed, The Rev. Frederick Samuel Attenborough, a Congregationalist minister who was one of Joseph Arch's strongest supporters on the NALU advisory committee, wrote in the *Labourers' Union Chronicle* on 7 June 1873, that 'neither he, nor the leaders of the union thought that the sixteen women had done either a wise or a womanly thing in attempting to influence the two lads in Mr Hambidge's employ, they would have been far better at home minding their families, and he trusted the lesson they had received would not be lost upon them.'[30]

It is true that much the same thing was said to the Tolpuddle men, but they of course did not suffer from misogyny. The lot of the Ascott women in the 19th century certainly owes a great deal to the fact that the unions were male dominated (the NALU didn't even accept female members) until the mid-20th century; they were also weak institutions (especially financially). As the 20th century developed there was less reliance on 'martyrs to the cause' because the Labour Party emerged as a political force and is still today essentially for the worker versus the establishment. Nevertheless, the Ascott women played their part in the process of challenging the injustices of 19th century Victorian society, paving the way for the extension of citizenship in the 20th century, and this should not be forgotten.

3

'Bold, imprudent, scandalmongers': rural women's work and the case of the Ascott Martyrs in mid-Victorian England

NICOLA VERDON

'**M**rs Walter Huckens',[1] an Oxfordshire agricultural labourer's wife from Combe, was one of several women interviewed by parliamentary commissioner George Culley when he visited the county in the late 1860s to survey women's and children's work on the land for the government. She told Culley that she had been 'out to fieldwork' from the age of 12 but with two small children, aged six and three, she had only been able to labour in the harvest fields in the last year. She worked alongside her husband and explained that 'if I can help him with a little boy, we can cut and tie an acre a day, and we got 9s. an acre... we had a fortnight at this'. While piecework at harvest was a boon to the family income, across the year her husband's work was precarious. He earned 10 shillings a week full time, wet weather often curtailing the working week by a day or two in winter.

63

The family paid 1s 4d a week in rent and, unlike some of their neighbours, had no allotment. Mrs Huckens was keen for her children to receive schooling up to the age of 12, something she had not benefitted from, but knew this was unlikely as they began to learn glove-making at eight years old. On the day of this encounter with Culley, Mrs Huckens had spent all day at gloving herself, but had only made 5d, a paltry financial return for what she described as a 'hard' day's work.[2]

In many ways Mrs Huckens' life corresponded with those of the Ascott Martyrs and was also typical of women of the rural labouring class in mid-Victorian England more widely, with poverty, poor housing and lack of education defining experiences. Young rural girls grew up with limited employment choices, usually compelled into agricultural labour or, more likely, domestic service. Married women were confronted with the dilemma of balancing domestic and childcare responsibilities with contributing financially towards the meagre household income. They were employed on a range of seasonal agricultural tasks connected to 'cleaning' the land, such as weeding, hoeing and stone-picking and in the planting, picking and sorting of root crops. Women also followed the reapers in the hay and harvest fields, turning, tying and stacking the cut crops. Studies by historians using a range of primary sources have shown that the employment of women on farms differed from region to region according to local labour demand, market conditions, and families' needs.[3] In some parts of the English countryside, women (and children) had an alternative to farm work in the form of cottage industries with pillow lace-making, glove-making, straw-plaiting and button-making the most significant in the second half of the 19th century. As in agriculture, women who worked in these industries were exploited as a cheap source of local labour. Rural women endured hard lives in Victorian England, managing tight budgets in difficult economic circumstances. They were examined, judged and criticised by their social superiors, the government and the press but were rarely allowed space to stand up for their rights or to speak for themselves. This makes the case of the Ascott Martyrs all the more significant.

In 1873, when the events at Ascott unfolded, English agriculture was at the tail end of a period of 'high farming', which had been dominated by high rents and prices (see essay 4). Farm labourers did not share in this prosperity however, and agriculture was a low-wage, low-status occupation throughout the Victorian era. Men who worked with animals, particularly shepherds and horsemen, often enjoyed a 'constant' contract across the year, but the vast majority of agricultural labourers were 'ordinary' men, engaged by the week on a daily wage, which could be topped up by task work at different times of the year, such as haymaking and harvest. Wage rates differed across counties although by the mid-19th century there was an established broad regional distinction between the higher-wage north, where industry vied with agriculture for workers, and the lower-wage south, where rates reached their nadir in the south-west.[4] When Culley visited Oxfordshire in November 1868 he found the regular male wage in the north of the county to be between 12 and 14 shillings a week, and in the south between 13 and 15 shillings, although some farmers 'sank' this wage in winter by a shilling or two.[5]

Women worked in agriculture where there was local demand and supply. In some areas of northern England their labour was year round and essential to the cultivation of the land; in other areas, it was more seasonal. The casualisation of women's work reached its peak in the Fenland counties of the east, where the employment of women and children in agricultural gangs had aroused much comment and alarm in the mid-1860s, resulting in parliamentary legislation to curb the worst abuses.[6] Despite their obvious presence, it is difficult to determine how many women worked in agriculture. The census tells us that in 1871 women made up just under 6 per cent of the agricultural workforce in England and Wales as a whole, although in Northumberland, Cumberland and Durham it was much higher. Oxfordshire matched the national average, with women forming 6 per cent of agricultural labourers (outdoor) in 1871. Yet a survey of 35 farms in the county in Culley's report a few years earlier found that in spring and summer women formed 17 per cent of the workforce, dropping slightly to 15 per cent in autumn and 11 per cent in the winter months. He concluded that women usually worked in Oxfordshire for seven months a year, including harvest, and that the vast majority of these were married women performing the 'lighter' work of the farm. Very few girls and comparatively few unmarried women worked in the fields in Oxfordshire, except in family units at harvest.[7]

Women who worked seasonally or casually in agriculture tended to be ignored by the census enumerators because their focus was on tabulating full-time, regular work. Also, the census was usually taken on a night in the early months

Women haymaking.

of the year when demand for women workers wasn't as great as it was in the summer; between 1851 and 1911 it was always taken in March or April.[8] Using a large sample of farm account books to measure the employment of female outdoor labourers in agriculture, Joyce Burnette has estimated that the census of 1851 recorded fewer than half of the female outdoor labourers working in agriculture at that time because it failed to capture those who worked on an irregular basis.[9] Other historians have found plenty of examples where women, especially married women, were employed on farms as day labourers and recorded in farm account and labour books but were classified as 'unoccupied' in the census.[10] Of the seven Ascott Martyrs who were described as farm labourers/fieldworkers in the charge sheet of May 1873, none had been classified as such in the 1871 census.

Regional variation in the employment of women was reflected in wage rates, with women workers based in the northern counties of Durham, Northumberland,

Cumberland and Westmorland earning two or three times their southern counterparts. Everywhere women earned between a half and a third of the male daily wage. In Oxfordshire Culley reported that women were paid 8d for an eight-hour day in the fields, with an increase of 1d per hour for extra time, and where they worked alongside men, for example at the threshing machine, they were paid 1s a day. Working as part of a family team at harvest, as outlined by Mrs Huckens at the beginning of this essay, could contribute £6 to £8. Earnings from female agricultural labour, modest, intermittent and fitted around housework and childcare, were nevertheless a valuable contribution to the household income at a time when men's wages were so low.

The numbers of women employed in agriculture dropped where there were alternative employment opportunities and cottage industries were particularly important in parts of rural southern and midland England. Outside London the glove-making industry was concentrated in three forested areas – the Quantock Hills of Somerset, the Malvern Hills of Worcestershire and Wychwood Royal Forest in west Oxfordshire. Woodstock was the most important gloving centre in Oxfordshire, but this industry also extended to Charlbury, a few miles east of Ascott. There is some debate about why certain domestic industries were established in different rural areas. In some regions it may have been because of the pastoral nature of farming gave little work for local women, who thus formed a ready labour supply; in others, such as the case of straw-plaiting, it was linked to local raw materials and proximity to London, while in other areas it was more closely related to poverty and male under-employment.[11] Gloving was introduced in the Charlbury region following the Napoleonic wars in an attempt to relieve distress caused by economic depression and although it had to weather renewed competition when prohibition on French gloves was removed in the 1820s, in the middle of the 19th century it was a thriving industry.[12] By 1851 Samuel Pritchett's glove manufactory in Charlbury employed 1,000 people, the vast majority of them sewing women. In the late 1860s a manufacturer in Woodstock told Culley that a 'good' sewer in his factory could make a dozen gloves per week, earning 5 to 7 shillings, while an 'average' woman worker could earn 4 to 5 shillings.[13]

Significantly gloves were also 'put out' to be sewn at home by women and girls living within a few miles' radius of Woodstock and Charlbury. The Workshop Regulation Act of 1867, which restricted hours for women and children working in certain settings, may have encouraged this practice. The Woodstock manufacturer quoted above told Culley the Act was 'so troublesome' that he no longer employed girls under 13 except 'in their own homes'.[14]

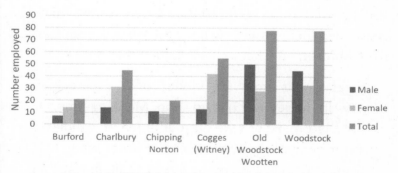

West Oxfordshire gloving industry, 1871.

Gloves were treated and cut out in factories before being distributed and collected in the villages on behalf of the manufacturers by an intermediary, usually a woman called a 'carrierwoman' or 'packwoman'. Gloving was an attractive occupation as it was flexible, fitted around domestic duties and could be done by rural women throughout the seasons and across the life cycle. Girls began learning the art of gloving from their mothers at a young age, which interrupted any rudimentary schooling they may have received, although they didn't usually begin earning money until they were more proficient. Wage rates were based on the number of completed gloves (usually by the dozen). 'Gloveress' appeared frequently as an occupational category in the mid-Victorian censuses in the villages of west Oxfordshire and in the charge sheet of 1873 half of the Ascott Martyrs were described in this way.

Although gloving was important to the women of rural west Oxfordshire in the 1870s, like agriculture it was an occupation that was susceptible to trade fluctuations, exploitation and sharp practice. Women were reliant on the intermediary for work and had little or no bargaining power in that relationship. Culley found that three out of five manufacturers he interviewed kept stores which they compelled their workers to use. One witness, Mrs Gardner, from Shipton on Cherwell, explained this system:

> I get gloves from Mr Money of Woodstock; he pays in money and has no shop. Mr Dagget and Mr Pritchett make us take out our in tea, or candles, or sugar etc, within a few pence of what we get. If I want 1s 6d. they make me spend 1s 3d. in the shop, or they would 'sack' me, i.e., give me no more work.

Gloveress Mrs Brackenborough outside
her home in Woodstock.

They sell sugar at 5½d. a pound when we could get
it at 4½d. if we had ready money. Candles they
charge at 6½d. instead of 6d etc.[15]

Demand was not constant, and competition undercut
profit margins so that the wages paid to rural women were
variable and often very scant. Culley found that a girl of 16
working in a factory would earn from 3s to 5s a week but
working at home women and girls received between 2s 6d
and 3s. Paid on completion, wages also depended on time
and skill. Mrs Wood of Wootton did 'a little glove sewing'
but with five children aged 11 and under, she only had
'time to earn about 1s 6d a week'.[16] Gloving was sedentary
work, and many hours a day stooped over gloves in poor
light weakened eyesight and physical health.

Women's motivations for working in agriculture and gloving were varied. For most wives of agricultural labourers, it was poverty and economic need which drove them (and their daughters) to work. Gloving held some advantages over agricultural work as mothers did not need to find childcare to cover their absence from the home. Nor did it take such a toll on already threadbare clothing or footwear as fieldwork. Culley described 'the miserable dress' worn by Oxfordshire women in the fields, which consisted of 'their husband's coat and an apron cut from an old manure bag'. This was clearly inadequate given the physical work and exposure to the elements. It may have kept 'out a certain amount of rain from the upper part of their person,' he explained, 'but the slipshod feet can rarely remain dry for half an hour on an ordinary winter's day.'[17] But some women preferred agricultural work because it was better paid and less restrictive. Culley found eight women working in the fields at Shipton on Cherwell on his visit, picking grass from newly sown wheat. They were paid 9d for an eight-hour day. They reported to him that 'they could not make 1d an hour at gloving, and they liked the farm work best'.[18] Although women were exploited, we should not forget they could also enjoy their work. In agriculture women often worked in groups alongside other women or family members, where they could chat, gossip and eat together. Home-working, on the other hand, could be isolating and unrelenting. In west Oxfordshire rural women therefore had some, albeit limited, choice about the type of work they undertook depending on personal circumstances and preference.

Village elites and government commissioners, men of education and social standing, frequently criticised working women whatever the industry. Reverend Jordan of Enstone believed that gloving 'spoiled' young women for domestic duties, while Rev. Hoskyns Abrahall of Combe argued it led to immoral behaviour 'from the fact that the girls, when it is dark... walk out and meet the youths, who are then returning from their work'. Rev. Tyrwhitt of Lockinge echoed many when he told Culley that field work was the 'ruin' of women. He went on:

> They become bold, imprudent, scandalmongers, hardened against religion, careless of their homes and children, most untidy, given to drink, coarse-minded, debased, depravers of any virtuous girls who work with them, having no pride in their home or their children, and few home feelings. Their children are ragged and quite untaught, and a dirty home often drives the husband to the public house.[19]

This is quite a range of accusations! Such evidence reveals unease about women who, through their work, transgressed middle-class ideals of femininity, respectability and womanhood. In their incursions into the countryside in the late 1860s, government commissioners like Culley tended to rely on the evidence of landowners, farmers, land agents, Poor Law guardians, clergymen and medical practitioners. These were all men who shared a common understanding about women as domestic beings, with the breadwinner husband/non-working wife the 'proper' model for society. Such evidence doesn't tell us much about the reality of rural women's working lives, which was beyond the experience and understanding of these male commentators.

Like the women who worked in agricultural gangs, the Ascott Martyrs' case became a cause célèbre in mid-Victorian England, when rural working-class women became national news. Unlike the gang women, who remained largely shadowy and anonymous, the 16 convicted women from Ascott were named, recognised individuals and they provide, as Karen Sayer has argued, 'a valuable example of the response of the public to women as political actors'.[20] Sayer's analysis reveals the ambiguity of the press reporting and parliamentary discussion of the case because the actions of women contravened dominant ideologies of women as domestic, apolitical and submissive. Although some accounts highlighted threatening behaviour and abusive language, the radical press represented the women as respectable, well dressed and non-violent, protecting the jobs of their husbands. Commentators emphasised that the women were wives and mothers rather than workers. This was particularly important for the National Union of Agricultural Labourers (NALU), who, although they sympathised with the cause the women were defending, believed cheap female labour undercut the wages of men and had barred women from joining the union at its inception in 1872. The NALU leader Joseph Arch argued that women 'should have been minding their houses, or should have been in domestic service, or working at some trade suited to women' rather than working in the fields.[21] The NALU's voice, *The Labourers' Union Chronicle*, therefore painted the women as martyrs, as passive victims, a depiction which, Sayer argues, 'was acceptable within the bounds of respectability'.[22] The Ascott Martyrs' case is a unique one which allows us to explore the experiences of rural women as workers, as family members and as public actors.

Conclusion

When and how frequently rural women entered the labour market depended upon several factors: where she lived, how old she was, her marital status, the number and age of her children, the occupation of her husband and local custom regarding the employment of women. Rural women moved in and out of work throughout their lives as male wages barely met subsistence needs. This was certainly the case in Oxfordshire, where male agricultural wage rates remained low throughout the Victorian years. The middle-class ideal of the male breadwinner/domestic housewife, one adopted by the agricultural trade unions in the 1870s, was rarely achieved in rural families. But women were always at a disadvantage in the labour force, and despite their skills and proficiencies, be it in fieldwork or in glove-sewing, they were poorly paid and inadequately protected. The instances where rural women fought back to achieve better pay and conditions for themselves or their husbands are few and far between. Thus while the women of Ascott are, in many ways, representative of poor working-class rural families in mid-Victorian England, what happened in May 1873 and the aftermath of the events was unique.

4

The economics and structure of farming in Oxfordshire in the 19th century

JOHN MARTIN

> Since 1862, the tide of agricultural prosperity had ceased to flow, after 1874 it turned and rapidly ebbed.
>
> Lord Ernle, *English Farming Past and Present* (1922)[1]

In 1837, when Queen Victoria came to the throne, more than half of the population of Great Britain worked in the countryside, principally in agriculture and allied industries. By the end of her reign in 1901, the sector accounted for less than 10 per cent of the workforce with the interests of manufacturing taking precedence over those of agriculture. A pivotal moment in this transformation was the Anti-Corn Law League's success in repealing the Corn Laws in 1846. The most infamous Corn Laws were protectionist measures brought in by the British government in 1815, which restricted the amount of foreign grain that could be imported into the country.

Farming in the field.

The repeal of the Corn Laws in 1846 heralded the adoption of a free-trade dominated system whereby Britain's manufacturing industries had unfettered access to overseas markets in return for allowing tariff-free imports of agricultural produce. It was not until the early 1870s, following the opening-up of American prairies, coupled with the development of railways and the use of steam-driven ships, that large-scale imports of agricultural produce occurred. Imports of cheap agricultural produce, and in its wake, price falls for home-grown produce, became increasingly evident after 1874. The Anti-Corn League's campaign had portrayed the farmer as a rustic dullard, an ignoramus and servile retainer who unthinkingly followed the landowners' lead in politics and country affairs.[2] As Richard Hoyle has astutely reminded us, 'In writings on agricultural history, farmers are so often the bridesmaid and so rarely the bride.'[3] The aim of this article is to explore the changing structure and economics of agriculture, with particular reference to way it impinged on the role and attitudes of farmers, nationally and more specifically to those which prevailed in west Oxfordshire.[4]

Throughout the Victorian era, agriculture was in a process of transition. The agrarian changes which took place between the end of the French and Napoleonic wars in 1815 and the 1880s were so significant that, according to the social historian F.M.L. Thompson, they constituted a 'second agricultural revolution'. The changes 'made the farmer more like a manufacturer', using inputs from outside the agricultural sector.[5]

Prior to that date the prevailing system of mixed farming was in effect a closed-circuit system. This meant that wheat, barley, meat and some wools were produced for sale off the farm because the roots, clover and even possibly the pulses as well as the hay grown on the farm were consumed on the spot to support livestock production and the horses which worked the farm. Improvements in output were not necessarily that great but agriculture performed moderately efficiently compared with other industries.

The mid-Victorian period, spanning the 1850s up to the early years of the 1870s is widely regarded as a golden age for English agriculture a period of sustained prosperity for the landowning classes and their tenant farmers. Concerns about the possible threat of overseas competition following the repeal of the Corn Laws encouraged the shift in favour of what James Caird denoted as high farming.[6] In the context of the 19th century, this entailed the adoption of intensive farming particularly in respect of cereal and root production and the intensification of livestock husbandry. Those who under-drained their land, introduced new and innovative crop rotations, and introduced the most up-to-date ways of fertilising their land, were considered to be high farmers, while those who still followed the older methods were low farmers. In its more extravagant form, high farming was a system which required costly inputs which could only be justified when prices were good and seasons favourable. As Lord Ernle reminds us, since 1862, the tide of agricultural prosperity had ceased to flow; after 1874 it turned and rapidly ebbed.[7]

The repeal of the Corn Laws in 1846 was the most obvious manifestation of the relative and absolute decline which was taking place in the power and influence of the landed interest in the House of Commons, their position being superseded by those representing manufacturers and industrialists.[8] The repeal of the legislation which had prohibited the importation of wheat had changed the balance of power at the national level for the Corn Laws had revealed the control which landed society had previously exerted. Indeed, these laws ensured that it was only possible to import grain free from import duties if the price of wheat reached 80 shillings per quarter (about one fifth of a ton), a price which was never achieved in the 30 years that the laws applied. That rural control was now gone as the industrialists took control of the nation. Industrial and social change was afoot. Nevertheless, in contrast to the national scene, there was still a remarkable degree of stability in terms of the hierarchical and authoritarian, occupationally segregated nature of rural communities.

At its apex were the aristocracy and gentry who owned most of the land, renting it to farmers, a system which enabled them to distance themselves from the more mundane day-to day farming activities. Lower down were the tenants, who provided the working capital, expertise and business acumen to deal with the variations in yields and prices which occurred in accordance with the weather and the state of the economy. Collectively farmers in turn presided over the lower echelons of the pyramid, consisting of vast numbers of landless labourers who were engaged to work the land and look after the livestock. There were considerable differences not only between one area and another but between one estate and another, in the conditions which prevailed in the countryside and the relationships between these three groups. One of the areas where the class distinction was most pronounced was west Oxfordshire, particularly on the Duke of Marlborough estate. According to James Caird: 'The country exhibits a poverty-stricken and neglected look, and there is no confidence of a friendly or even of a feudal character between land and tenant.'[9]

As there was no statutory regulation of landlord–tenant relations until the final quarter of the 19th century, in those regions which had not developed effective local arrangements tenants could be dismissed without being able to receive any customary compensation. As one witness to the Select Committee on Agricultural Customs explained:

the landlord who lets his farm from year to year... is at liberty at any time to dismiss his tenant; and if there be any misunderstanding... or in any other way offend the landlord, he can be got rid of him, and there is no call upon him for compensation; the landlord can get rid of him with perfect impunity at the end of six months.[10]

Another important factor influencing the prosperity of agriculture was that of soil type. Lighter soils were much more amenable to growing a variety of crops including turnips and clover, which had been instrumental in transforming farming practice during the agricultural revolution of the 18th and early 19th centuries. Conversely it was much more problematic to grow these crops on heavier soils which were difficult and costly to cultivate. Although officially Ascott is located on the map as being a district of 'miscellaneous loams', an area in which no particular or common characteristic can be assigned, it includes all sorts of soils from sand to heavy clay conditions.[11] The surrounding farms, including Church Farm, consisted of slightly heavier soil which placed

Ascott panorama showing position of Crown Farm land.

limitations on the way the farm could be cropped and in turn its profitability. The land having been recently enclosed and reclaimed from woodland, involving the removal of trees and shrubs, the process had exposed infertile and difficult to work patches of subsoil which were distributed in the newly enclosed fields. As a result, the soils were considerably more variable than if the land had not been reclaimed in this way. In addition, being a newly established farm, the traditional customary ties between farmers who had farmed in the area for a long time and their men were considerably less evident than those in other areas. As John Kibble, the working-man historian of north-west Oxfordshire had noted: 'when the forest (of Wychwood) was enclosed it was a sad blow to many who had lived on its borders, for some of them had got a great party of their living, out of the Forest. Burdens of wood for firing, fallen branches and furze were brought and sold to those who could buy. In spring wild bird's eggs helped to make many a nice pudding.'[12] (See map, page vi.)

This gulf between the farmer and his workforce was particularly evident in the case of ambitious, enterprising and aspiring farmers such Robert Hambidge (1827–1892), who had taken over the tenancy of Crown Farm after the deforestation of Wychwood.

ASCOTT-UNDER-WYCHWOOD, OXON,
5 miles from Chipping-Norton, 5 from Burford, and 300 yards from a Railway Station.

UNEXPIRED Term of 23 years, from Michaelmas last, in a good SHEEP and TURNIP FARM; consisting of about 360 Acres of dry healthy Arable and about 30½ of Pasture Land, with a suitable Farm House, and convenient and roomy Homestead.

The Farm lies well together, and the valuable Lease to be disposed of for the remainder of the term, subject to the approval of the Agents of the Crown. The Farm is now in the occupation of Mr. George Yapp, who will furnish particulars, and, on application, shew the farm.

To treat apply to Lyne and Son, land agents, Oddington, Stow-on-the-Wold.

Advertisement for Crown Farm, 1864.

In 1864 he had acquired the outstanding 23-year lease of 390½-acre Crown Farm, following its termination by the previous tenant George Yapp. Born in Icomb, Robert went to school in Stow-on-the-Wold. At the time of the 1851 census, aged 24 he was visiting his older brother George who at the time was farming 200 acres at Guiting Power, near Winchcombe in Gloucestershire. In 1853 Robert appears on the electoral register for the Stow-on-the-Wold district, qualifying by virtue of occupying land at Lower Farm, Icomb as does his brother Leonard, with his father holding the freehold. At the age of about 30 Robert married Rose Hannah Godfrey, a farmer's daughter from the adjoining parish of Great Rissington. By the time of the 1861 Census, he was farming 150 acres at Westcote, near Icomb and employing four labourers and three boys. His eldest son Leonard was also born in Westcote in 1861, so it's likely he had taken over the farm some time prior to 1861. Another son, John Godfrey, was baptised in Westcote in July 1866, by which time Robert and his wife were described as living in 'Ascott, Oxon' and being 'late of Westcote'.

At the time of the move to Ascott, Robert had two sons and a daughter, his third son arriving shortly after the move to Crown Farm. Hambidge was seen as a man of some substance, perhaps as something of a leader in respect of the local farmers.[13] He came from a locally significant extended farming family (his father owned much of his land as opposed to renting it). He was part of the local social set, being a committee member of the local Conservative Association and a church warden, and he rode with the hounds. Under the circumstances he followed the interests of the landowning classes, which he saw as being synonymous with his own. His farm was two to three times the size of the other farms in the village and he employed proportionately more workers than any of the other farmers.

The profitability of his farming was determined by his managerial ability to ensure that crucially important seasonal tasks such as planting, hoeing root crops and harvesting were undertaken as far as possible at the optimum time. Farmers' income varied significantly between one year and the next, out of which they had to pay rent, a variety of local rates and, more importantly, to pay their labour force. There was considerable pressure for farmers to be economical with the labour bill, one of the few items of expenditure over which they had direct influence.

As a tenant of the Crown Estate, Hambidge was less constrained in the way he was allowed to farm than his peers who rented their farms from resident landlords, who tended to more closely monitor the activities of their tenants in the way they were expected to farm and behave. As for the latter, as the Select Committee on Parliamentary and Municipal Elections observed in the late 1860s, the inducement to endorse the landlord's wishes in issues such as voting might frequently proceed rather from the hope of future advantages to be conferred than the fear of injuries to be inflicted.[14] Tenant farmers, despite their enfranchisement and the secret ballot introduced in 1872 (see essay 10), still tended to follow their voting instructions and to support their views in respect of village administration. Although the degree to which the ruling classes were benevolent to their lower orders varied considerably between one estate owner an another, such manifestations of overt kindness were usually the reward for obedience and conformity. Victorian paternalistic benevolence was tinged with a strong sense of condescension and even contempt for what were deemed to be the lower orders.

Tenant farmers were often forced by necessity to accept their position of relative powerlessness in relation to that of their aristocratic estate owner. This was further reinforced by the power structure of village life, landowners and their relatives having multiple occupancy of authoritarian roles not only as employers but as magistrates, councillors and school governors, as well as patronage in terms of, for example, the allocation of the church living.[15] According to John Calvertt, an Oxfordshire farmer who like Hambidge rented his farm from the Crown Estate, the organisation had a very light touch approach (administered by Mr Clutton from the office of the Crown Commissioners of Woods, Forests and Land Revenue in Whitehall Place, London) apart from the very occasional visit, as long as they made their rent payments. When economic conditions deteriorated in the later 1870s the Crown Estate was, according to Calvertt, prepared to be far more generous in the treatment of its leaseholders than Lord Churchill was able to in respect of his tenants. Calvertt and Hambidge having successfully petitioned the Crown Estate,[16] it returned a significant portion of the rents paid, 'to assist me through the depressed seasons'.[17]

Hambidge, having taken the tenancy at a time when agriculture was prosperous and rents relatively high, was also under considerable pressure to farm in acceptance of the prevailing norm. He was also farming at a time when what were once customary rights over common land, woodland

and game were being enshrined in law as property rights favouring landowners. This process was particularly evident in terms of legislation which protected pheasants and partridges, and included ground game, hares and rabbits.

Farmers were under particular pressure to endorse, virtually without question, the landlords' interest in game preservation, which might take precedence over agricultural activities. 'To talk too freely of the injury of game, or in any other way offend the landlord... can be got rid of.'[18] Game preservation, encompassing the management, protection and production of game for shooting, was an increasingly important activity on many estates, particularly those in the southern and eastern counties. Indeed, on the more famed shooting estates, such as Blenheim, game preservation became little short of an obsession which was achieved by prosecution and restricting access to the land, with bailiffs, gamekeepers and watchers being tasked with ensuring that the birds were protected. A high density of game birds on shooting estates was essential for battue or driven shooting where the birds were driven by beaters to the waiting guns. The shoot, particularly in terms of the size of bag, provided the opportunity for landowners to display their propertied wealth and status to their guests.

In order to achieve a high density of game birds it was deemed necessary for gamekeepers to focus their activities on not only controlling but, in reality, making efforts to exterminate, almost indiscriminately, all the feathered and furred species which they considered might pose a threat to pheasants and partridges. Vermin control on shooting estates focused on eliminating weasels, stoats, foxes and hawks, which had helped to keep the rabbit population in check. In respect of birds of prey, hawks, falcons and eagles which had been historically protected at best, or tolerated at worst, were by the mid-18th century now deemed vermin. In the words of the Earl of Wilton, 'A consequence of this wholesale preservation and destruction is that while game is slaughtered in one case (for sport) all other birds are being massacred under the common title of vermin.'[19]

Gamekeepers also protected rabbits from poachers while legislation imposed draconian penalties, including transportation, on those found guilty. The existence of such savage penal legislation is evidence of the strong element of compulsion which underpinned the bonds of deference in rural society.

Game conservation of this magnitude clearly had an adverse impact on agricultural productivity and, in turn, the profitability of the farm. The rabbit population and the damage they caused to growing crops was a particular source of friction. Instances were recorded of crops not only extensively damaged, but in some cases completely destroyed by rabbits.[20] Complaints from tenants almost invariably fell on deaf ears of both the estate owners and the land agents who administered the land on their behalf. It was not until the landmark legislation of the Ground Game Act of 1880 that tenant farmers were finally granted permission to kill rabbits and hares which were damaging their crops. Game preservation was particularly important on the Blenheim estate where as early as the late 18th century the duke's gamekeepers were making extensive use of cooped broody hens to incubate collected pheasants' eggs.[21]

Those farmers who did not complain too openly about the damage caused by game preservation were treated far more sympathetically than those who voiced their concerns. This was a symbiotic relationship; owners who were magnanimous may have thought it inappropriate to increase farm rents by squeezing long-established hard-working tenants who farmed according to their established conventions.

In a similar way during periods of low prices or unfavourable seasons, supportive tenants might be favoured with rent reductions or existing arrears being tolerated. Conversely, such favours might not be extended to those tenants who either deliberately or inadvertently infringed on the patronage of their landlord. Knowing your place in the social hierarchy remained throughout the Victorian period an accepted, deeply entrenched and established convention to which those farmers who did not endorse the community norms risked the wrath of their landlord and being ostracised by their peers. Although perhaps not quite as high up the social ladder as his neighbour Calvertt, both men almost certainly had similar social aspirations, and so Hambidge is likely always to have acted in a manner approved by the establishment, and as befitted what he regarded as his social, political and religious 'station in life'.

Given the demographic revolution which was taking place in the 19th century, population growth ensured that there was an abundant supply of agricultural workers in relation to the relatively fixed demand for their labour. As such agricultural workers were forced to endure low wages, underemployment and widespread poverty, particularly in the more rural areas such as west Oxfordshire, where there was little alternative form of employment. The harsh economics of supply and demand determined that in those areas, where employment opportunities were mainly under the jurisdiction and patronage of farmers, wages were usually barely sufficient for subsistence. As wage costs were one of the few expenses which farmers had control over, it was tempting for them to pay as low a rate as possible. This was particularly evident among those who endorsed the religious view that God had ordained their position in life and that it was a sin to envy others or even for them to try to change their lot in life.

This was evident in the southern part of England, particularly in Oxfordshire where there was a large surplus of labour available for work and few opportunities for the labour force to complement their meagre incomes with non-agricultural work. Agriculture was subject to minimal state intervention, with legislation being confined principally to issues relating to more rigorous regulation of animal diseases and landlord–tenant rights. Such intervention was not however extended to introducing legislation to fix wage levels between masters and their workforce.

In almost all west Oxfordshire parishes in the 19th and early 20th century, one or two landowners owned upwards of half the land in the parish and sometimes one landlord owned most of the land in more than one parish. However, in west Oxfordshire there appears to have been a mix of settlements, some of which are not easy to define. For example, Milton-under-Wychwood did not have a dispersed landownership pattern, but was an open village in character, with a large surplus of labour available for work. Stonesfield, however, was a classic open village. There were very few gentry or grand houses in the village, it had a mixed economy based on agriculture and a slate industry, which meant that labourers were not totally dependent on the land. In consequence it '... seems to have bred an independent spirit, disliking the calling of any man "Sir" except the parson...'[22] Ascott was an open village in that there was no resident lord of the manor but the majority of the village and the land surrounding was owned by Lord Churchill of Cornbury and Wychwood, a relative of the Duke of Marlborough who resided at the nearby Blenheim estate, the latter being famed for its game shooting, an activity which took priority over the interests of farming.

By the 1860s the changing fortunes of agriculture which Lord Ernle had drawn attention to were pressurising farmers to become more efficient, particularly in terms of controlling costs. Despite the abnormally low wages which prevailed for farm workers collectively, labour costs constituted a significant item of farm expenditure. Farmers were also often directed by their landlords, such as the Duke of Marlborough, to hold firm against the fast-rising and newly formed Agricultural Workers' Union, which was considered to be responsible for undermining 'the well-being of this hitherto peaceful and orderly place'.[23]

The strike at Ascott, which began in April 1873, followed a union meeting where it was agreed to demand 14 shillings per week, which Hambidge the principal farmer was willing to concede to his most 'efficient' men, but declined to grant it to them all. On Monday 14 April his men walked out. On the following Monday, 21 April, all the men in village who belonged to the union joined the strike.

Proceedings were formally initiated in the domestic setting of Sarsden rectory on Monday 19 May 1873 where Hambidge made a complaint against 17 women (see essay 1), the walkout having taken place at the crucial time in the farming calendar the middle of barley sowing, when it was essential to complete the task as soon as possible. Late-sown barley, colloquially known as cuckoo barley, planted when the first cuckoo had arrived, yielded considerably less and was of considerably inferior quality to that planted earlier in the spring. Moreover, it was reported that Hambidge still had 500 sheep being folded on roots, land which still needed to be cleared, prior to being ploughed and planted with barley if time allowed. Hambidge had 12 agricultural horses, four working bullocks, milking cows, bullocks and young livestock, and only a head shepherd and a youth (who were on weekly contracts) to help him.[24] Whether or not the walkout by the labour force had been deliberately undertaken to coincide with the spring labour peak remains a moot point – it is however evident as Alun Howkins' analysis has shown that in a labour market in which the supply of labour was usually more than equal to demand it was only at specific and limited periods of the year, such as the need for hoeing to take or for crops to planted or harvested, that the worker had a temporary advantage in wage negotiations.[25]

The magistrates' fears of social disruption reflected the views of the farmers, who became increasingly vocal in response to the outcry on the women's behalf. A letter (see appendix A) from the parochial officers and tenant farmers of Ascott, including Hambidge, written on 30 May and published on the day of the Hyde Park demonstration (see appendix B),[26] set out the narrative of the dispute, but also described the state of the village, where those known to be opposed to the union 'from the highest to the lowest' were heckled in the street. They believed the strike was only sustained by this collective social pressure, and denounced the 'outrageous and unseemly conduct of women, the wives and daughters of Unionist labourers, the major part being the exceptional females of the place' – 'exceptional' being an ill-disguised, offensive public slur. Meanwhile, Mrs Hambidge was described as 'a kind and sympathetic friend in the time of sorrow, sickness, and need'. Hambidge denied that he sought to destroy the union, and asserted that he was on good terms with his men (recalling 'a cheerful, contented countenance' and the hearty 'Good night, master; thank you kindly'), despite acknowledging that until recently he had been a paying a pittance of 9 shillings per week.

The magistrates asked Hambidge not to proceed with the prosecution, but he refused. Magistrate Carter then took alarm at the prospect of having to impose a sentence of imprisonment. He appealed directly to Hambidge not to press the case 'as it was a most painful affair', given the number of the women and the fact of two of them having babies, and that the afternoon's proceedings were sufficient warning as to their future conduct. Hambidge insisted, stating that 'I am not able to get any one to work', presumably because of the intimidation.[27] After what was described as a lengthy consultation between the two magistrates, Harris 'announced that the case had been clearly proved against the defendants' and the sentences were given out, those 'who appeared to be the ringleaders' receiving the longer periods. **It was Hambidge's insistence on pursuing the case which resulted in the women being imprisoned.**

Conclusion

With the benefit of hindsight, and now living in considerably more enlightened times, the imprisonment of the 16 women appears a vindictive response by Hambidge, whose insistence on proceeding with the prosecution set in train what is now widely recognised as a complete miscarriage of justice and abuse of the legal system. While not trying in any way to exonerate farmers in general and Hambidge in particular from the deplorable way they treated farm labourers in the Victorian period, it is nevertheless important to appreciate that they were not the only possible villains. Their responses were severely constrained by the prevailing structure of rural society and their subordinate position in a rigidly differentiated occupational hierarchy which was committed to a free trade, free enterprise system.

How far Hambidge's action reflected his personal views in deciding to prosecute the Ascott Martyrs or was simply indicative of what the local agricultural interest, consisting of estate owners and tenant farmers, expected of him remains an unresolved issue. It is important to note that Lord Churchill is reported to have organised tenant farmers to hold firm against the fast rising and newly formed National Agricultural Workers' Union. Under the circumstances, it is highly likely that Robert Hambidge would have been encouraged by his peers to endorse this approach. While not necessarily exonerating him, it is evident that there were at least mitigating circumstances which should be taken into account when evaluating his actions.

5

All things bright and beautiful? Church and chapel in the Wychwoods

JOHN BENNETT

> The rich man in his castle,
> The poor man at his gate,
> God made them, high or lowly,
> And ordered their estate.
>> Cecil Frances Alexander, 1848[1]

> The labourer is as respectable as the farmer, because
> God made him, and to trample upon the labourer is
> to trample upon God's property.
>
>> Joseph Arch, July 1873[2]

The verse above, from the popular hymn 'All Things Bright and Beautiful', illustrates a still rarely contested world view in mid-19th century England. It encapsulates the establishment view of the divinely ordained relationship between the agricultural labourer ('the poor man') and the landowner ('the rich man') at the time of the Ascott Martyrs' story. The second quote, from a speech given in Milton-under-Wychwood by

Joseph Arch, illustrates the challenge to this world view by the champion of the agricultural labourer and sometime Primitive Methodist preacher – but a challenge still citing a Christian God in support of his cause.

This essay considers the relationship between landowners, farmers, agricultural labourers and their shared God in the Wychwoods area at the time of the Ascott Martyrs' story. Central to this is the question often asked of the relationship between the agricultural worker and Christian church in all its forms – how far did the ethos and authority of those institutions hinder or support the workers' plight?

In the Oxford Prison charge sheet (see pages 22–3 and 162), each of the jailed women gives their religion. Eight identified as Church of England, seven as Baptists, and one as Methodist. These bald facts show that half of the women declared an allegiance with the established Church and half identified as belonging to one of the common Nonconformist denominations in the Wychwoods area. This division is broadly in line with national estimates for the religious divide in mid-19th century England.[3] Of course, the selection of a religious allegiance on a charge sheet may not be entirely reflective of actual affiliation. Having been convicted by clerical magistrates from the Anglican Church, the Ascott women might be inclined to favour an identification with the established church in the hope of more lenient treatment from those in such positions of power. We also know that religious affiliation was, even in the 1870s, a more fluid affair than a box-ticking exercise on a charge sheet might suggest.[4]

Other than this we know nothing about the personal

spiritual lives of these 16 women. However, we can build some picture of the role of religious institutions in rural lives of the working classes in rural Oxfordshire and the Wychwoods in particular. It is also possible to look at the attitudes of the various religious denominations towards the worker. These two themes will form the main content of this study, alongside a particular consideration of the significance of Nonconformism for the birth and growth of the NALU in the Wychwoods area. For the purposes of this essay the geographical area under consideration comprises the three Wychwood villages, Shipton, Milton and Ascott, and the other local townships within their hinterland.

The Church of England

The Church of England, as the established church, had a long-held hegemony in the religious, social and political lives of the English citizenry. However, it was having to cope with significant challenges to that position throughout the 19th century, and was also having to contend for membership with the rapid growth of a number of Nonconformist Christian sects who were now able to operate in a much more liberal religious environment. This challenge is visible in the religious life of the Wychwoods from the early years of the 19th century.

St Mary the Virgin, Shipton-under-Wychwood (Figure 1), was the historic mother church of the area, once forming the centre of an ecclesiastical and administrative parish comprising the townships of Ascott-under-Wych-wood,[5] Milton-under-Wychwood, Lyneham, Leafield, Langley and Ramsden. However, by the mid-19th century these townships had begun to achieve some independent parochial status.

Figure 1: View of Shipton-under-Wychwood in a photograph of the early 1900s showing the parish church, St Mary the Virgin.

Besides St Mary's in Shipton, there were a number of historic parish churches within the region with deep social and religious roots. Ascott had Holy Trinity, dating back to the 12th century (Figure 2); Leafield had an old Church of England chapel dateable back to the 15th century;[6] and Fifield had the medieval church of John the Baptist dating back at least to the 14th century. There were other historic parish churches in nearby Chadlington, Fulbrook and Burford. However, from the later 18th century and into the 19th century, a steep rise in population in rural Oxfordshire was putting pressure on parishes to increase their provision of church accommodation. For the Church of England the situation was made more urgent by the growth of Nonconformist groups, who were making particular inroads in areas where there was no parish church, or the parish church was

Figure 2: Holy Trinity, Ascott-under-Wychwood, in a photograph from the early 1900s.

remote. Shipton parish encompassed a number of such areas.

The government had also recognised this need for increased church accommodation and the Church Building Act of 1818 established the Church Building Commission with a budget of one million pounds to build new churches particularly in growing urban areas. The budget was increased by another half a million pounds in 1828.[7] This programme increased provision in the growing urban areas from the 1820s to 1850s. In rural areas there was a continued expectation that the lay community would provide additional accommodation. In Oxfordshire it was often the rural gentry who stepped in to fill this void.

The squire of Sarsden, James Haughton Langston (1796–1863), was a key local benefactor. Langston (Figure 3) inherited considerable wealth from his father along

**Figure 3: Portrait of James Haughton Langston MP
(1796–1863), squire of Sarsden Estate and
important local benefactor.**

with the Sarsden estate and increased his land holdings
to include extensive acreages in Churchill, Lyneham,
Milton-under-Wychwood and Chadlington. He was by all
accounts a progressive and beneficent local estate manager
and farmer.[8] He instigated and fully-funded the build of
All Saints, a brand new parish church in nearby Churchill
in 1825–27. He provided land and largely funded the build
of SS Simon and Jude (Figure 4) and adjoining school and
schoolmaster's house in Milton-under-Wychwood in
1853–54. He had also offered to build and endow a new
church for Lyneham around 1850, but this was vetoed by
the vicar of Shipton;[9] however, Langston provided a new
school room in Lyneham in 1862, which was also licensed

to hold regular Church of England services.[10] Langston was a popular local squire. There was even a plan to erect a statue of him on the recreation ground in Milton, but Langston objected to this: 'It would be only for the boys to throw stones at the old Squire.' The money raised, was put towards the provision of a new water supply to Milton village.[11]

Other significant new churches were provided or subsidised by other local landowners. The land for the building in 1841 of the church of Holy Trinity in nearby Finstock was donated by Francis Almeric Churchill (1779–1845), the first Baron Churchill, built just one year

Figure 4: Church of SS Simon and Jude, Milton-under-Wychwood, 1853–54, funded by James Haughton Langston. Fanny Honeybone is buried here with her husband. She had specified as Baptist on the charge sheet.

after the Finstock Methodist Chapel had opened. The old chapel in Leafield was demolished and supplanted by St Michael and All Angels in 1859–60, the stone provided by Francis George Spencer (1802–1886), the second Baron Churchill, while the build costs were covered by the Crown. A new parish church was built in Ramsden in 1841–42; this was again replaced in 1853–54 with the building of St James, largely funded by the incumbent, Robert Lowbridge Baker, and other local benefactors, the builder being Groves of Milton.[12] All these churches are still in use.

Thus, by the 1870s the Wychwoods area was well provisioned with Anglican churches, both old and new. The Church of England as the established church of course had distinct advantages in terms of longevity, status and resources that were not available to the non-established Nonconformist sects. But by the mid-19th century various Nonconformist missions had made significant inroads into the Wychwoods area, especially those peripheral to the location of the parish church in Shipton. The build of new Anglican churches was one response to this challenge, but both sides had to up their game to win and keep their congregations.

While the Anglican Church might be perceived as in league with the landowners and the build of brand-new churches can be seen as a countermeasure to the Nonconformists, it does not mean to say that they were insensitive to the plight of the agricultural labourer. The clergy sat on Poor Law Unions, on boards of guardians for workhouses, and administering to the poor in other, more informal ways. A local example of church charity occurs in 1871: 'the Rev. R. Tweed, the Incumbent of Ascott, has, with his usual kindness and liberality, presented 4 cwts of coal to each of the poor families living in the village.'[13] This kind of *ad hoc* charity was not unusual; however, the donation was probably to those unable to work through disability and infirmity rather than to the underpaid agricultural labourer.

The Church of England would have been a significant presence in the lives of the Ascott Martyrs, whether they were regular attendees or not, because of its administrative, religious and political control within the parish. Essay 8, on the clerical magistrates, offers a further illustration of the church's continuing religious and judicial authority. The Church of England still had a virtual monopoly on the sacraments and rites including births, marriages and deaths. We know that all the Ascott Martyrs were baptised in the Church of England, despite what other congregations they may have joined in later life. Most of the Ascott Martyrs who remained in the area were buried in Church of England graveyards.

The Ascott Martyrs, as already noted, had identified as eight Church of England, seven Baptist and one Methodist. The choice of a religious denomination was not necessarily an 'either/or' option; parishioners were often to be seen at the church in the morning and chapel in the evening.[14] The church's aim was to provide a seat for every parishioner, though this was a constant battle against a rapidly growing population. The Anglican Church did have 'establishment' and history on their side; the familiarity of the old parish church with its accompanying graveyard where villagers could find their relatives buried was a symbol of stability, continuity, patrimony and identity – a strong idea in the minds of all parishioners. No wonder that new parish churches were invariably built in a neo-gothic style: the style embodied these notions.[15]

The rapid growth of Nonconformist churches, however, now meant that the Church of England had to compete for attendees. A key strategy in winning over hearts and minds was the provision of Sunday school education, and in particular the Sunday school treat. Newspapers of the period feature frequent reports on Sunday school events by all denominations. The following report of an event in Shipton in 1869 gives a flavour of such occasions:

> On Thursday 29th ult., a most liberal treat was given to the children both of the Sunday and Day School on the lawn in front of the vicarage. At 3 o'clock the children with their teachers, numbering 200, assembled and amused themselves until four, when a most sumptuous repast was served to them by their teachers and other ladies of the village... they then proceeded to the amusements provided for them, such as racing, cricketing, jingling, Aunt Sally, and with various other games for the females, which was heartily enjoyed by all present.[16]

In the 1870s the vicar of Ascott complained that the Shipton farmer John Fowler Maddox, a committed Baptist, was 'bribing' local children to attend the Baptist Sunday School rather than the Anglican one.[17] It seems that both sides were not above providing 'incentives' to their parishioners.

It is also important to note that despite the Anglican Church's identification with the gentry, some ministers

Figure 5: Baptist Chapel Milton, erected 1839 (front porch added 20th century). The Baptists were the most successful of the Nonconformist groups in the Wychwoods, Milton being the most important of their local chapels.

were more proactive in wanting to alleviate the plight of the farm worker. The renowned cleric Edward Girdlestone (1805–1884) was one such example. He became known as 'The Agricultural Labourer's Friend' when he took up a curacy in the parish of Halberton, Devon in 1862, and was moved to action when he witnessed the impoverished state of the farm labourers there. He proposed the formation of an agricultural labourers union as early as 1868, while he also helped over 600 agricultural families to move from the west of England to secure more lucrative work in the industrial areas of the north.[18] However, he was the exception rather than the rule.

Nonconformists in the Wychwoods: the Baptists

There had been large growth of the so-called new Dissent from the early 19th century despite the frequent hostile opposition from local squires and the established Church. In the Wychwoods and wider area there could be found Quakers, Baptists, Wesleyan Methodists, Primitive Methodists, Congregationalists and Plymouth Brethren. However, the two sects most visible in the Wychwoods were the Baptists and the Primitive Methodists.

A flourishing Baptist community existed in the Wychwoods and wider region by the mid-19th century. The Baptists first found a foothold in Milton in the very early years of the 19th century and built their first chapel there in 1808.[19] They were patronised by the important Milton family of Groves (Figure 8), who were successful masons, quarry owners and builders, and were already well established in Milton from the early 18th century.[20] The

Figure 6: Interior of the Zoar Baptist Chapel, The Terrace, Milton, built 1841/1883. The modest interiors and exteriors of the Nonconformist chapels were a marked contrast to the more ornate architectural grandeur of the Anglican churches.

Figure 7: Ascott Baptist Chapel, built circa 1812. Seven of the Ascott Martyrs identified themselves as Baptists.

Groves' connection was important, bringing influence, money and respectability to the Baptist cause.[21] There was additionally a Particular Baptist congregation in Milton, established in the 1840s and well attended into the 20th century (Figure 6). Their presence is a further illustration of how fertile this area was for the establishment of Nonconformist congregations, Milton being able to support two Baptist chapels and a Primitive Methodist chapel by the mid-19th century, the population in 1851 being 800 persons.

The Milton Baptists rebuilt their chapel in 1839 (Figure 7), and in 1867 they had resources to add a substantial school room next to the chapel. It should be recalled that before 1853 there was no Church of England presence in the village, which now exceeded the size of Shipton in population. The Baptist cause spread to neighbouring villages though Milton remained the hub of local organisation throughout the 19th century.

A Baptist chapel in Ascott was apparently first built in 1812 (Figure 7).[22] The 1851 religious census return for this chapel reports free sittings of 100 and an average congregation of 25.[23] However, the congregation faltered in the 1850s but reopened and revived in 1862 with the Scottish tailor William Irvine as the resident minister.[24] The Bishop of Oxford, Samuel Wilberforce, writing of Ascott in 1855 described them as a 'rough impressible set',[25] suggesting disapproval of a tendency to Dissent.

The Shipton Baptist chapel was opened in 1861, the build financed by the local farmer and Baptist John Fowler Maddox (1824–1920), who we have already seen bribing children to attend the Ascott Baptist Chapel.

Maddox had considerable status in the Wychwoods,[26] but though a Baptist he was also a farmer and a member of the Oxfordshire Association of Agriculturalists which had been expressly formed to challenge the Agricultural Labourers' Union. At a meeting of the Association in July 1872 he is reported to have said:

All who joined the union from his farm had been discharged, and he was determined that so long as he supplied the money to pay those he employed, he should be the master. The farmers must admit that to an extent

Figure 8: A Groves family wedding group in front of the Milton Baptist Chapel in 1910. The photograph illustrates the continuing association of the Groves family with the Baptists. The Groves family continued to make a significant trading contribution to the community, as they still do.

the labourers had been paid at a somewhat low rate. He had plenty of work for the men he employed, and he should always pay them well, and endeavour to maintain the good feelings which ought to exist between master and men. Rather than employ union men, he would permit every acre of turnips on his lands to remain untouched.[27]

Maddox had influence in Shipton, and one suspects he would not tolerate the local Baptists, whose chapel he had paid for, agitating on behalf of the union, though he does betray some sympathy for the depressed state of wages. The build of the chapel was no doubt an act of philanthropy, but intended more as an agency of temperance, stability and spiritual welfare than of revolution.

The Baptists associated with the chapels in Ascott, Shipton and Milton were, despite some early hostility, generally respectable Christian congregations within these villages. The evidence of their patronage by the local Groves family (Figure 8), and by farmers such as J. F. Maddox and other tradespeople gave them respectability and sufficient means to play a beneficent role within the parish, providing resource for the spiritual, moral and educational welfare to all classes within the community. The identification of seven of the Ascott women with the Baptists also demonstrates their success in finding adherents among the agricultural workers.

By the 1860s the Baptists were also tolerated, if not directly supported, by the local gentry. Their main asset in this regard was the charismatic Baptist preacher Charles Haddon Spurgeon (1834–1892) (Figure 9). C. H. Spurgeon was something of a national celebrity in the 1860s and 1870s. His audiences often numbered in the thousands,

Figure 9: Charles Haddon Spurgeon, the charismatic Baptist preacher who preached nearby at Minster Lovell.

and Queen Victoria is said to have gone incognito to hear him preach. He travelled widely to speak and preach, and his influence was felt in the Wychwoods area. He also held a number of outdoor services in Minster Lovell, just five miles from Ascott, in the 1870s. The *Oxfordshire Weekly News* for 19 June 1872 advertises two sermons by Charles Spurgeon to be delivered at Ringwood Farm, Minster Lovell; tickets were 1 shilling each, a half day's pay for an agricultural labourer.[28] The local farmer and diarist John Calvertt also records several encounters with Charles Spurgeon; in 1877 he records in his diary having 'heard Spurgeon preach to about 3000 persons under the Oaks at Ringwood'.[29]

Spurgeon did express sympathy for the agricultural workers' cause. A press report from April 1872 records: 'Mr Spurgeon referred with satisfaction to the strike of the agricultural labourers as an unexpected sign of life amongst a long-neglected class.'[30] But there is no evidence for Spurgeon extending this support beyond occasional pronouncements from the pulpit.

The Nonconformists in the Wychwoods: the Primitive Methodists

The meteoric rise of the Primitive Methodists from their foundation around 1810 to the mid-19th century is a remarkable story. Their spread and influence throughout Britain by the 1870s put them on an equal footing to many of the other Nonconformist denominations with much longer histories. They began as a secession from the Wesleyan Methodists in north Staffordshire, adopting the name 'Primitive Methodism' as an expression of their

Figure 10: The former Primitive Methodist Chapel, Milton, 1860, now a private residence, was once a nucleus of NALU activity in the Wychwoods.

desire to return to what they saw as the more authentic evangelical roots of John Wesley's early missions. They spread their word via a network of travelling preachers and tended to target working class communities. In Britain the Primitive Methodists joined with the Wesleyan and United Methodists in 1932 to form the Methodist Church.

The Primitive Methodists had begun to establish congregations in Oxfordshire from the 1820s and had a flourishing circuit in existence covering the Wychwood area by the mid-19th century. They were established in Milton by the 1830s, having built their first chapel in 1834.[31] The 1851 religious census records an average morning congregation of 110.[32] They had built their second, presumably larger, chapel in 1860 (Figure 10) in a significant location facing the extensive village green.

The Primitive Methodist Chapel in Milton was sited in a prominent location facing the village green. Though there was no Primitive Methodist chapel in Shipton or Ascott, there were a number of other chapels in the area with circuits covering Chipping Norton and Witney. The Charlbury stonemason and amateur chronicler of local history John Kibble (1866–1951), writes:

Primitive Methodism got a strong footing at Milton. A chapel was built [1834] and glorious camp meetings were held upon the Green. The late Mr Isaac Castle was a tower of strength. His tent was a feature for all good work, both religious and temperance, and he built a house with a room for a coffee tavern, so that there should be somewhere besides the public house as a place of call and refreshment.[33]

Kibble's words highlight the appeal of the Primitive Methodists, and the name of Isaac Castle reveals a connection between the Primitive Methodists and the NALU.

The 'camp meetings' were mass outdoor preaching events which could last all day. While ostensibly being an opportunity for Christian evangelism, they were also popular social events accessible to all within the local area, and a powerful recruitment opportunity. The provision of food, music, singing and charismatic sermons would have made them lively social events, with sometimes thousands of people in attendance; camp meetings are known to have taken place in Milton and other local villages.[34]

There are no Primitive Methodist chapels recorded for Ascott and Shipton; however, the proximity of the Milton chapel made the denomination accessible to these villages, and the camp meetings enabled the Primitive Methodists' voice to extend widely in the local area, without the need for bricks and mortar chapels. While we have no evidence to know that the Ascott Martyrs attended these camp meetings, it is more than likely that they were familiar with such events.[35]

A significant feature of the Nonconformist chapels, of all denominations, is that their organisation and management, and even the building and maintenance

Figure 11: Photograph of Annie Arch.

of their buildings, was largely supplied from their own congregations. This connection with the local community made them more accessible to the labouring class and gave these members the opportunity to participate in the administration and delivery of their religion, and, through its Sunday school, its key educational role.[36]

The Primitives were also not averse to using female preachers. In about 1870 Joseph Arch's own daughter, Annie (1851–1904), became a Primitive Methodist preacher on the Leamington circuit when she was 19 years old.[37] To see their sex in such a position of trust and authority alongside their male counterparts must have given confidence to the women of the Wychwoods (Figure 11).

The name of Isaac Castle (1824–1891) also connects us to the NALU. He was a signatory on the deeds of the Milton Primitive Methodist chapel, and we also find his name as a regular committee member in the minute book of the NALU during the 1870s.[38] He appears to have begun working life as an agricultural labourer but by the 1870s is described as a 'wood dealer' with property interests in the area. He was well known as promoter of Primitive Methodism, temperance and the Agricultural Labourers' Union. His marquee was available to all three for the promotion of their cause and was also certainly used for meetings promoting emigration opportunities to the agricultural workers of the Wychwoods (see essay 9, which deals with emigration). There is a plaque to Isaac Castle's memory inside the Milton Primitive Methodist Chapel.

The link between membership of the Primitive Methodist church and membership of the NALU is well known.[39] Joseph Arch was himself a Primitive Methodist lay preacher, and many of the key leaders in the early NALU such as Joseph Leggett, Christopher Holloway and George Banbury all had key roles in their respective Methodist and Primitive Methodist churches. An explicit connection between the early formation of the Union and the Milton chapel is recorded in the Oxford District minute book for 7 May 1872, where the secretary was ordered '...to request of the Trustees and Minister, the use of the Primitive Methodist Chapel Milton for the purpose of holding a Meeting of delegates from the Branches, such Meeting to be held when Mr. Arch or other Friends shall be among us...'[40] This is despite the fact that the rules of Primitive Methodist chapels expressly forbade the use of chapels for political purposes.[41]

The evangelical flavour of many of the union meetings, which were often accompanied by bands and the singing of Union songs,[42] is another indicator of the allegiance between the Primitive Methodists and the Union. In her preface to Arch's autobiography, of 1898, the Countess of Warwick quotes an anonymous source:

> Another thing that appealed to the imagination was the extent to which the meetings of the strikers were inspired by song. The hymn tunes were easily linked to the verses in which the labourers expressed their hopes, and embodied their demands. The industrial revolt had in it some of the elements of a religious revival, and one of the most conspicuous of these was the resort to singing as a relief of emotions otherwise too difficult to articulate.[43]

Press reports of these meetings often comment on the number of women and children present.[44] It is almost certain that the 16 Ascott women must have seen Arch speaking at one of the meetings he attended in the Wychwood area, reportedly attended by thousands, even before their release from prison. His name was a big draw.

Arch's speeches often included an appeal to the gospels and a Christian morality in support of the labourers' cause, as evidenced by the quote at the head of this essay. He was often referred to as 'the apostle of the labourers' movement'.[45]

A number of early mass rallies for the promotion of the NALU and establishment of Oxfordshire branches took place in the Wychwoods area. Large meetings of agricultural labourers took place on the Milton recreation ground in 1872, which led to the formation of what became known as the Milton Union, soon after becoming the nucleus of the Oxfordshire District branch of the NALU.[46] It seems that the organisational structures of the Methodists in general and the Primitive Methodists in particular provided a ready-made 'infrastructure' upon which the NALU could piggyback for the building of the Union. The hierarchical networks of branch, district and region were duplicated within both organisations.[47] When the NALU spread into the Gloucestershire district of Cirencester, the local branches all coincided with the location of an already existing Primitive Methodist chapel.[48]

We know that the Primitive Methodists targeted the poorer classes of society, and their core membership was undoubtedly working class. However, they also relied on some of the more professional members of their communities to help set up congregations in agricultural areas, to help with the administrative and organisational skills required to purchase land, build chapels and establish trusteeships for the sustaining of these chapels.

Summary

The religious institutions in the Wychwoods area provided a mixed set of Christian offerings to the agricultural labourer and their families in the 1870s. The principal denominations – the Church of England, the Baptists and the Primitive Methodists – were all familiar institutions by the 1870s. The Baptists and the Primitive Methodists had established chapels in the local villages at least from the 1830s and the Ascott Martyrs and their families who attended these chapels in the 1870s would have been second- or third-generation worshippers. The Church of England, in the face of this competition, had increased its provision and had raised its game in the preceding decades. Through its inherited wealth and through its establishment connections, and with the explicit support of benevolent landowners, it had built architecturally ambitious new parish churches in the area. While the incumbents of these churches were often of the same class as the local landowners, they were not always indifferent to the plight of the poorer classes in their parish and needed to fill these new pews. There was undoubtedly a tug of war to win over souls.

The Anglican Church represented the political interests of its incumbents from the bishop and vicar and downwards, and their officers were of the same class as the landed gentry. The Nonconformists, their preachers and their congregations were much closer to the agricultural worker, and their officials were often drawn from this class because they represented the interest of the congregation, often voting on who would be their ministers. However, while the Baptists could express sympathy for the downtrodden worker they never, at this period, espoused radical political reform in terms of promoting unionism or extension of the franchise. Indeed, some of their officials, such as John Fowler Maddox, actively worked against it. The Primitive Methodists were more overtly aligned with the agricultural worker and provided many of the 'determined and lively minded men of independent and radical spirit' who promoted and led the Oxfordshire branch of the NALU. Without the support of the Primitive Methodists the Agricultural Union would not have been established so rapidly.

For the Ascott women, the chapel, Baptist or Methodist, would have given them more opportunity for involvement in chapel affairs. In some of the Primitive Methodist chapels and at the popular camp meetings they would have also seen and heard women preachers, thus seeing their sex given a voice and mission beyond the domestic. Whatever their religious commitment and denomination, nominal or real, they were part of a religious society where the Anglican Church was attempting to reassert its control in the face of the advance of dissent and Nonconformity. The courage the women found to support their striking menfolk must have been, at least in part, kindled by the self-reliance and confidence they discovered in their dissenting chapels, their resolve further strengthened by the compelling oratory of charismatic union men, and sometime Nonconformist preachers, such as Joseph Arch.

6

Rural society in the 1870s: poverty, injustice, ignorance and inequality

BRIAN COX

> ...the plight of the Victorian agricultural labourer: low wages, poor food and inferior cottage accommodation.
>
> Reginald Groves, *Sharpen the Sickle*[1]

> The majority of the cottages that exist in rural parishes are deficient in every requisite that should constitute a home for a Christian family in a civilised community.
>
> The Rev. James Fraser, member of the Royal Commission on the Employment of Children, Young Persons and Women in Agriculture, 1867-9[2]

During the latter part of the 19th century, English agricultural society in Oxfordshire was polarised between the 'haves' and the 'have nots', although there were nuanced relationships between the extremes. Families of agricultural labourers, living barely above

Evicted cottagers.

subsistence level, were the 'have nots'. The men of such families were battered by the changing fortune of the availability of agricultural work; women either helped in the fields at harvest time or were in engaged in 'cottage industries' (see essay 3). Although the children of the family had access to education, the needs of the family often meant they did not attend school but helped in the fields. This essay explores the plight of the labourer and shows that the conditions under which the agricultural labourers lived were perceived by them as becoming intolerable and without hope.

The changing nature of land use and the growth of tenant farmers reduced security of tenure for labourers. This detrimentally affected the relationship between labourer, landowner and farmer. The historian J. V. Beckett describes the earlier long-standing stability that was the hallmark of the English aristocracy being based in the countryside, and cites James Caird, a 19th-century commentator writing about the national picture, as saying 'the landowner is necessarily concerned in the general prosperity and good management of his estate, and the welfare of those who live upon it with which he is so closely involved'. Caird added that this welfare meant that 'from his [aristocratic] class the magistrates, the management of the roads, public buildings and charitable institutions' were selected, as well as influencing 'the church, the school, the farm and the cottage'.[3] Beckett comments that, in contrast to the challenge that was experienced by their continental counterparts, all parts of English society accepted the *status quo*.[4] He continued that 'as a general rule, the landowners of Oxfordshire interest themselves very little in agriculture. Few of them are practically engaged with farming.'[5] This lack of interest and the growth of tenant farmers became one of the factors that started to undermine earlier stability in Oxfordshire and resulted in neglect of those whose living was dependent on the land. Poverty and insecurity increased. Once the economics of falling profits began to bite, farmers and landowners hired labourers only for short periods of time and often did not supply free accommodation, meaning that settled, trusting relationships were not established. Pamela Horn summed up the plight of the Victorian agricultural labourer: 'low wages, poor food and inferior cottage accommodation were the only rewards for long days spent in continuous toil.'[6]

Regarding the work of women in rural Oxfordshire, the 16 women convicted following the Ascott incident were a mix of labourers, helping on farms, and workers in the glove industry. Wychwood Royal Forest in west

Oxfordshire ran west from the town of Woodstock, and later, particularly in Charlbury, was one of only three areas outside London producing gloves. This area was known for its finer work and ornamental gloves for the aristocracy, as well as large contracts for military gloves.[7] Again economic depression caused by cheaper imports brought about distress to workers in the industry from time to time.

The plight of the poor was nothing new. During a debate on the Corn Laws in the House of Commons on 17 February 1819, Sir Robert Wilson expressed exasperation that the 'agriculturalists' in the country sought continually to prevent the imports of cheap grain and added that 'they do not know or will not consider the temper and condition of the labouring classes'. He further upbraided the landowners by adding,

> What claims have the Agriculturalists to this special favour from the House at the expense of the labouring classes? [...] do they not still confine them to insufficient wages, which they are obliged to eke out with scant subsistence and parish relief?[8]

This statement from some 50 years before the Ascott events brings home that those agricultural labourers were both hard pressed by poverty and seen by some as the victims of those seeking to make a profit from the land. This situation did not improve over the intervening years and life remained hard for the labourers. This raises the question: who was responsible for the welfare of the labourer?

Barry Reay, who has written on the risings of agricultural labourers, points out that they 'were essentially a socially static group... most were condemned to the same life as their parents.'[9] His use of the word 'condemned' is telling. The prospects for improvement in life were grim. Reay writes, 'There is a tendency in some studies of rural life to gloss over tensions and conflict and emphasise social harmony.' In the following decades, tensions continued to grow between concerns over the plight of the agricultural labourer and efforts to maintain the *status quo*. Some even gave the wider public a misleadingly positive view of rural life. For example George Wallis, a landowner in Oxfordshire, writing in the same year as the Ascott incident to Hugh Hammersley (chair of the Oxfordshire quarter sessions) about the rise of the National Agricultural Labourers' Union (NALU) stated, 'I cannot doubt that you will feel with us great regret that the good feeling which has, till last year, existed between farmers and their labourers should be so thoroughly swept away by outside agitators.'[10] In England, farmers and landowners generally had a good relationship whereas farmers and labourers had been growing steadily apart.[11]

It can be argued that there was a great deal of 'unresolved ideological and social conflict'[12] in the minds of the farmers and labourers in Oxfordshire at the local level. Labourers knew that conditions were unlikely to improve if their ability to influence them remained ineffectual. In this time of social and economic change, they were unrepresented. It is ironic, however, that it was the Union that attempted to manage that change non-violently through support, protection and negotiation on behalf of the labourer.

The use of machinery to replace labour is a subject that is often mentioned as being a cause of rural poverty and unrest, as in the Swing Riots of the 1830s. However,

Gordon Mingay challenges this link. He writes that 'There was... relatively little concern with raising the productivity of labour. Labour was cheap and plentiful, while effective factory-made machines were not available until well into the nineteenth century.' He adds that as late as 1870 as much as three quarters of the corn harvest was still cut by hand. Thus, although there may have been a growing concern by the labourers as to the negative effect of mechanisation on their livelihood, the real danger lay in the farmers' expectation of paying cheaply for labour and disposing of it almost on a daily basis. The expected security of tenure had been lost.[13] This reliance on disposable, cheap labour also contributed to the poverty of the Oxfordshire labourer.

A significant hardship experienced by labourers related to their living conditions. The Rev. James Fraser, a member of the Royal Commission on the Employment of Children, Young Persons and Women in Agriculture in 1867–69, reported that only two parishes out of 300 had acceptable cottages in terms of quality and quantity (see the quote at the start of this essay).[14] Similarly, Canon Girdlestone wrote in 1863 of North Devon labourers 'getting no pay at all when sick or injured and living in cottages not fit to house pigs in'.[15] However, when he tried to get the farmers to improve the labourers' lot, they refused.

Labourers also had aspirations to own land for producing their own food and livestock. Nigel Scotland reports on the early speeches of Joseph Arch 'put the blame for the depressed state of agriculture on the land laws that allowed wealthy families to monopolise large tracts of land without any commitment to cultivate

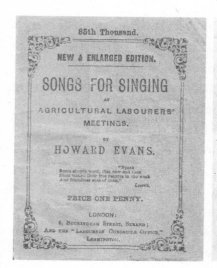

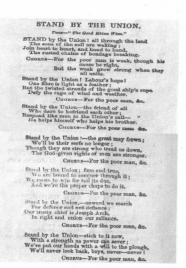

Song book and 'Union' song.

them'. Arch maintained that labourers should be given the right to own and cultivate their own land.[16] The demand for land was not new. What was new was the manifesto of the recently formed NALU. So although the plight of the labourers had been seen at various times, no effective action had been taken by those in power to rectify the problems of labourers' poverty, representation, housing, employment and security. In contrast, the NALU took up the labourers' cause.

Although some landlords and farmers were sympathetic to the demands of labourers, many were not. The demands of the NALU were not seen as legitimate by landowners or farmers and were met with suspicion and distrust. The farmers in Oxfordshire created the Farmers' Defence Association once union-organised protests and strikes started.[17] The establishment reacted to maintain the *status quo*. The Duke of Marlborough wrote in August 1872 in a letter to *Jackson's Oxford Journal* stating that 'there will be one consequence... gained by bitter experience by the labourer, that he has quarrelled with his best friend and followed a mischievous agitation in the hopes of bettering his condition'.[18] Conversely, publishing the Union viewpoint, the *Bee-Hive* journal believed that the establishment held that 'the working classes are not fully incorporated into the nation as part of society'.[19] In Oxfordshire, the establishment was not just the aristocracy, landowners and farmers but also included many Anglican clergy. An example of the clergy supporting the establishment and casting suspicion on the union is seen in an emotive letter to the *Jackson's Oxford Journal*, written by a local clergyman, and referring to 'the [union] agitators – the harpies, that have preyed on the pockets of the poor' and added that the farmers have had the victory, by forming their own union, and 'that now there is such a complete collapse of the Agricultural Labourers' Union'.[20] The reported collapse, at the date of the letter, was not true.

There were attempts to give relief to those living in poverty, but often this responsibility, designed at the national level, was exercised locally by those with wealth and status. Money was raised through local taxes and because the poverty was often extreme, those charged with local administration of relief were concerned about the potential for (what they saw as) excessive local taxation. The main methods of relief were various systems of 'poor law'; the effectiveness of this relief has been a matter of historical debate. The Old Poor Law and the New Poor Law could both be seen as both failing to address poverty, and being an inmate of a the poorhouse denoted destitution.[21]

The New Poor Law, which came into being following the Poor Law Act of 1834, was greatly influenced by the problem of surplus labour in the countryside. It aimed to thin the ranks of persistent able-bodied paupers and reduce the financial burden of ratepayers by giving relief only to those resident in the workhouse. As Keith Snell writes, one example of providing a temptation to abuse power was the formation of the new boards of guardians which 'placed administration more firmly in the hands of the employing and tenant farmers'. Snell states that the employers used their new position to compel acceptance of low wages and used their power against those they found 'obnoxious', which effectively intensified rural class hostility.[22] In the case of the incident at Ascott, it is interesting to note that the farmer, Richard Hambidge, who brought the charges against the women was one of the local church wardens. He was supported by the other parish officials.[23] The local elite worked together to keep order. Snell adds that tenant farmers were most likely to use the threat of the workhouse against relief applications.[24]

The other effect of the New Poor Law, much as occurred under the Old Poor Law, was that continued payment of outdoor relief depressed wages. As far as the Poor Laws in Oxfordshire were concerned, George James Dew, a relieving officer in the Bicester Poor Law Union wrote in October 1870, 'It is a melancholy sight to see so many poor creatures applying for relief, which, after all, is just sufficient to keep body and soul together.' He also wrote in his diary that he had no illusions about the 'petty tyranny and discrimination which was central to the poor law at local level'.[25] In a parallel study, Arthur Brown, looking at Essex villages, points out

Chipping Norton Union Workhouse 1836–1948. Fanny Honeybone became an inmate here.

the families were under increased pressure as some of the traditional forms of female employment started to contract during the years 1851 to 1871. This included indoor farm servants that in Essex, for instance, 'reduced from 2,543 to 693'.[26] He continues that noting that in nearly all Essex villages, that as well as enduring 'acute poverty... labourers' wives or widows were likely to have to subsist on the lowest possible allowance from the Relieving Officer before entering the workhouse to die'.[27] Interestingly, the statistical appendix to the *Report* of the 1911 Royal Commission on the Poor Laws and Relief of Distress displayed a steady climb of paupers receiving both indoor and outdoor relief from 1,893,000 in 1860 to 2,314,000 in 1870.[28] So, the figures in the decade leading up to the events in Oxfordshire indicated that poverty was getting worse – although it is not possible to split urban figures from those in rural settings.

The establishment may have intended these Poor Laws as providing support for those in need, but in practice they were another means of suppression.

Another example of unwelcome charitable provision recorded by A. F. J. Brown was education. He states that when the plight of the labourer was noticed, the form of charity given was not what the labourer wanted – 'a living wage and a kindly system of poor relief'[29] – but sought the strengthening of education. However, the motivation for this was to strengthen religious influence in local communities. He adds, 'The clergy saw it as a duty to bring Anglican Christianity into every corner of their parish and every public activity taking place.'[30] Locally, some clergy did seek to improve the educational conditions of labourers, and we also know from the Ascott-under-Wychwood church school logbook[31] that many children of labourers attended, but Brown brings out that this education was often substandard and their overall aim was to inculcate 'habits of obedience... and promoted attitudes appropriate to people of their lowly status'.[32]

This was reflected in a comment in the *Reynolds' Newspaper*, a radical newspaper which in 1870 stated that 'The education obtained in church schools is of no lasting benefit... many people regard secular knowledge as dangerous... and much prefer... they be subjected to... divine doctrines of respectful obedience to superiors.'[33] The parson as part of local hierarchy also sought to keep the *status quo* by ensuring the 'respectful obedience' of labourers. In the case of Ascott Church School, the school logbook paints a mixed picture of its importance to the labourers. The logbook for 2 June 1873 records that attendance was very bad due to the Whitsuntide cricket match. Similarly on the 16 June 1873 attendance was bad due to 'outdoor attractions such as stalls... and the agricultural labourers meeting on the green'. The logbook for 11 August 1873 records, 'Harvest work is very general, very few have attended school this week.' Then after six weeks' holiday in the week commencing 29 September 1873, the logbook records, 'the attendance through this week was very thin'. The same record also notes that the following week the attendance was still bad as many children were helping their parents with the allotments. The writer concludes that they will have to make the lessons easier than they were before the holiday. Perhaps most telling, on 2 January 1874 the logbook states, 'Very small numbers... but I am sure the school would be fuller if parents were less indifferent in the practice of sending their children.' There are also two brief entries relating to the arrest of the women in Ascott: 'Wednesday's attendance was bad owing to... the excitement caused by the summoning of nearly 20 women...by Mr Hambidge', adding that 'attendance diminished through the parents of some of the absent children being included in the sixteen women of the village committed to prison'.[34] The writer makes no judgement on the case apart from it being 'excitement' and that it affected attendance and no judgement on the children's engagement in harvest, even though that would have been visible to the local farmers.

As the historian Eugenio Biagini points out, 'the crucial issue was not so much government intervention, as *who* would control and administer those institutions which affected working-class lifestyles – regardless of whether... secular or religious.'[35] He adds that political control was the crucial issue. In Oxfordshire, the move from church to secular educators was seen with trepidation by the establishment. *Jackson's Oxford Journal* published an article on 'the dangers of the new year' and the introduction of secular-run education was the sole subject of the article. The article was concerned with the attempt of the National Education League to secularise the 'humbler classes'. Although education must have benefitted the children, this was also seen by some as being at the cost to them of remaining the humbler classes. The National Education League sought state provision of education while the National Education Union supported the continuation of the existing voluntary system supported by government grants. The 1870 Education Act was a compromise, giving local choice. The Cowper-Temple clause in the Act, however, demanded a non-denominational religious service, which Church of England schools were not happy with, although it was supported by non-denominational, Nonconformist and School Board schools.

Edward Barber, the General Inspector of Schools for the Oxford Diocese, in his *General Report for the Year 1880*, points to previous year's comments that the Education Act 1876 was 'proving somewhat unequal in its working, and that the uniformity which was so desirable was far from being attained'.[36] He added that 'the absence of bye-laws in many of our parishes was the chief cause of this'.[37] He wrote that the new 1880 Education Act (the Mundella Act) would now include universal byelaws to overcome these deficiencies and that unemployed 'children between 10 and 13 years... [and] all other children must have reached the Standard fixed by the bye-laws of their district before they go to work, and anyone employing them without a certificate will become liable for a penalty'.[38] Later in the same report he admits that 'The dull and stupid (or it may be nervous) children who fail to pass in their Examination will no doubt suffer...'.[39] He also adds 'that there must be a greater readiness... on the part of magistrates to carry out the provisions made'.[40] This shows that the local establishment, up until the new Act, worked to its own ends at the cost of the working class – especially where the role of magistrate and employer was often fulfilled by the same individual. The fact that the Ascott school logbook shows that children were absent due to the harvest also indicates that farmers were happy to use children in this work, regardless of the byelaws (if there were any) or effect on the child's education.

In explaining the context to the Ascott-under-Wych-wood incident in 1873, it can be seen that there were long-term issues with poverty in England, especially in rural settings. The changed use of land and the abandonment of the care for the labourers by employers had led to extreme poverty among the agricultural labourers. There was also a surplus of labour in the south of England. This is alongside the reduction in profits for farmers, the use of day hiring (and firing) linked to a lack of long-term concern for the welfare of the labourer, which led to a breakdown in trust between farmers and labourers especially, and a lack of representation on their behalf except through the NALU. The Union empowered the labourer. As David Kent has pointed out, the apparent ease with the *status quo* masked an undercurrent of social unrest. This social unrest was not perceived as threatening the nation's stability and therefore the local establishment became more empowered to act against disruption at the local level. But as it was left to the local establishment to preserve order, together with providing local support, these provisions were varied at best.[41] This did not mean that some in government were unaware of their plight. Some contemporary observers deplored the conditions faced by agricultural labourers which led to poverty and hardship among rural families. Mr A. P. Taylor, speaking in the debate on the Second Reading of the Game Laws Abolition Bill in 1871, stated

> I will now say a few words about the agricultural labourers; ... that the whole class are suffering under a condition of existence which is a disgrace to our civilization... in hundreds of our villages the social condition of man is below that of any country of which I have ever read... great injury was inflicted on the agricultural labouring class in respect of their food and dwellings.[42]

Ascott-under-Wychwood schoolchildren, 1873.

But it was left mainly to the union to support the labourers' plight in practical ways, such as when they were laid off or when labourers needed to move to other areas where work was still to be found, including emigration to Australia, New Zealand or Canada.[43] Ultimately there was little prospect for men or women staying in rural Oxfordshire to break out of the poverty into which they were born.

The demand for the enfranchisement of the working class raised the prospect of some type of representation for agricultural workers, but in effect only a limited widening of the franchise occurred for the urban or the rural worker when the Second Reform Bill (Representation of the People Bill) was passed in 1867. In rural England, including Oxfordshire, all the modest extension did was to raise concern among the rural hierarchy, the landlords and the farmers that their domination of the countryside would be challenged. During the passage of the Representation of the People Bill in 1866 and 1867, for instance, concerns were expressed that working-class voters might be able to cause harm to the well-being of those in positions of privilege. Viscount Cranbourne during the debate on this Bill said, 'I have heard much on the subject of the working classes in this house which, I confess, has filled me with feelings of some apprehension', adding that workers would be tempted to pass 'laws with respect to taxation and property especially favourable to them, and therefore dangerous to all other classes'.[44]

Other political debates on the plight of the working class surfaced from time to time in Parliament. Even though there was clear sight of their plight, nothing actually changed. For instance, during 1867 there was a question tabled on the Law of Master and Servant Act by Lord Elcho, MP for Haddingtonshire. He said that it was objectionable that an employer (or a group of employers) who breached contracts was dealt with as a civil matter but an employee 'was liable to a criminal prosecution and might be imprisoned with hard labour'.[45] He continued that this was harsh, unjust, and uncalled for – and required remedy at the hands of Parliament. Spencer Walpole as Home Secretary answered on behalf of the government, stating that he could see the issue but due to the pressure of other government business a bill would not be forthcoming in the short term. The plight of the labourers' lack of effective equality was acknowledged but not given sufficient importance by those in power. Another example can be seen when Mr Sealy, the MP for Lincoln, put forward an amendment that labourers be given compensation if they had improved their property before eviction. This was defeated by 56 votes.

Conclusion

In the 1870s rural society in Oxfordshire remained one deeply divided between the 'haves' and the 'have nots'. The landlords and the tenant farmers retained economic, social and political control of the countryside, denying agricultural labourers, and their families, representation. Agricultural labourers were therefore mostly denied decent wages, a proper education and equal treatment in law, which can be seen in the arrest and sentencing of several ordinary working-class women. Somehow it touched the nation's nerve regarding injustice and inequality but, despite the noise, as so often happens it was some decades before any real changes occurred that were beneficial to the rural labourer.

7

The Criminal Law Amendment Act 1871

KEITH D. EWING

> By... Parliamentary escamotage the means which
> labourers could use in a strike or lockout were
> withdrawn from the locus of all common citizens,
> and placed under exceptional penal legislation
> the interpretation of which fell to the masters
> themselves in their capacity as justices of the peace.
>
> Karl Marx, *Das Kapital*, 1867[1]

Imprisonment with hard labour for strike-related
activity is a remarkable occasion, and raises questions
about the nature of the legal framework within
which it is possible. In the case of the 16 women from
Ascott-under-Wychwood, they were convicted under
the Criminal Law Amendment Act 1871, which occupied
a brief interregnum between two phases of labour law,
one represented by the repressive Combination Act 1825,
and the other by what is perceived to be the more liberal
Conspiracy and Protection of Property Act 1875. At a time
when contemporary trade unionists were struggling for
legal recognition and political acceptance, the 1871 Act was

deeply resented, the resentment growing when the Act was used subsequently by employers faced with a rising tide of trade union activity.[2] Although the full extent of the Act's use is unknown, there is sufficient evidence of its deployment in the *Report* of the Royal Commission on Labour in 1874 to suggest that there was good reason for trade union bitterness.[3]

Clearly a very controversial measure at the time, the 1871 Act was sufficiently notorious to justify mention in one of the most influential books of the 19th century, Karl Marx's *Das Kapital* (see quote at the start of this chapter). Marx's writing was typically colourful – though not wholly inaccurate – and it is remarkable that the 1871 Act should attract his attention in this way. It is not necessary to be a disciple of Marx to appreciate the points being made. The 1871 Act retained liabilities applying unfairly to workers; there was bias in the enforcement of the law by local magistrates who made common cause with employers; and the criminal law was being used not to protect the public interest, but to protect private commercial interests.

Criminal Law Amendment Act 1871

The Criminal Law Amendment Act 1871 was a product of the Royal Commission on Trade Unions, appointed by the then Liberal government in 1867. Chaired by Sir William Erle, who had adjudicated in a number of the leading cases under the Combination Act 1825,[4] the Royal Commission had been established to address two questions in relation to trade unionism. One was the decision in *Hornby v Close*,[5] a civil case which threatened the very existence of workers' organisations. It was held in that case that because trade unions were bodies in restraint of trade at common law, they could not sue to recover money that had been embezzled by a dishonest official. The second was the so-called 'Sheffield outrages', which were 'the culmination of a long series' of coercive measures taken by union supporters 'against non-unionists in the Sheffield cutlery trades'. These included the practice of 'rattening', whereby workers 'not in good relations with the union' would have their tools removed, this escalating in some cases to life-threatening acts of violence.[6] Accounts of the practice and its different forms make sobering reading.

The outcome of the Royal Commission was the Trade Union Act 1871, which provided a measure of legal protection for trade union organisations, and the Criminal Law Amendment Act 1871, which re-enacted in a modified form criminal liability for certain trade union activities. These latter were already contained in the Combination Act 1825, the provisions of which were analysed in a Memorandum prepared for the Royal Commission by Sir William Erle personally.[7] There he explained that the law is 'described in terms of wide generality, in order that there may be comprehended therein a wide class of actions which from their nature do not admit of precise definition'.[8] Guided by Sir William, the Royal Commission appeared to be untroubled by such restrictions, concluding that it was 'of the highest moment that the law, so far as it aims at repressing all coercion of the will of others in the disposal of their labour or capital, should be in no degree relaxed'.[9] Although the Liberal government accepted the need for the retention of criminal liability, the 1825 Act was repealed and replaced albeit with variations.

Acknowledged judicially as not having been 'conceived

in any weak spirit of tenderness to workmen',[10] the Criminal Law Amendment Act 1871 followed the example of the 1825 Act by focusing on two questions: (i) unlawful means to secure (ii) unlawful purposes. Both unlawful means and unlawful purposes were similar but not identical to the provisions of the 1825 Act they replaced. So far as the unlawful means are concerned, these applied to the following:

- The use of violence to any person or property;
- Threats or intimidation of any person in such manner as would justify a justice of the peace to bind over to keep the peace the person making the threats; and
- The molestation or obstruction of any person 'in the manner defined by this section'.

Molestation or obstruction was thus no longer drafted in terms of 'wide generality,' as Sir William Erle had described the position under the 1825 Act. [11] Thus 'a person shall, for the purposes of this Act, be deemed to molest or obstruct another person in any of the following cases'. These cases appear to have been informed in part by Sheffield 'rattening', and were listed as meaning (i) persistently following another person from place to place; (ii) hiding tools, clothes or other property of the other person; (iii) watching or besetting the house or other place where that other person resides, works, carries on business or happens to be; and (iv) with two or more other people persistently following someone in a disorderly manner in or through any street or road.

So far as the unlawful purposes are concerned, it was necessary under the 1871 Act for the offending conduct to have been undertaken with a view 'to coerce' the respondent for one of the following five purposes (as paraphrased from the original):

- In the case of an employer as respondent, to dismiss a worker; or in the case of a worker as respondent, to quit employment. This was designed to prohibit action taken to enforce union membership, or as in the Ascott case to prohibit action taken to ensure that workers did not work during a strike or lockout;
- In the case of an employer as respondent, to refuse to employ a worker; or in the case of a worker as respondent, to refuse to accept employment. This was the flip side of the previous purpose, designed again to prohibit steps taken by workers to enforce union membership, or ensure that workers do not replace those on strike;
- In the case of an employer as respondent, to belong to or not belong to an employers' federation whether temporary or permanent; and in the case of a worker as respondent, to belong to or not belong to a trade union. This again seems directed mainly at action by workers designed to encourage others to join a union;
- In the case of both employers or workers as respondents, to pay a fine imposed by an employers' association or a trade union. This seems to be addressed mainly to trade unions, designed to protect workers who failed to comply with the disciplinary procedures of the union, such as financial penalties imposed for strike-breaking; and
- In the case of an employer as respondent, to change the way of carrying out their business, or the number or description of people they employ. This would

protect employers from unlawful pressure designed to stop a business reorganisation or making people redundant, for example because of the introduction of new machinery.

It is important to note that – like the 1825 Act – the 1871 Act was addressed to the use of unlawful means for unlawful purposes by 'any person', and not only by the direct protagonists in any particular dispute, a consideration relevant in the Ascott case.[12]

As pointed out, however, the unlawful means used had to be designed to 'coerce' the respondent in order to secure one of the unlawful purposes.[13] The question of what amounted to coercion was considered in *R. v Hibbert*,[14] where the employer announced that he was changing his wage payment system. This led to a strike, a five-week picket outside the workplace, and eventually to charges being brought under the 1871 Act for conspiracy to molest and obstruct (i) workmen with a view to inducing them to quit, and (ii) an employer with a view to inducing it to change its mode of business. It was said by Baron Cleasby in the Court of Exchequer that it was for the jury to decide where persuasion ends and coercion begins, but that coercion could be affected either by physical force or 'the operation of fear upon the mind'. He continued by saying that there 'might be such a molestation by watching and besetting premises as might be expected to and would operate upon the mind so as to take away liberty of will, by *giving rise to a fear of violence by threats, or to some apprehension of loss or ruin, or to feelings of annoyance.*'[15]

It is notable that Baron Cleasby considered that peaceful picketing need not necessarily be 'coercive', making clear that 'watching and speaking to the workman, as they come and go from their employment, to induce them to leave their service, is not necessarily unlawful; nor is it unlawful to use terms of persuasion towards them to accomplish that object'.[16] Although the defendants were found guilty (and jailed), this was a notably more liberal position than that which had been adopted in *R. v Druitt* under the Combination Act 1825 (as it had been amended by the Molestation of Workman Act 1859).[17] As such it tended to confound the claim by the Webbs that it was 'a criminal offence for two Trade Unionists to stand quietly in the street opposite the works of an employer against whom they had struck, in order to communicate peacefully the fact of the strike to any workman who might be ignorant of it'.[18] Nevertheless, there was little room for error: it was made clear that picketing would be unlawful 'if carried on to such a length and to such an extent that it occasions a dread of loss'.[19]

Apart from maintaining criminal liability, the 1871 Act also made provision for the prosecution of offenders in courts of summary jurisdiction, before either a stipendiary magistrate or two justices of the peace. As with the 1825 Act, the only penalty on conviction was imprisonment with or without hard labour for up to three months. There was no power to impose a fine instead, 'as it was believed that a fine would be paid collectively, and would therefore carry no deterrent'.[20] Complex provision was made for appeals, which could be heard only 14 days after conviction. The appellant would be required to enter into a recognisance (bond) before a justice of the peace to the tune of £10 to abide by the judgment of the court, and to pay any costs awarded by the court. Moreover, two people would be required to stand as surety for the £10 in the event of any default by the appellant. The justice of the peace before whom the recognisance was entered had a power 'if he thinks fit' to release the appellant from custody, perhaps one way to circumvent the restriction that no appeal would be heard until 14 days had passed following conviction.

In relation to prosecution, it is notable that the 1871 Act addressed the possibility of bias on the part of magistrates, acknowledging that local justice in Victorian England was not a conflict between equals. Section 5 disqualified from sitting in a court of summary jurisdiction anyone who was a 'master, father, son, or brother of a master' in the particular 'manufacture, trade, or business' in which or in connection with which the charge related.[21] But as the Ascott case revealed, section 5 fell far short of what was required. The problem of bias that Marx alluded to was not just one of close family members but the wider social circles from which magistrates were drawn, which would bring them into contact with business owners with whom they would share common interests and common outlooks. This was an issue in rural communities as well as in the towns and cities, where the 'farmers and the squires' received the 'cordial support' of the 'rural clergy' who dispensed criminal justice in their role as magistrates.[22]

Ascott prosecutions

Turning to the operation of the 1871 Act in the Ascott case, there are four issues to consider. The first is to identify the conduct of the defendants for which they were charged.

The best information suggests that the basis of the charge is that they

> ...unlawfully did molest and obstruct John Hodgkins and John Millin, being workmen in the employment of the said John Hambidge, with a view to coerce the said John Hodgkins and John Millin to quit the said employment contrary to the Act made in the 34th and 35th years of the reign of Queen Victoria, intituled An Act to amend the Criminal Law relating to Violence, Threats, and Molestation.[23]

> [It is to be emphasised that the defendants were not themselves participants in the strike, but that they were acting in support of those who were participating. Repeating the point previously made, the Act made it an offence 'for every person' to do one or more of the unlawful acts, including the workers directly involved as well as third parties, as in this case.[24]]

As already pointed out, however, there was no longer a generic offence of molestation and obstruction in the 1871 Act as there had been in the 1825 Act. This was a significant difference, with the 1871 Act deeming molestation and obstruction to *be* (not to *include*) persistently following; hiding tools; watching and besetting; and disorderly following. This was a potentially significant limitation of the scope of the offence.

The Ascott women could have been lawfully convicted of molestation and obstruction only if they had committed one of the foregoing four statutory forms of molestation or obstruction. In this case we must presume that the unlawful means was 'watching and besetting', though it was not specifically mentioned. Admittedly the position is not helped by the jurisprudence under the 1825 Act which had suggested that when a charge of molestation is laid, it was not necessary to specify in detail the nature of the conduct said to constitute the molestation:

> The principal ground of objection was that they do not set out the means of obstruction, the nature of the molestation, or what the threats were. We conceive that that is quite unnecessary. Those counts are framed under the Act of Parliament, using the words of the Legislature with a view to show that the enactment of the Legislature had been violated.[25]

By s. 2(2), the 1871 Act appeared expressly to cover this point by providing that 'the description of any offence under this Act in the words of such Act shall be sufficient in law'. Nevertheless, the position was now different, in the sense that the form of molestation used was integral to the offence committed. It would have been good practice under the new regime introduced in 1871 to have specified the molestation and obstruction with greater particularity, for example by persistently following, or watching and besetting, as the case may have been.

Assuming that the molestation and obstruction were the unlawful means used, a second question is whether it was done for an unlawful purpose. Here, one issue would be whether the conduct was coercive as that term was later to be explained in *R. v Hibbert*.[26] As already seen, it was said there that coercion could take the form of physical force or 'the operation of fear upon the mind', and that there 'might be such a molestation by watching and besetting premises as might be expected to and would operate upon the mind so as to take away liberty of will, by giving rise to a fear of violence by threats, or to some apprehension of loss or ruin, or to feelings of annoyance'.[27] Although the 'facts' are disputed and the defendants were neither legally advised nor legally represented, the account of the case in the *Oxfordshire Weekly News* relied on by the Home Secretary suggests that the behaviour alleged by the prosecutor and accepted by the magistrates would probably have been coercive as that term was understood by lawyers at the time.[28] According to the foregoing:

> Some 30 women, a few of whom were armed with sticks, went to a gate and waylaid two men, who had accepted employment from a farmer named Hambidge, *threatening that if the men went back to work they would beat them*; and after some parley the men retired, when the women followed them, *hustled them, pushed them into a hedge, and declared they would duck them in a pond if they attempted to return to work*. The men in about half-an-hour attempted to go back to work, when they again met the women, some of whom asked them to go to the public house to have beer, and some tried to get them to join the Union. The men refused, and on their refusal *the same threats of ill-treatment were repeated* if they returned to work. Charges were afterwards brought against 16 of the 30 women for a breach of the Criminal Law Amendment Act, in having used violence, threats and intimidation to prevent those men from working.[29]

It will be noted that there is no mention in the foregoing passage to the molestation and obstruction with which the women were charged, but that there is mention of 'violence, threats and intimidation', which were separate offences with which the women were not charged. It would be hard to deny that on the 'facts' italicised above that the 'violence, threats and intimidation' found by the magistrates are likely to have met the threshold of coercive behaviour. Whether it would have been enough to have sustained charges for intimidation designed to coerce rather than molestation and obstruction by watching and besetting designed to coerce is a different question. Although not implausible, it is to be noted that for the purposes of a charge based on intimidation, the Act required threats or intimidation 'as implied a threat of personal violence'.[30] Nevertheless, the threshold for a threat of violence was not very high, and the foregoing account of what happened reveals allegations of violence and threats thereof, albeit of a minor nature.[31]

A third question relates to the penalty imposed by the justices, about which there was much criticism. It is to be recalled, however, that – as in the case of the 1825 Act – imprisonment was the only penalty provided for by the Act. There was no opportunity for a fine to be imposed, despite the fact that Joseph Arch later claimed that the National Agricultural Labourers' Union (NALU) had been 'prepared for the infliction of a fine', and that a union official was in court with 'the necessary money all ready'. [32]

Ignorance of the law was not confined to the Union, with the Home Secretary (Henry Bruce) telling the Commons on 6 June 1873 that the magistrates had inflicted an excessive punishment, before adding that

Henry Austin Bruce, 1st Baron Aberdare, Home Secretary.

...there was no doubt they might have passed a lighter sentence, and have bound the women over in their own recognizances to appear and submit to the sentence; or, on the other hand, it would have been quite competent for the magistrates, on the evidence before them, to convict those who had taken the most active part in the disturbance for an assault, and to fine them, enforcing the fine, if necessary, by imprisonment. Neither of those courses, however, appeared to have occurred to the magistrates, and the case did seem to show a very grave want of discretion; because, although the women undoubtedly had committed an offence, the extent to which their punishment was carried had a tendency to enlist the sympathy of the public on the side of those who had broken the law, whereas a moderate punishment would have been accepted by all as a suitable penalty.[33]

By modern standards, the Home Secretary's was a remarkable intervention, apparently crossing the line designed to protect judges from political criticism for decisions they make or sentences they impose.[34] It was all the more remarkable for the fact that Bruce appeared unaware of the powers available under the 1871 Act, despite being an experienced magistrate,[35] and despite the claim that he 'did not make [his] statement on this subject without consulting one of the most eminent and experienced of the London Police Magistrates as to the Law, and as to the practice of the Magistrates in similar cases'.[36]

The Home Secretary was, however, correct in his assessment that the sentences were excessive, a view shared by the Lord Chancellor (Roundell Palmer, 1st Earl of Selborne). Although the latter accepted that 'unlawful combination involved danger to society and thus required repression by law', he was alert nevertheless to the dangers of unnecessarily creating martyrs by heavy-handed and disproportionate sentencing.[37]

A fourth, and final, question for our purposes related to the right to appeal, as mentioned above. It is true that the appeal could not be heard until the 15th day after conviction, which – given the sentences of seven and ten days respectively – may have been a disincentive for the 16 women convicted in the Ascott case. As already established, in order to lodge an appeal it would have been necessary for the appellants to enter into a recognisance before a justice of the peace of £10, to abide by the judgment of the court, and to pay any costs awarded by the court. It was also necessary to find two people willing to stand as surety for the £10 in the event of any default by the appellant. But this ought not to have been a problem,

Roundell Palmer, 1st Earl of Selborne, Lord Chancellor.

if it is true as Joseph Arch later claimed that the union had been ready to pay any fines that it had wrongly expected to be imposed. If it had been willing to pay the fines, it is difficult to understand why it would not have been able to make a different financial commitment on behalf of the women, particularly in such a high-profile case.

It is not known why an appeal was not lodged, or whether it was even considered.[38] As we have seen, the justice of the peace before whom the appeal would be lodged and the recognisance given had the power to release the women pending the hearing of an appeal. The appeal court then had wide powers to (i) confirm, reverse or modify the decision of the magistrates, (ii) remit the matter to the magistrates for a re-hearing in accordance with the opinion of the appeal court, or (iii) make 'such other order in the matter as the court thinks just' (s. 3). At the very least this would have provided an opportunity to address the conviction, the sentence, as well as wider concerns about the administration of justice then being ventilated in the national press but which would require a political solution.[39] Particularly eye catching in this respect was Frederic Harrison's Letter to *The Times*, where he wrote that

> Masters and men alike have to thank you for your powerful criticism on the recent sentence at Chipping Norton. But I wish to point out that this gross miscarriage of justice is no solitary case, since the Act is responsible for constant cases of similar harshness, and gives permanent cause for the same indignation. The two magistrates whom you rebuke may have brought the Act into discredit; but it is the Act which led the two magistrates into their blunder.[40]

Conclusion

The statutory offence of 'obstruction and molestation' for which the Ascott women were convicted was transformed again by the Conspiracy and Protection of Property Act 1875, s. 7, the essential features of which remain on the statute book to this day.[41] It continued to be an offence to use violence or intimidation towards another person 'or his wife or children' or injure that person's property. And now without the epithet 'molestation and obstruction', it was an offence (i) persistently to follow other persons from place to place; (ii) hide tools, clothes, or other property owned by another person or hinder the use thereof; (iii) watch or beset the house or other place where a person, resides, works or happens to be; or (iv) follow another person with two or more others in a disorderly manner in or through any street or road. The offences under the CPPA 1875 would be committed where the offending conduct was done with a view to 'compel' those to whom it was directed not to refrain from exercising their 'legal rights', in a manner which was 'wrongful and without legal authority'.

The key significance of the 1875 Act was the universal application of these offences, being no longer about preventing coercion in the disposal of labour or capital, but about penalising steps taken to compel anyone to do or refrain from doing anything they had a legal right to do. In this perverse sense the 1875 Act addressed a major trade union grievance about 'class' legislation,[42] which criminalised only trade unionists. Perhaps ironically,[43] the Ascott defendants were as likely to have been convicted under the 1875 Act as under the 1871 Act,[44] even though it was now expressly provided that 'attending at or near a place where a person resides, or works, or carries on business, or happens to be... in order merely to obtain or communicate information, shall not be deemed a watching or besetting within the meaning of this section.'[45] But the Ascott women were probably not present for these limited purposes, though they might well have been affected by the new sentencing options under the 1875 Act of three months or a fine of up to £20.

8

'The cross in one hand, the gibbet in the other': clerical magistrates and the impact of the Ascott Martyrs' case on their future[1]

CHRISTINE GOWING

> The time is coming when there will be a cry to which the Legislature cannot turn a deaf ear for the reorganisation of the Magistracy, and the squires, with their clerical allies, have themselves to thank for the revolution that will eject them from the last stronghold of their power.
>
> *The Spectator*, 31 May 1873 (see appendix B)

'The shameful Chipping Norton affair which roused the whole country.'[2] That was how Joseph Arch, president of the National Agricultural Labourers' Union (NALU), described the case of the Ascott Martyrs, and it was, without a doubt, high profile in every respect, prompting public outrage, wide newspaper coverage and parliamentary scrutiny. And central to the anger was the role that the magistrates had played in the event. Indeed, the popular narrative goes so far as to portray these JPs as the villains of the piece with their harsh sentencing of the Ascott women. The fact that they were local clergymen intensified a controversial public perception of their judgment as cruel and incompetent, and their sentencing as unfair. In his scathing criticism of the magistrates, the journalist Archibald Forbes was the first to claim the women as 'martyrs', declaring that it had been the magistrates who had qualified them for this classification.[3] Additionally, a popular theory has emerged that this case was responsible for the decline, or even termination, of clerical magistracy in Britain in the late 19th century, for the harsh punishment caused a national storm which resulted in pressure to curtail the appointment of clerics as magistrates.[4] However, the evidence suggests otherwise.

The focus of this essay is on the aftermath of the court case, the history of clerical magistrates nationally, and their appointment and governance. And, principally, it addresses the question: what was the impact of the Ascott Martyrs incident on the future of the clerical magistracy in Britain? This will be explored through both secondary and primary evidence and by a statistical analysis of nominal data relating to Oxfordshire justices of the peace in calculating and comparing the patterns and percentages of clerics during the 19th century and into the 20th. The terms 'magistrate', 'justice of the peace' and 'JP' will be used interchangeably. The events leading to the court case are detailed elsewhere in this collection of essays.

In 1873, striking was not illegal, and neither was picketing, but it was almost impossible to achieve under the

Figure 1: Rev. William Edward Dickson Carter, JP,
rector of Sarsden.

existing legislation. The Ascott women were summonsed
and charged with using violence, threats and intimidation
to prevent men from working,[5] and taken to the Chipping
Norton Police Station where the petty sessions were held,
and of which the magistrates trying the case were Rev.
William Carter, rector of Sarsden, and Rev. Thomas Harris,
rector of Swerford. The evidence that was presented gave
them no option other than to find the women guilty of the
crime of which they were accused under the Criminal Law

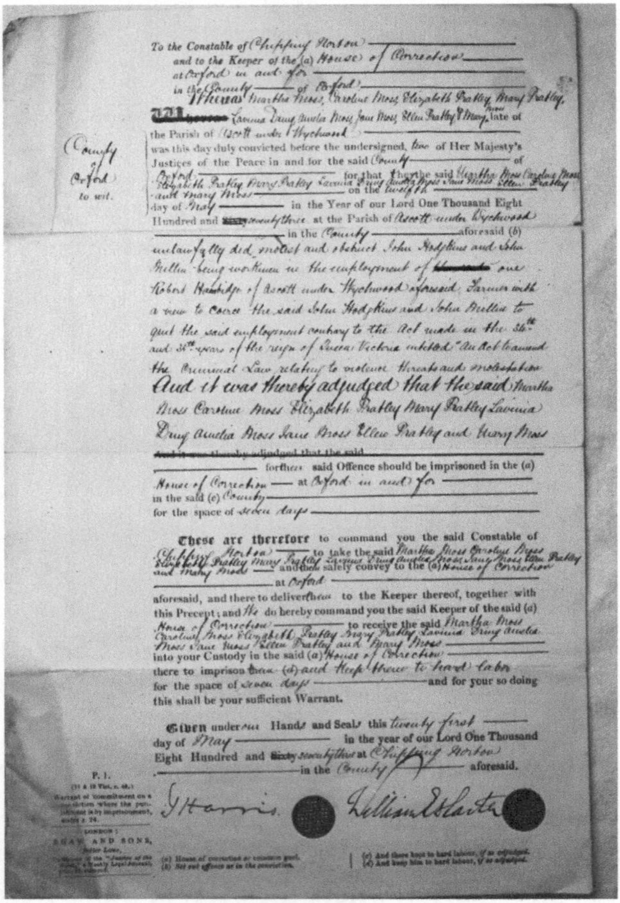

County of Oxford to wit.

To the Constable of Chipping Norton and to the Keeper of the (a) House of Correction at Oxford in and for in the County of Oxford

Whereas Martha Moss, Caroline Moss, Elizabeth Pratley, Mary Pratley, Lavinia Dring, Amelia Moss, Jane Moss, Ellen Pratley & Mary Moss late of the Parish of Ascott under Wychwood was this day duly convicted before the undersigned, two of Her Majesty's Justices of the Peace in and for the said County of Oxford for that they the said Martha Moss, Caroline Moss, Elizabeth Pratley, Mary Pratley, Lavinia Dring, Amelia Moss, Jane Moss, Ellen Pratley and Mary Moss on the twelfth day of May in the Year of our Lord One Thousand Eight Hundred and ~~Sixty~~ seventy three at the Parish of Ascott under Wychwood in the County aforesaid (b) unlawfully did molest and obstruct John Hodgkins and John Millin being workmen in the employment of one Robert Hambidge of Ascott under Wychwood aforesaid, Farmer with a view to coerce the said John Hodgkins and John Millin to quit the said employment contrary to the Act made in the 34th and 35th years of the reign of Queen Victoria intituled "An Act to amend the Criminal Law relating to violence threats and molestation. And it was thereby adjudged that the said Martha Moss, Caroline Moss, Elizabeth Pratley, Mary Pratley, Lavinia Dring, Amelia Moss, Jane Moss, Ellen Pratley and Mary Moss

~~And it was thereby adjudged that the said~~ for their said Offence should be imprisoned in the (a) House of Correction at Oxford in and for in the said (c) County for the space of seven days

These are therefore to command you the said Constable of Chipping Norton to take the said Martha Moss, Caroline Moss, Elizabeth Pratley, Mary Pratley, Lavinia Dring, Amelia Moss, Jane Moss, Ellen Pratley and Mary Moss and them safely convey to the (a) House of Correction at Oxford aforesaid, and there to deliver them to the Keeper thereof, together with this Precept; and We do hereby command you the said Keeper of the said (a) House of Correction to receive the said Martha Moss, Caroline Moss, Elizabeth Pratley, Mary Pratley, Lavinia Dring, Amelia Moss, Jane Moss, Ellen Pratley and Mary Moss into your Custody in the said (a) House of Correction there to imprison them (d) and keep them to hard labor for the space of seven days and for your so doing this shall be your sufficient Warrant.

Given under our Hands and Seals this twenty first day of May in the year of our Lord One Thousand Eight Hundred and ~~Sixty~~ seventy three at Chipping Norton in the County aforesaid.

J Harris. William E Carter

P. 1.

Figure 2: One of the committal documents for the Ascott women.

Amendment Act 1871 (see essay 7).

The women were in a weak position: they were given no legal advice, nor representation (nor was there later any attempt to appeal).[6] Was Carter sensitive to this? Reports of the trial record that he appeared particularly uncomfortable with the situation and the limited options with which he and Harris were faced. He asked the farmer, Robert Hambidge, who had brought the action, if he was sure he wanted to proceed with the prosecution, and newspaper reports claim that Carter shifted uneasily on his seat due to apparent distress with how the case was proceeding. However, on the legal counsel of Abram Rawlinson, the clerk to the justices and the legal adviser, the sentence was pronounced: imprisonment with hard labour for terms ranging from seven to ten days. Later William Dickins, chairman of a Warwickshire bench (and previously a barrister) wrote, 'In my judgment and experience, I do not see how you could have refrained from sending these women to prison, especially after the complainant pressed for a decision.'[7]

A conditional pardon to commute the hard labour element of the sentence (Figure 3) was later granted by the Home Secretary on 29 May 1873. However, it was too late to be effective, as the women had already served the sentence. The pardon read:

I have advised Her Majesty to remit that part of the sentence of the women still in custody under committal by the Chadlington bench of magistrates which imposed hard labour in addition to imprisonment they are not therefore to be kept any longer at hard labour an official authority will follow in due course.

Figure 3: Telegram to Oxford Prison from Home
Secretary granting conditional pardon 29 May 1873.

After the sentencing, word spread quickly and a hostile crowd gathered outside the building. And so began a campaign of protest and antagonism against the clerics' decision and their position as justices: riots followed, and the media took up the cause. *The Times* sent a special correspondent to follow the case and the liberal barrister and journalist Leonard Courtney called for the dismissal of the bench chairman, the Rev. Harris.[8] *The Spectator* contributed to the adverse reaction with a scathing article, stating that,

> The Lord Chancellor has the power to remove magistrates who have shown themselves unfit to exercise authority from the commission of the peace, and in the present instance this power ought certainly to be used... Labourers are beginning to feel that they cannot count on an impartial trial by magistrates of the temper of the clerical Shallows of Chipping Norton... [9]

A number of regional newspapers also covered the story with not only a concern about the justices' ruling but a challenge to the policy of clerics in the judiciary. Much of the criticism centred on the perceived ignorance of the magistrates, particularly their lack of training and legal knowledge. They were often critically referred to as being 'unpaid', as if this made them amateur officials; but so were all provincial magistrates. These accusations were disingenuous – Carter and Harris were no more or no less trained and knowledgeable than any other JP across Britain's counties. In fact, in 1873 they had 18 and 21 years' respective experience as magistrates. And, as in all court cases, magistrates were guided and advised by a legal clerk to the justices, who *was* trained and paid. A letter written to *The Times* by Frederic Harrison, the English positivist and lawyer, supported the magistrates but blamed the legislation: 'It is the Act which led the two magistrates into their blunder; they simply did what was done twenty times before under its provisions...'[10]

The official correspondence that followed the trial demonstrates the discomfort of the magistrates and the concern of the legal and political hierarchy. The Home Secretary reported to Parliament that 'the Lord Chancellor had thought it proper to write to the Lord Lieutenant of the county with regard to the conduct of the magistrates in the matter, and to call on them for an explanation of that conduct; and after receiving such an explanation, he would take the course which he thought necessary'.[11] For it was the Duke of Marlborough, as Lord Lieutenant of Oxfordshire, who officially nominated candidates for inclusion in the commission of the peace – prior to approval by the Lord

HIS GRACE THE DUKE OF MARLBOROUGH

Figure 4: The 7th Duke of Marlborough (1822–1883).

Chancellor – and who was responsible for them.[12]

In his explanatory response to the Duke of Marlborough, Carter explained that 'my colleague remained unshaken in his opinion' and defended the decision, arguing that there was 'no alternative of punishment... It amounts to no illegal judgement... had I refused to convict the case was dismissed and this I could not allow when it was proved and a manifest injustice would have been inflicted on the prosecution. The case did not warrant a remission of punishment.'[13] The Duke's reply to the Lord Chancellor suggested that the same judgment would have been made by any magistrate, clerical or not:

> They [Carter and Harris] conscientiously assure me that they could not have awarded punishment with greater discrimination than they did... The fact of these magistrates being clergymen has been adduced as a reflection on their judgment. While admitting that owing to the peculiar relationship in which clergymen not unfrequently stand with regard to persons brought before them in their magisterial capacity, there may be some objections on general grounds to their appointment to magisterial offices, I am entirely of opinion that in the present instance the same judgment would have been arrived at if the magistrates deciding the case had been laymen instead of clergymen and while the necessity for a conviction must have been singularly repugnant to their feelings, that they acted solely under a strong and imperative sense of their public duty.[14]

However 'repugnant' to Carter and Harris it may have felt, their sentencing decision had the support of local farmers. A petition with nearly 300 signatures compiled by 'owners, occupiers of land and others' was presented to Carter and Harris and it, not unnaturally, defended the magistrates:

> We... being fully aware of the circumstances brought before the bench... respecting the case of intimidation at Ascott, desire to express our entire approval of the course adopted by you and hope that the sentence passed upon the offenders will check any further attempts to interfere with the freedom

of labour. We beg to tender our thanks for your able and impartial administration of justice on the bench for so many years past.

It was forwarded by The Duke of Marlborough to the Lord Chancellor as supporting evidence of 'the irreproachable character which they both bear'.[15] The Lord Chancellor however, still maintained that 'the authority of the law would have been in this case better vindicated by a different and more lenient course'. Nevertheless, no course of official action against the two magistrates followed.

Magistrates: lay, clerical, stipendiary

Justices of the peace were first appointed in the reign of Edward III under a statute of 1361. In 1745 a land ownership requirement was introduced in order to qualify, and was raised in 1774 from £40 to £100, for which an oath of qualification was sworn. Clerical magistrates had to qualify too. In 1874–5, a survey of landowners in Buckinghamshire revealed that 28 clergymen owned between 300 and 1000 acres, and 54 owned between 10 and 300 acres,[16] and this was likely also to be typical of Oxfordshire clergy. For example, the 1873 Return of Owners of Land shows Carter owned 300 acres and Harris owned almost 250 acres. This was glebe land attached to their rectories, provided by the church as part of their parish livings. The clerical magistrates, therefore, could understandably be accused, as could their fellow lay magistrates, of having a vested interest in cases that involved agricultural labourers' disputes. This may have been the cause of much of the resentment against Harris and Carter.

It was not only land qualification, however, that enabled

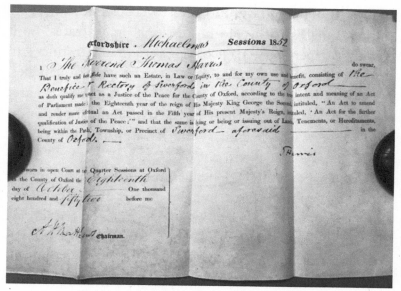

Figure 5: Justice of the peace oath of
Rev. Thomas Harris JP (1852).

their appointment, but the pragmatic issue that in rural areas, there were few candidates and clergymen were most likely to have the educational and social background that was required for magisterial work. Clerical magistrates were thus among their peers of the landed elite who, inevitably, held the cultural influence and political authority in communities and are defined by the legal historian Thomas Skyrme as 'an oligarchy composed of the leading men of their locality, most of them wealthy and all of them influential'.[17] In his diary, Rev. Francis Witts in a parish 15 miles from Ascott describes his work as a magistrate, explaining, 'Other magistrates were generally nobleman or landed gentry, with a few exceptions from the commercial or manufacturing class.'[18] There were simply not enough non-clerics to do the work and, by the beginning of the 19th century, there were calls for enlarging the pool of JPs with paid professional magistrates. So it was that stipendiary magistrates were first introduced in London but were not appointed to the county benches, hence the need for clerics to swell the numbers.[19] Later the NALU would campaign for the replacement of clerical magistrates with stipendiary magistrates in counties, but this was never achieved.

In terms of training for magistrates, there is no evidence of any formal procedure, but the official lists of seniority that were issued imply that new magistrates were trained 'in post' by more senior colleagues. Guidebooks such as Burn's *Justices of the Peace* and the annually updated *The Justices' Manual*[20] provided instruction, together with the guidance of legal advisers – as in the case in question, when solicitor Abram Rawlinson gave counsel in his position as clerk to the justices.

Clerical magistrates and their decline

John Tomlinson's work on the clerical magistracy in the Midlands in the 19th century concludes that, following the peak of the 1830s, the number of clerical magistrates in England and Wales fell dramatically, 'marking the emergence of a more exclusively religious clerical profession uneasy with the antagonisms associated with local law enforcement'. He sees it as an early indicator of clerics' withdrawal from secular activities, which included other roles such as appointments on hospital and asylum boards, and as school governors, Poor Law guardians and charity administrators. Each of the Ascott case JPs was involved in other ways in secular community life – Harris was chairman of the Board of Guardians of the Chipping

Norton Union for 27 years and Carter ran a night school. An additional factor was the increase in the number of other potential candidates who were becoming more available through the development of industry and urban areas.[21]

Carl Zangeri's work calculates that the number of clerical magistrates nationally, as a percentage of all magistrates, was at a peak of over 25 per cent in the 1830s and dropped sharply to around 6 per cent in the 1870s.[22] Other studies vary in detail, depending on the urban or rural nature of the district, and the availability of other social groups to take up the judicial role.[23] But did the Ascott events of 1873 radically affect the rate of this decline?

It did not take long for judgement of Harris and Carter's 'very grave want of discretion', as it was described in Parliament, to mutate from criticism of the two Oxfordshire justices into intense public protest against the appointment in general of clerics as magistrates.[24] For example, an article in *Reynold's News* described the magistrates as 'men so utterly incapable, so dull in comprehension, so warped in judgment, so devoid of sympathy, so singularly stupid...' adding, 'We emphatically denounce the employment of clerical justices as being most unwise, impolitic and conflicting in their religious calling'.[25] This view of a potential conflict of interest extended to the church itself:

> The Bishop of Durham does not approve of clerical magistrates... he argues that the duties of the magistrate frequently interfered with the usefulness of the minister... a minister may have fined a parishioner on Saturday 5 shillings and costs for some

trifling offence, and so deprived him possibly of a meal is not likely to see the offender at church on the Sunday to listen to the message of love and mercy. It is not a question of fitness for clerical magistrates do their work quite as well and often better...[26]

The Liberal Prime Minister, William Gladstone, in response to a general question, spoke in the House of Commons of his reluctance on the matter and that he thought it a salutary tendency to restrict the number of such magistrates.[27] Unsurprisingly, Joseph Arch of the NALU was severe in his criticism: 'these clerical magistrates had thoroughly disgraced themselves... clergymen have no business on the Bench... they are always hardest and most severe.'[28]

The media storm and public criticism of the two magistrates and the call for reform of the county JP benches was high profile, forceful and vociferous and it is unsurprising therefore that the myth has developed that, as a result of the Ascott Martyrs' case, clerical magistrates were dropped from the judiciary.

In response to the Lord Chancellor's request for background information, the clerk to the county justices, John Davenport, briefed the Duke of Marlborough for a defensive response:

The whole number of acting Magistrates in Oxfordshire is 112. And of this number 12 only are clergymen, if you exclude 4 who are upwards of 80 years of age and can scarcely be said to be 'acting' Magistrates. And of the 12 and 4 (16) Clerical Magistrates, 6 are in the west part of the County, where there is a paucity of Squires, and within which part the Chipping Norton District is situate. And of the 16 also, 5 only were appointed to the Commission of the Peace at your Grace's instance.[29]

This exemplifies the difficulty in filling appointments and illustrates that there was no evident preponderance of clerics as magistrates in Oxfordshire. In justifying the appointment of those in post, Davenport emphasised that this was because of a lack of other eligible men.[30] Records show that Oxfordshire magistrates in 1873 totalled 114 JPs, 14 of whom were clerical. Other social categories include nobility, military and political men, and squires.

Debate continued to flourish and, in the House of Lords during consideration of the second reading of the Qualification of Justices of the Peace Bill in 1875, several significant comments on the topic reflected the mood of the time and illustrated the appetite for change in the judiciary. The arguments again were particularly focused on the point that, however one viewed the merits or demerits of clerical magistrates, they were generally appointed only when there were no other suitable candidates.

In Oxfordshire, the percentage of clerics as magistrates had already been falling steadily. Diana McClatchey's work in 1960 shows that in 1816, 36.8 per cent of Oxfordshire magistrates were clerics, but by 1837 the percentage had dropped to 27 per cent and in 1857 to 21 per cent.[31] Tomlinson's calculation demonstrates that in the 1870s, the percentage of clerical magistrates had declined to 6 per cent throughout England and Wales [32] although this was, in fact, exceeded in Oxfordshire with a percentage of 13 per cent in 1873. Nevertheless, clerical magistracy in the county had evidently already started on its decline well before the controversial Ascott Martyrs case. Why was this? Tomlinson summarised it as relating to 'contemporary considerations regarding the appropriate roles and character of clergy and the fear that it was damaging for the church to be involved so directly in legal enforcement' and 'It has been argued that the clerical magistracy created conflict between clergy and many people, particularly non-Anglicans and the poor and ultimately damaged the church, adding weight to a process of secularization.'[33]

Secularisation and a withdrawal from involvement in local affairs was linked with a possible growing moral discomfort at the combining of the roles of cleric and magistrate. Other church influences may also have been involved. Both the 19th century Oxford Movement (a High Church movement beginning in the 1830s which developed into Anglo-Catholicism) and the evangelical movement may have made a cleric naturally less likely to aspire to non-clerical duties – although it is not known what pressure may have been exerted on an individual cleric to become a magistrate.

New analysis

Little scholarly attention has been given to the position of clerical magistrates in the later decades of the 19th century, and in order to address the claim that the Ascott case brought an end to the appointment of clergy as magistrates, an analysis has been undertaken of Oxfordshire magistrate data beyond 1873.[34] This plotted the incidence of clerics among members of the bench as a percentage. Nine nominal data sets were analysed from published lists of magistrates in 1873,[35] 1879, 1884, 1890, 1895, 1901, 1905, 1911 and 1915.[36]

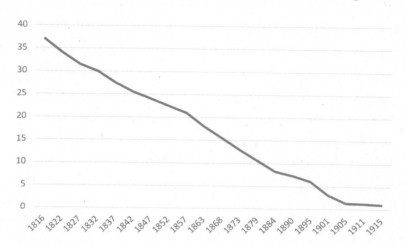

Figure 6: Clerical magistrates as a percentage of Oxfordshire JPs, 1816–1915. The graph is smoothed between the available data points for 1816–1873.

The chart in Figure 6 shows the percentage of clerics as JPs between 1816 and 1915. (This includes data from Diana McClatchey's calculations of the percentage of clerical magistrates in the earlier period of 1816, 1837, 1857, plus new analysis.)

It is evident that the decline had started well before the Ascott event and remained constant throughout the 19th century.

Two observations from the analysis reveal additional points of interest. First, and importantly for the debate surrounding whether there was an end to clerical magistrates following 1873, the records show that at least six new Oxfordshire clerical justices were appointed *after* the case of the Ascott Martyrs. Secondly, it was noted that in Rev. Carter's final listing as a magistrate, he was the fourth most senior justice on the bench and the most senior cleric.

Conclusion: what was the impact of the case on the future of clerical magistrates?

On 21 June 1873, a letter from 'all classes' of Sarsden parishioners was published in *Jackson's Oxford Journal* in support of Rev. Carter. As well as expressing their sympathy for their rector, they focused on his work as a magistrate: 'What you did in the discharge of a public duty was as painful to you as to any person concerned... We quite believe that a more just, fair, upright and honourable gentleman has never filled that important office...' Carter and Harris were as experienced magistrates as their colleagues. Nevertheless, because of the high-profile Ascott case, they were easy targets for those who sought to change the judicial system. All county magistrates had to qualify by land ownership (which continued until 1906) and country parsons were often landowners *ex officio* by virtue of glebe land. So it was not only their personal or professional qualities (or lack of them), but their part in the authority and influence of the landed elite that encouraged protest. That would not be changed until the following century.

Undoubtedly, the Ascott Martyrs case brought public attention to the appointment of clergy as JPs as had never occurred before. Across the country, newspapers ran persuasive articles on the subject and politicians discussed alternatives. However, despite debate about legislation to curtail the appointment of clerics as magistrates, nothing reached the statute book. In fact, Harris and Carter continued in post for another 23 and 30 years, accompanied by other clerical colleagues. Harris's appointment ended in 1896 after 44 years and Carter's in 1903 on his death – after 48 years serving as a county magistrate. And clerical magistrates continued to be appointed. Two of the last Oxfordshire clerical magistrates in post were Rev. Hart Hart-Davis in the Henley Petty Sessions Division, who was appointed in 1906, and Rev. John Magrath in Bullingdon Petty Session Division, who served until 1925.[37]

The role of the two clergymen in the Ascott Martyrs case was undoubtedly controversial and it provoked divisive debate at the time. But the controversy was caused by systemic rather than by individual failings. The downward trend of the clerical magistracy, which had already been well under way in 1873, continued thereafter and at a steady rate so the popular theory about the end of clerical magistrates is evidently erroneous. Clergymen continued to serve as justices of the peace into the following century,[38] as demonstrated by a report of a 1948 Royal Commission, which commented:

> There may be reasons personal to himself, which make a clergyman or other minister particularly suitable for the bench, and if such a man is able and willing to undertake the duties of a magistrate, we think that it would be wrong to treat him as disqualified for appointment by reason of his office.[39]

Seventy-five years previously, intense hostile reaction following the controversial trial of the Ascott Martyrs had tried to bring about such a disqualification for clerical magistrates as part of 'the revolution that will eject the squires from the last stronghold of their power'. However, while there was public protest, there was press outcry and there was political scrutiny, the expectation of a change in legislation to end the appointment of clerical magistrates simply did not materialise.

9

'The promised land': the story of emigration, 1850–1911

MARTIN GREENWOOD

B y 1870, the farming boom of the 1860s was over, and agricultural families in the Wychwood villages were beginning to see the attractions of emigration. Significant numbers emigrated from them to New Zealand, including some of the Ascott Martyrs, such as Jane and Mary Pratley, and Amelia Moss. Two other Martyrs also emigrated: Elizabeth Pratley to Canada with her husband, Eli, and Ann Moss to the United States with her husband, Caleb.[1] Although the 'Great Exodus' had started in 1850, the exodus from the Wychwood villages dates from the early 1870s, and it reached its peak in 1874.[2] Most of these emigrants were agricultural labourers, shepherds, gardeners and carters, the majority going to New Zealand. Most of the local villages had their peak populations before then, with a few, like Milton and Shipton, not until 1871 (Table 1).

Between 1851 and 1911, the population of rural Oxfordshire declined from 131,818 to 123,047 or 6 per cent (Table 2).

Village	1801	1851	1871	1891	1911	Decline (Note 2)
THE WYCHWOODS						
Ascott (Note 3)	410	456	462	430	365	21%
Milton	495	799	**962**	898	707	26%
Shipton	406	616	**761**	743	654	14%
	<u>1311</u>	<u>1871</u>	<u>2185</u>	<u>2071</u>	<u>1726</u>	<u>21%</u>
OTHER LOCAL VILLAGES						
Burford (Note 3)	1,725	1,819	1,648	1,605	1,047	43%
Charlbury (Note 3)	965	1,477	335	1,478	1,307	11%
Churchill (Note 3)	491	645	562	548	515	22%
Enstone	912	**1,249**	1,094	1,144	932	25%
Hook Norton (Note 3)	1,032	1,496	1.259	1,265	1,349	11%
Leafield	487	837	**896**	734	671	25%
Tackley (Note 3)	368	558	570	906	451	27%
Taynton (Note 3)	315	379	335	290	184	51%
Woodstock (Note 3)	1,322	1,262	1,195	1,136	1,012	30%
TOWN						Growth %
Banbury	3,810	8,206	9,863	9,792	**13,458**	253%
Chipping Norton	1,812	2,932	3,641	**4,222**	3,972	119%
Oxford	13,421	27,843	31,404	45,742	**52,979**	294%
Oxfordshire	111,977	170,434	177,96	185,274	**189,484**	69%

Notes

1. **Bold type** = peak population, 1801-1911.

2. Decline % from peak population.

3. Other peak dates:

1821	Churchill 665	1841	Hook Norton 1,525
	Woodstock 1,455		Taynton 381
1841	Ascott 463		Burford 1,862
	Churchill 651	1861	Tackley 626
	Charlbury 3,027		

Table 1: Wychwood area populations, 1801–1911.

In the same period, the declines in many village populations from their peaks were significantly greater; for example, 21 per cent in the three Wychwood villages and 25 per cent in neighbouring Enstone and Leafield. In Burford and Taynton, the declines were much higher, 43 per cent and 51 per cent respectively.[3]

	1801	1851	Growth %	1911	Growth %
Oxfordshire	111,977	170,434	52.2	189,484	11
Oxford, inc. suburbs	13,421	30,410	122.8	52,979	74
Banbury, inc. suburbs	3,810	8,206	115.4	13,458	64
Urban Oxfordshire (Oxford + Banbury)	17,231	38,616	124.1	66,437	72
Rural Oxfordshire (inc. small towns*)	94,746	131,818	39.1	123,047	−6

* The small towns were Bampton, Bicester, Burford, Charlbury, Chipping Norton, Deddington, Eynsham, Henley-on-Thames, Thame, Watlington, and Woodstock.

Table 2: Population growth in Oxfordshire, 1801–1911.

The Great Exodus, 1850–1914

Between 1850 and 1914, some 13 million people emigrated from the UK, most of them agricultural labourers. The decade from 1871 to 1881 saw a 140 per cent rise in farm labourers, shepherds, gardeners and carters who moved abroad.[4] Whole families and groups of families went together, spurred on by the posters and advertisements which had long decorated their cottage walls. Many of the emigrants saw it as a search for the 'Promised Land', and land was generally on offer in New Zealand and other colonies.[5] Until after 1850, poverty, custom and ignorance kept country labourers set in their ways. Their ignorance was profound and this limited migration. However, a large number of country folk moved into towns, mainly the large northern industrial ones, like Bradford, Liverpool and Manchester. By 1851, only about a quarter of their adult inhabitants had been born there; the rest were immigrants.[6] By the 1870s, however, the farming boom of the 1860s was over and the first agricultural depression, 1874–1884, was causing severe rural poverty. 'It couldn't get any worse' must have been the thought of many agricultural labourers and similar low-paid workers in the Wychwoods and elsewhere. They were faced with the terrifying prospect of the Chipping Norton workhouse, or 'bastille' as it was often called, if they lost their jobs.

This led to the peak in emigration from the Wychwoods to New Zealand in 1872–75. A study of New Zealand Immigration Department passenger lists shows that about two thirds of the assisted immigrants who left Oxfordshire for the colony in the 1870s sailed in 1874.[7] During this year, 81 immigrant ships were dispatched from London and Plymouth, and 67 of these carried some immigrants from Oxfordshire.[8] If a villager emigrated, made good and wrote back to relatives and friends, the impact could be considerable. This was the case in the Wychwoods, where many positive letters were received from emigrants to New Zealand. After the peak in emigration from the Wychwoods in 1874, there was a decline, partly due to the loss of interest by the National Agricultural Labourers' Union and increasing economic difficulties in New Zealand, and partially because the 20–30 per cent increase in wages secured by many labourers by the mid-1870s was sufficient to keep them on the land.[9] There was also the loss of life in the *Cospatrick* disaster in November 1874 (see below) but there is evidence of subsequent emigration from Ascott to Perth and Western Australia.

Agricultural depressions

In 1851, agriculture employed over one-fifth of the working population and produced about the same proportion of the national income.[10] The agricultural depression of 1874–84 brought an end to the farming boom of the 1860s and caused severe rural poverty. This had struck the Wychwoods well before 1874, the area's peak year of emigration. In Joseph Ashby's Tysoe, Warwickshire, 'After 1877, the exodus became slower but did not cease but went by twos and threes after the Great Exodus. Emigrants' letters spoke of "free growing fruits" in Vermont, the "land of liberty," the States, where every man can speak his thoughts, of Australia's plentiful meat. Sometimes the men in Australia would comment on the wasteful, unskilled farm work they saw – it wanted more of the Tysoe men!'[11]

The problem was aggravated by a second agricultural depression from 1891 to 1899, partly caused by foreign competition, with frozen meat coming in from Australia, New Zealand and South America. Even in Flora Thompson's fictionalised Oxfordshire community Lark Rise (Juniper Hill), after the Golden Jubilee of 1887, 'nothing ever seemed quite the same.' and 'The Innkeeper's wife got in cases of salmon from Australia and Australian rabbit.'[12] There was also growing competition from mass-produced goods and declining local markets, which affected, for example, boot-makers, blacksmiths, tailors and wheelwrights. It also affected women's employment. In 1901, the novelist H. Rider Haggard was told by the schoolmaster in Greater Rollright, near Chipping Norton, that 'three quarters of the young men and all the young women left the village at nineteen or twenty years of age, only the dullest staying at home.'[13] By 1901, agriculture employed less than a tenth of the labour force and its share of national income was less than a fifteenth. The consequent lack of demand for farm labourers meant low wages and, by 1907, the Oxfordshire weekly agricultural wage was the lowest in England and Wales at 14s 11d (75p in modern currency but worth about £320 at 2022 values).

Agricultural trade unionism

In April 1872, Milton-under-Wychwood formed its own agricultural trade union and by Whit Monday it was described as 'an independent movement with thirteen branches and over 500 members'.[14] The main aim of the new agricultural trade unions was to secure an extension of the franchise to rural householders (not achieved until 1884), and improved wages and conditions of employment. Joseph Arch and other leaders of the new NALU came to see that, by emigration, local surpluses of labour could be eliminated, and the bargaining position of those who remained behind would be strengthened. So, this led to the development of union-sponsored emigration, and in 1872–3 real interest in emigration among farm workers became apparent.

In July 1872, Charles Carter, an emigration agent for New Zealand, held a meeting in Shipton and he recruited ten families, who embarked on the *Chile*. The close links between the Oxfordshire rural unions, particularly the Milton one, and emigration to New Zealand date from the recruitment of this party. The *Chile* sailed from London on 12 September 1872, reaching Napier (Hawkes Bay) on 29 December 1872, with 220 assisted emigrants, of whom 192 had been recruited for Brogdens, the rail contractors, mainly from Cornwall.[15]

In late 1873, New Zealand offered free passages for suitable emigrants, and there was an immediate response in the Wychwood villages. Two thirds of assisted emigrants who left for New Zealand in the 1870s sailed in 1874 (Table 3).[16]

Departure date	Ship	From	To	Arrival
12 Sep 1872	Chile	London	Napier	29-Dec-72
22 Nov 1873	Invererne	London	Hawkes Bay	08-Mar-74
23 Dec 1873	Mongol	Plymouth	Port Chalmers	13-Feb-74
26 Dec 1873	Scimitar	Plymouth	Canterbury	05-Mar-74
04 Mar 1874	Ballochmyle	Plymouth	Canterbury	01-Jun-74
24 Mar 1874	Halcione	London	Hawkes Bay	06-Jul-74
1 Sep 1874	Assaye	London	Auckland	26-Dec-74
12 Sep 1874	Cospatrick	London	Auckland	Note
25 Sep 1874	Crusader	Plymouth	Canterbury	31-Dec-74
27 Oct 1874	Waimate	London	Canterbury	25-Jan-75
31 Oct 1874	Michael Angelo	London	Nelson	22-Jan-75
3 Nov 1874	Lady Jocelyn	Plymouth	Canterbury	21-Jan-75
20 Nov 1874	Hudson	Plymouth	Hawkes Bay	12-Feb-75

Note: The Cospatrick was destroyed by fire in the Bass Straits, Australia, on 17 Novemebr 1874.

Table 3: Wychwood emigrant ships to New Zealand 1872–1875.

In 1872, Wootton, close to the Wychwoods, was also a centre of agricultural unrest, with an early branch of the NALU formed in May 1872 under the chairmanship of Christopher Holloway, a staunch Methodist and lay preacher. He helped Milton form its branch, and in October 1872, he was elected chairman of the Oxford District of the NALU. The New Zealand authorities hired him and Henry Taylor to act as agents to select suitable migrants and accompany them all the way to New Zealand. They used their standing among the agricultural communities of Warwickshire and Oxfordshire to attract migrants.

On 4 November 1873, Holloway invited Carter to address a meeting of labourers at Milton. The meeting was held in Isaac Castle's large new marquee and 500–600 were present. Castle was a committed Primitive Methodist. A collection of £17 was made to help a group of about 80 leave from London on the *Invererne* on 22 November 1873.They reached Napier (Hawkes Bay) on 8 March 1874. The group included John Ireland with his large family, also several large interrelated families, all from the Wychwoods and many of them active in the agricultural union movement and Nonconformist chapels.

On 29 November 1873, the *Labourers' Union Chronicle* published an article encouraging emigration, including the following: 'Away, then, farm labourers, away! New Zealand is the promised land for you, and the Moses that will lead you is ready.'[17] Such was the response that the New Zealand government chartered the *Scimitar* the same day. On 13 December 1873, the Holloway and Taylor contingent set off from Leamington, picking up a further group of 43 from Tysoe at Banbury, and yet more emigrants at Oxford, including villagers from Wootton and the Wychwoods. By the time they reached Plymouth by train, there were 700 men, women and children in the party. They set sail in two vessels of the New Zealand Shipping Company, the steamer *Mongol* and the sailing ship *Scimitar* on 23 and 26 December 1873 to Canterbury and Dunedin, where the *Mongol* arrived in a record 51 days and the *Scimitar* in 71 days, a sailing ship record which stood for 25 years.

The county's staunch support for the NALU is apparent in the substantial groups that joined each party that left the midland counties under the leadership of a delegate of the union. Four such parties left during 1874, all for Canterbury, with a total of 315 Oxfordshire emigrants. Thomas Osborne led the last union party of 1874, on the *Lady Jocelyn* on 3 November. Among her 72 Oxfordshire emigrants were at least 19 from the Wychwood villages of Milton and Lyneham. The ships dispatched to Hawkes Bay during 1874 took 150 Oxfordshire emigrants, including nearly 40 from the Wychwood villages, and many from villages in the area. By autumn 1874, New Zealand must have been a household name in the Wychwood villages, particularly in Milton, which had sent about 140 emigrants there, and must have had links with the colony as strong as any place in England.[18]

By 1874, farmers were replying to union demands with lockouts, blackleg labour and eviction of union supporters from their cottages. From this point onwards union membership began to decline and by 1879 little remained of the enthusiasm seven years before. 'The Revolt of the Field' had failed and its leaders turned to political action. The NALU's membership had fallen from over 86,000 in 1874 to 15,000 by the end of 1881 and by 1889 was a mere 4,254. During the period 1872–81 an estimated 40,000 to 45,000 trade unionists and their families might be accepted for total NALU-sponsored emigration. This assumes that each male emigrant would, on average, be accompanied by three dependents.[19] It seems that most of the emigrants were satisfied with their move and they soon wrote to their families to tell them so. Furthermore, some of the union officials who escorted parties out to the colonies also decided to settle there, notably Joseph Leggett in New Zealand and Henry Taylor in South Australia. As for the NALU and the agricultural unions, after 1881 they virtually ceased to play any part at all in the sponsored emigration of their members.[20]

Passages

Between 1860 and 1900, an estimated 1,500,000 farm workers emigrated from Britain and most of them found a better standard of living and a less divided society. As noted above, this included a sizable number from the Wychwoods. There must have been an element of excitement among those headed for (say) Australia or New Zealand but the prospect of the long, uncomfortable and dangerous passages in sailing ships must have been very daunting for potential emigrants. Most of them were agricultural labourers, who had barely even left their parishes. For a start, it was a long train journey to London or Plymouth. The hustle and bustle of a big city must have been terrifying. There were all sorts of risks from rogue sellers of lodgings and passages, and all the supposed requirements for the journey.

By the 1850s, the length of the journeys and the conditions on board were improving. After the mid-1850s, a new non-stop route to Australia picked up the Roaring Forties for a high-speed dash across the Southern Ocean. By then many sailing ships also had auxiliary steam engines powered by a single screw, so that they did not get becalmed in the doldrums and made 75–80 days a realistic target. By the 1870s, steamships were regularly carrying emigrants to Australia, although sailing ships continued to the end of the 19th century. Improved engines allowed ships to maintain speeds of 15 knots, cutting the journey down to 40–50 days.

It was easier for people arriving in Australia than the United States. Unlike the United States, Canada, Australia, New Zealand and Argentina continued to operate liberal

Tackley memorial to the *Cataraqui* disaster.

The *Cospatrick* at Gravesend in 1856
and the Shipton memorial to the disaster.

immigration policies and to encourage immigration with assisted passages well into the 1930s. The 1852 Passenger Act allowed emigrants to stay on board free of charge for 48 hours after arrival, which gave them more time to find somewhere decent to live and even a chance to find a job.[21] There were also immigrant depots at Melbourne, Sydney and Port Phillip, where they could stay free of charge. Often all the emigrants had been engaged within 48 hours after the inspection was over. There was a scramble for housemaids, because of the scarcity of servants, the result of most young eligible women finding husbands quickly. Young females were warned against marrying the first settler they met. One young woman from Newcastle on arrival in Port Phillip was more sensible and turned down an offer of marriage with the comment, 'Nay, nay hinney,' she said very cavalierly, 'nay, my hinney, I'se to wait a wee and see what turns up.'[22]

Disasters

In 1847-52, 43 emigrant ships were lost out of the 6,877 which left British ports and, out of 1,400,000 passengers on them, 1,043 died as result of shipwreck or fire.[23] Many fell victim to the epidemics rife on the emigrant ships, which were the true killers. There were two disasters where there was serious loss of local lives.

First, on 4 August 1845, the wreck of the *Cataraqui* occurred off King Island, just one day short of their destination in Port Phillip: the ship sank and broke up, leaving 399 dead and only nine survivors (eight of them crewmen). The dead included 42 villagers from Tackley and 15 from Stonesfield among the 96 from Oxfordshire.[24] Fortunately, David Howie, who was on the island collecting animal furs was able to help the survivors. They were eventually picked up and delivered to Melbourne on 13 September. On 2 August 2020, to mark the 175th anniversary of the shipwreck, a cairn with a ship's bell and a plaque listing all the names of the dead, was unveiled on King Island, South Australia, by Greta Robinson, great-granddaughter of David Howie. There is also a beautifully carved oak door in St Nicholas' Church, Tackley, dedicated to the 42 villagers who died in the shipwreck.[25]

Secondly, on 17 November 1874, the *Cospatrick* disaster occurred. The ship embarked at the Blackwall emigrant depot near London with 470 passengers and crew and sailed for Auckland on 11 September 1874. There were only three survivors, members of the crew, when the ship caught fire on 17 November 1874, 250 miles west of the Cape of Good Hope. Seventeen Shipton residents were lost, all members of the families of Richard Hedges and Henry Townsend. Four years later, a stone memorial fountain was erected on the village green at Shipton to commemorate the community's tragic loss.[26]

Epidemic diseases

Nevertheless, it was the epidemic diseases, not the disasters, which were the real killers. In 1848, of those who left England for Quebec, 5,293 died of typhus during the voyage, and a further 10,037 in Canadian hospitals. Many were fleeing the Irish potato famine or the Scottish Highland clearances.[27] In 1852, the *Ticonderogo* sailed from Liverpool to Melbourne with 795 emigrants, of whom 100 died of typhus, and an equal number of cases of the fever were still suffering when the ship went into quarantine at Port Phillip Heads. A quarantine ship was sent alongside with stores for three months. The citizens of Melbourne were appalled.[28] Cholera was even more malignant and inspired greater fear. In 1853, for example, of the 77 ships that set sail from Liverpool for New York, 46 were stricken with cholera and 1,328 emigrants died of it.[29]

By the mid-19th century, however, every European maritime nation and every country receiving emigrants had built up an elaborate code of regulations, covering the limited numbers to be carried, specified amount of food and water to be carried and issued and minimum standards of ventilation and sanitation. The regulatory framework of assisted passages to Australia and New Zealand meant a higher chance of survival than on the shorter, unregulated crossing to North America. New Zealand was late in establishing quarantine stations, only designating Somes Island, or Matiu, in 1869. Even then it was not used as such until 1872.[30] In 1874, the voyages of the *Mongol* and the *Scimitar*, which carried a sizable number from the Wychwoods, both had epidemics of measles and scarlet fever, with 15 and 26 deaths, all children except for two. Both ships were quarantined and were the subjects of Royal Commission enquiries. However, there is no evidence of typhus or cholera on the Wychwood ships 1872–75.

Emigrants to New Zealand in the 1870s

On 28 December 1872, as noted above, the first Brogden shipment on the *Chile* arrived in Hawkes Bay, to be met by John Brogden. By August 1873, 2,172 immigrants had been brought out under this scheme. They included 1,299 working-age men, who were contracted to work for Brogdens for two years but, by August, only 287 were still working for them. Most of these men were agricultural

Map of New Zealand.

labourers, rather than true navvies, and they preferred agricultural work.[31]

On 28 February 1874, a group of 111 Oxfordshire labourers sailed from Plymouth to Canterbury, New Zealand, on the *Ballochmyle*, led by Joseph Leggett, secretary of the Oxford District of the NALU, and a former carpenter from Milton. Apart from the large Leggett family, the group included three other large families from Milton, the Groves, Stringers and Wilks. Eli Pratley, who married Elizabeth, one of the Ascott Martyrs, emigrated to Canada; sadly she died shortly afterwards, and, in November 1873, he returned to Ascott with his children, all in wretched condition. His half-brother, John, was married to Ellen, also one of the Ascott Martyrs. In December 1873, John's son Philip left for New Zealand with his wife, Jane and three children, on the *Mongol*. Eli himself remarried on 16 May 1874 and emigrated for the second time from Plymouth on the *Crusader* on 26 September, with a group of 101 led by George Allington (a regular member of delegate meetings of the NALU). Eli's brother, Frederick Pratley, was on the same ship, with his wife, Mary Ann, another of the Ascott Martyrs, and six children. Both prospered farming on the South Island (see below).[32]

After the arrival of the *Mongol* and *Scimitar* in February and March 1874, local Union representative Christopher Holloway (see essay 1) spent several months touring all parts of New Zealand. In a letter of March 1874, he wrote, 'New Zealand is now in a very prosperous condition. Labourers get 8s for a day of 8 hours, and there is likely to be plenty of work for some years… Provisions cheap, clothing slightly dearer than at home; religious privileges great, and education within reach of everyone'. Joseph Leggett 'spent the first night in his new abode' (in Nelson) with Christopher, and the latter was at once able to 'procure a situation of 12s per day for him'. He also had an interview with the Premier (the Hon. Julius Vogel) and mixed 'pretty freely with all classes of the community'. In spring 1875, after his delayed return to England, he became 'a special travelling agent' of the New Zealand government.[33]

Four NALU parties left in 1874, all for Canterbury, carrying 315 emigrants. In general, all of them were impressed by the care and attention paid to them on board ship. Their welfare was the constant concern of a surgeon-superintendent appointed by the Agent General. They were so well fed that one emigrant said that he had never lived so well. On arrival the New Zealand government inspectors came on board and asked whether the captain and doctor had treated them well. They also sent them a boatload of bread and other provisions. There was similar care and attention at other depots as they moved up country. In some communities, like New Plymouth, the local community was so thrilled at the reappearance of immigrant ships, after a lapse of nearly 20 years, that they provided a public banquet for each party while they were at the depot. There were, of course, often also relatives and old friends waiting to welcome them.

As each party arrived, the local immigration officer advertised the date on which they would be available for engagement. Henry Kaill, a labourer from Dorset who arrived on the *Atrato* in June 1874, describes such an occasion at Christchurch barracks. 'The next day after landing was hiring day – it was like a fair, the men that were mostly wanted were ploughmen, and single couples to live in doors. There were plenty of masters; I engaged with a gentleman as ploughman, at £80 per year'. Most immigrants would have agreed with him that 'no working man in England has any idea what a good master is'.[34] The major benefits mentioned in letters home were good wages, good cheap food, short eight-hour days and the relief of easy trips to the local shop. They were also full of praise for their employers, who were often like a father and mother. As one immigrant put it, 'We live first class and dine with our master.'

As Alfred Simons, the Kent Union's leader, reported when he visited New Zealand in 1879: 'There are no poor laws and no poor law guardians! And there are no union workhouses and no starving poor!'[35] He also wrote of a widespread Good Samaritan spirit which meant that the travelling labourer was readily fed at almost any door. This unusual practice had developed in the convict settlements of Australia; the custom spread to meet the needs of any itinerant workman and crossed the Tasman Sea to New Zealand. Settlers benefited by being able to draw on the wandering work force. As the servant girl Harriet Herbert put it, 'There is no bitter oppression here – all are equal and free.'[36]

The New Zealand employers did not expect to be 'sired' or treated with any form of deference. The men also enjoyed riding out and the hunting of boars, rabbits, pigeons, ducks and goats in the bush 'but you must have a good horse and gun. Nearly all have a horse to ride to work.'[37] For women, the saddle was also important and the ability to dress suitably for the occasion. They could go to church on horseback and wearing silk dresses. For them, the enrichment which colonial emigration could bring to family life was the main inducement to women's emigration. For single women, emigration led swiftly to marriage. Everyone was much fitter, partly because most of them were young and fit and the number of aged immigrants was small. The drive of strong personal ambition also stands out as one of the potent shaping forces in 19th-century New Zealand society. No immigrant could remain unaffected by this prevailing atmosphere.[38]

Methodists in New Zealand

Many immigrants were religious and were quickly absorbed into their new environment. Methodists who arrived as strangers were soon made welcome by their co-religionists and convinced them, as one immigrant

expressed it, that 'there is the same God here as is at home'.
[39] George Mumby and John Borman, newly arrived from
Lincolnshire, went from the New Plymouth Immigration
Barracks to chapel on their first Sunday in Taranaki in
September 1875. They were welcomed by name from the
pulpit and Borman was engaged to take a lay preaching
assignment out in the country that afternoon. In June
1874, a Primitive Methodist enthusiast went to the
Ashburton barracks, asking if there were Methodist of any
kind among the new arrivals. He was quickly introduced
to George Aston, from Gloucestershire, who had enlivened
the voyage of the *Ballochmyle* with his hymn-singing. The
Astons had been Wesleyans but his welcome led to him
joining the Primitive Methodists in New Zealand. William
Philpott, aged 49, was one of the large groups from Tysoe
included in Holloway's party of 1873. He settled on an
18-acre bush station and sold firewood in neighbouring
Invercargill. Although Scots Presbyterians surrounded
him, he maintained his connections with the Methodists
by attending fortnightly meetings in a local farm.

Wychwood emigrants

a) To New Zealand

'We CAN LIVE here, but we only lingered in England.' So
wrote John Timms, late secretary of the Ascott branch of the
Union, as a pithy summary of his first nine months in New
Zealand.[40] He had sailed on the *Crusader* in September 1874,
among the two-thirds of assisted emigrants who left for New
Zealand in the 1870s. Sixty-seven of the 81 immigrant ships
which sailed in 1874 carried some Oxfordshire immigrants,
seven of them to Hawkes Bay. They included an Oxfordshire

group of about 80, who sailed on the *Invererne* to Hawkes Bay on 22 November 1873. Initially, they in the main took up and cleared forest country, and included the following Wychwood members:[41]

- John Mycock, 44, of Charlbury, his wife, Sarah, and six children. By 1882, he was farming 68 acres of his own worth £250 at Ormandville.
- Edward Harding of Taynton, his wife, Sarah, and five children. He was a staunch unionist. By 1882, he owned 144 acres of freehold at Woodville worth £1,136, on which he was running 295 sheep by 1883.
- John Ireland of Milton, wife, Phillis, and ten children and two grandchildren; owned 108 acres at Makaretu in 1882.
- John Pinfold, secretary of the Taynton branch of the NALU, sailed on the *SS Hudson* in November 1874, and settled in Woodville.

The Woodville Settlement, founded in 1875, had a strong Oxfordshire contingent, including the Hardings and others from the *Inverene*, among them their daughter and son-in-law, Henry and Frances Cox, and Edward and Eliza Groves, and their six children, all from Milton. By 1882, seven of the ten married men from Oxfordshire on the *Invererne* owned freehold land.

In 1874, the following also arrived from the Wychwoods:

- On *Crusader,* Peter and Millicent Honeybourne, of Ascott, with their eight-year-old son, Thomas. He quickly became a contractor, building roads and a portion of the Christchurch tramway. He settled in Waikiri in Canterbury, where he lived for 50 years and established a carrying business. Later, his son ran the business – with three waggons, two spring drays, a gig and a tip cart..

- On *Assaye*, Henry Hutt, six-year-old son of James and Esther Hutt of Charlbury, later appointed manager of Paeroa Creamery in Auckland in 1899.
- On *Waimate*, Charles Barnes, 14, came out with his parents, Thomas and Ann. By 1899, he was combining farming with running an agricultural contracting business for which he had a 'complete agricultural plant'.
- Eli Pratley emigrated on *Crusader* with his new wife, and a daughter aged five. (The photograph shows Eli Pratley and family.) His brother, Frederick, was on the same ship, with his wife, Mary Ann, who had been one of the Ascott Martyrs, and six children. Both brothers prospered farming on the South Island, initially on a joint lease, and later on separate farms. Eli had ten sons and one daughter.

All the above men were labourers and in a few years were freeholders – an impossible dream for their friends left in the Wychwoods.

Eli and Jane Pratley and their children.

b) To Western Australia [42]

After the decline in emigration to New Zealand, there is evidence of continuing local interest in emigration to Western Australia. In 1876, James Townsend sailed to Perth, as did George White in 1879. On 29 October 1880, Frank Gomm with Alfred and Edwin Townsend sailed on the *Potosi* to Perth. In June 1881, James and Albert Weaver, another George White and Henry Pratley with Thomas Ward and his new wife (formerly Sarah Ann Hone) sailed on the *Charlotte Padbury* for Perth. Mixed fortunes attended these Ascott lads. Edwin Townsend married Lucy Ann Drummond in 1887 but sadly died in 1900, aged only 36. Raymond and Henry Pratley married in 1884 but nothing more is known. Albert and James Weaver also married in 1884. Albert married Charlotte Staples in Fremantle. They had at least one son, born in 1889. Charlotte died in 1914, Albert in 1938. James married Sarah Hyde who died in the same year, aged only 18. Their son, James Albert, died the following year. James married again in 1888. George White married Jane McGowan in 1884 but died the following year, aged only 26.

Conclusion

This reveals how successful emigration could be for those brave enough to undertake the long journey to New Zealand in the 1870s. The significant numbers from the Wychwood villages included the Ascott Martyrs Jane and Mary Pratley, Amelia Moss, and Elizabeth Pratley, who went to Canada but sadly died there, plus Ann Moss to the United States. Many of these emigrants wrote home with glowing stories of life in New Zealand. Most were more than satisfied with their move and some of the union officials who escorted parties out to the colonies also decided to settle there, notably Joseph Leggett in New Zealand, and Henry Taylor in South Australia. Even after the peak in emigration from the Wychwoods to New Zealand in the 1870s, interest continued in Perth and Western Australia.

Emigration acted as an escape and was indeed the Promised Land but it was also a break with families at a time when communication was very difficult and the chances of meeting their family again virtually nil. They were brave and above average souls, built businesses and helped the fast-developing economies. If they had been treated better by English society, one can only imagine the positive contribution they could have made back in the Wychwoods.

10

Electoral reform, politics and the Ascott Martyrs

NICK MANSFIELD

'If the labourers' position was to improve, the franchise must be extended to households and individual men, so that they could be eligible to vote and represent the needs of labourers in Parliament.'

Christopher Holloway, NALU Oxfordshire activist, 1873

In 1873 none of the Ascott women were able to vote in local or parliamentary elections. While the women were excluded by virtue of their gender, their menfolk were also unable to vote on account of poverty. Their economic overlords dominated the political system by exercising their right to vote in the very restrictive franchise.

Nevertheless, the system was changing around them. This essay looks at the pattern of government and elections affecting the Ascott women in the late 19th and early 20th century as Britain evolved into a democracy. It outlines the parliamentary reform acts of 1832, 1867, 1884–5 and 1918, concentrating on legislation which applied especially to rural areas, such as the introduction of the secret ballot in

1872 and improvements in local government. It examines how these changes impacted on politics in the Wychwood district, particularly in relation to the National Agricultural Labourers' Union (NALU). The Liberalism of the NALU leader, Joseph Arch, was countered by the pervasive influence of the Conservative estates in an area where paternalism successfully incorporated self-help efforts among the rural poor. In all this, both the Ascott women and the striking farmworkers they attempted to support were politically powerless. This helps explain why support for the NALU was so intense, verging on a messianic crusade. Though the 1867 Reform Act had increased the overall numbers of electors, the household qualification introduced in towns did not apply to the countryside. The Ascott strikers of 1873 were excluded while those they saw as oppressors – landowners, farmers and professional men – dominated the electorate. The arrested women had no part in the political process. Forbidden to be actual members of the NALU, they resisted in a traditional way.

For several centuries, all over rural Britain, transgressors of established village mores were subject to traditional collective direct action. Offenders' effigies were paraded and ridiculed, accompanied by street bands of improvised musical instruments, in a boisterous charivari known as 'rough music'. Often the offenders were village men and women whose sexual activities were censured. But 'rough music' also applied to those seen as oppressors of the poor, like millers and grain dealers during early 19th century bread protests. They featured unpopular employers from the Captain Swing riots in the 1830s to farmers resisting NALU wage claims in the 1870s. The Ascott women would have been fully aware of this tradition. Their semi-humorous jostling of the two hapless strike-breaking youths from a neighbouring, possibly rival village clearly gained widespread community approval. As Fanny Rathband (née Honeybone) recalled in old age: 'There was something of the idea of fun in what we did – certainly no intention to harm them.'[1]

Early 19th century parliamentary reform

Parliamentary democracy was based on medieval precedents until the early 19th century, resulting in a grossly unfair and corrupt system, dominated by wealth. During the 17th century, Oliver Cromwell's republican government transferred seats from 'rotten boroughs' to some large towns and attempted to standardise voting qualifications. But this was reversed with the restoration of the monarchy in 1660.

Britain's changing needs as the world's first industrial country required a more serviceable system. This did not come about until the Reform Act of 1832, which established standardised voting qualification based on land ownership and abolished the worst abuses of the old system. Even this modest measure nearly led to civil war as opponents of reform equated any change with revolution and anarchy. To defeat these threats, the reforming Whigs mobilised radical working-class supporters, especially those from the emerging trade unions. They were bitterly disappointed when the modest franchise was revealed. In the generation from 1832, working-class radicals campaigned for one man, one vote, with the Chartist movement being the most significant element. By the 1840s, Chartism was mobilising thousands of supporters through mass meetings and collecting millions of signatures for its petitions to Parliament. The electorate was tiny by modern standards; for example Banbury Borough after 1832 had 329 voters. Henry Vincent, a prominent Chartist leader, stood for Banbury in 1841 but only secured 51 votes. There is little evidence that in Oxfordshire villages Chartism made any impact, though the Chartist Land Company briefly established a settlement at Minster Lovell in 1847. This was one of six colonies that the mercurial leader, Feargus O'Connor, established in southern England, with the objective of settling Chartists as self-sufficient peasants and enabling them to own enough land to qualify for the vote. But the financial underpinning of the Land Company was unsound. The 'spade husbandry' of the colonists was unequal to modern British agriculture and the scheme rapidly collapsed in debt and scandal.[2]

Deserving voters

This disaster led to the rapid decline of the Chartist movement, though demands for further electoral reform were still propagated by working-class movements. However, by the mid-century economic prosperity was improving. In particular, the pattern of boom and slump of early British capitalism was evened out. The grand spectacle of the Great Exhibition of 1851, highlighting British ingenuity and prosperity, seemed to turn its back on the 'hungry 40s'. It was visited by large numbers of working-class people, though it is unlikely that any of the rural poor of Ascott could afford to attend. A range of self-governing self-help organisations also prospered in this new climate. Trade unions developed from small, embattled, locally based societies to national organisations which were bureaucratic but professional. Initially comprising only skilled workers, and charging high subscriptions, 'New Model' unions found a niche role in the well-developed late Victorian industrial structure. Though these were found in Oxfordshire only in the market towns, the growing friendly society movement, based on large national 'affiliated' groups like the Foresters and Oddfellows, was active in many villages. It attracted the penny subscriptions of even poorly paid farmworkers, wishing to insure against sickness or accident.[3]

The country towns of the south Midlands saw the growth of consumer cooperatives based on the Rochdale principles of 1844. This accelerated after the formation of the Co-operative Wholesale Society in 1863, which facilitated large-scale and cheap wholesaling for local stores. By the end of the century, cooperatives dominated British working-class retailing with cradle-to-grave services.

Another working-class self-help movement which had already started a generation before 1873 was Primitive Methodism (see essay 5). From its origin in 1807, it experienced growth spurts in the 1830s and 1870s. As a member-led group its proponents gained organising and speaking skills which were to contribute much to the messianic flavour of the NALU (Joseph Arch was a Primitive Methodist). Together with the more middle-class Wesleyan Methodists it also contributed to the allied burgeoning temperance movement which campaigned against drinking alcohol, and numbered three million British members by the 1860s. All these self-help movements led to a more respectable, sober, considered and educated working class which deemed itself worthy of the right to vote.[4]

By contrast, gentry paternalism – still very significant in Oxfordshire – chose to provide and support improving activities for the deserving rural poor to distract them from demanding the right to vote. Landowners created village institutions like reading rooms and allotments which they could control. This even applied to cooperatives, as the late Malcolm Bee found evidence of paternalistic cooperatives in Oxfordshire. At Long Hanborough, the Duke of Marlborough instigated a branch of the Oxford Co-operative Society, presented the shop and gave his estate workers land to build cottages if they saved enough dividend towards a mortgage. In 1882 the Earl of Jersey of Middleton Hall (described as 'an excellent co-operator') founded the hundred-strong Middleton Stoney Society and subsidised it even when it ran into financial difficulties, until his death in 1913. Contemporaneously, the larger Steeple Aston Society built a well-stocked shop with a loan from the vicar which was run for 20 years by the village schoolmaster.[5]

The Reform Act of 1867

There was political division on the issue of extending the right to vote to the respectable working class. The Liberals, who espoused self-help values, wanted to press ahead, enfranchising what they saw as potential supporters to threaten Tory domination of rural heartlands. The Conservatives wanted to restrict the right to vote to those they patronised, while cautiously recognising that self-help cultural change made further reform inevitable.

During 1866 a series of mass meetings were held in

cities by the Reform League, mainly trade unionists backed by the Liberals. The government attempted to close Hyde Park in London to several hundred thousand protestors but was forced to back down when the immense crowds pulled down the park's railings, allowing the meeting to be held. Fearing more disturbances Benjamin Disraeli, leading a minority Conservative government, bowed to the pressure and introduced his own moderate Reform Act; 'A Leap in the Dark', in the title of Tenniel's famous *Punch* cartoon. The Liberal opposition unavoidably had to give their support and the act was passed in 1867.

In urban areas the vote was extended to all male householders, along with lodgers paying £10 a year in rent, but it did not apply to rural areas like Oxfordshire. While the Act added 983,000 voters nationally, including some working-class householders, this only represented 13 per cent of the adult population. The Act's conservative character was paramount, concentrating on enfranchising household heads and granting extra votes to the wealthy, based on property qualification. There were still only 1,524 qualified voters in the Banbury constituency in 1868. The 16 voters in Ascott (population 463) were part of the Oxfordshire County constituency, which returned three members of parliament, often unopposed, in a deal between the Whigs and Tories, usually two to one in favour of the latter. We can be in no doubt that many of these voters were part of the 'principal inhabitants' that publicly supported the beleaguered magistrates at Chadlington petty sessions on 18 June 1873, held at Chipping Norton.[6]

Voting was also still declared in public with the results published, allowing widespread opportunities for bribery, corruption and intimidation of voters by landlords and employers. However, continuing pressure from the Reform League led to a new Liberal government, with Gladstone as Prime Minister, passing an act to introduce the secret ballot in 1872, despite Conservative opposition, especially from the Tory dominated House of Lords. Thereafter corruption and intimidation, even in gentry-dominated rural heartlands, would become more difficult.

The National Agricultural Labourers' Union

The introduction of the secret ballot took place within months of Joseph Arch (1826–1919), a self-employed Warwickshire hedge-cutter, being approached to form a national union for farmworkers. Arch was typical of the independent, respectable working-class men discussed above, a Methodist lay preacher and a Liberal supporter. His ownership of a cottage freehold qualified him for the vote in 1867.[7]

In contrast to urban areas, Victorian affluence was slow to percolate down to working-class people in the countryside. Farmworkers continued to be poorly paid and often lived in great poverty, with only the workhouse at the end of their hard lives. They were pitied and patronised by a trade union movement growing in confidence, which also feared that the migrating rural poor would be prepared to provide cheap blackleg labour in the cities. As successive reforms of Parliament extended the franchise to more working-class men, the Liberal Party, the ally of the mid-Victorian trade unions, saw an opportunity to attract new voters in the countryside by offering reform and the promise of alleviation of poverty, thereby threatening Tory domination of the countryside. The Liberals supported Arch as one of their local activists in the creation of the NALU. Liberal MPs and grandees dominated the founding national conference at Leamington Spa in May 1872 and effectively bankrolled the early organisation.

From Warwickshire, the union spread quickly throughout southern England, using outdoor revivalist meetings based on Primitive Methodism. They attracted mass attendances, and quickly claimed 100,000 members, making it the largest British trade union. (Overall the miners' unions were larger but organised on a regional basis.) Arch was rapidly promoted by the Liberal press as a charismatic figure and his homespun but inspired oration to mass rallies was described as 'the Revolt of the Field'. The term was coined by the celebrated correspondent of the *Daily News*, Archibald Forbes, fresh from reporting on the Franco-Prussian War and Paris Commune.

Through aggressive local strike action, skilfully matched to the needs of the farming year, the NALU generally succeeded in raising wages.[8] The Ascott strike occurred when the union was still growing, and although the NALU – along with most trade unions – was lukewarm about recruiting female members, as demonstrated by the Ascott women, their action was clearly supported by the whole village community.[9]

Emigration was a key NALU policy, in response to rural overpopulation and subsequent low pay. Arch visited Canada and Australia to promote his migration scheme and persuaded Australian states, desperate for skilled agricultural labour, to pay the wages of NALU officials and to charter special migrant ships (see essay 9). At the end of 1873 Christopher Holloway personally conducted a party of 500 from Milton-under-Wychwood and Wootton to New Zealand with the support of the colony's government. In the neighbouring county of Buckinghamshire, Edward Richardson, schoolmaster and NALU activist, shipped the rural poor of whole villages to Tasmania and Queensland. Several of the Ascott women later joined the imperial diaspora for a better life.[10]

From the union's first meetings, Arch had emphasised the key objective of extending the right to vote to farmworkers and argued that economic and political improvements went hand in hand. In November 1872, he also spoke at meetings of the Electoral Reform Association arguing that the rural franchise needed to be the householder vote as established in the boroughs in 1867.[11]

The welcoming event for the women returning from prison was held at Chipping Norton and attracted several thousand, mostly wearing the blue colours of the NALU. Though the main speaker was Joseph Arch, it fell to the local NALU and Liberal activist and Wootton farmworker Christopher Holloway (chairman of the Oxford District) to demand that 'if the labourers' position was to improve, the franchise must be extended to households and individual men, so that they could be eligible to vote and represent the needs of the labourers in Parliament'. None of the Ascott women spoke at this or subsequent meetings nor was the NALU ever committed to female suffrage, which leaves the sense that the Union was exploiting the women for its own purposes. When he returned for the celebratory rally

Membership emblem of the National Agricultural Labourers' Union, 1872. Joseph Arch's founding speech for the union at Wellesbourne, Warwickshire forms the centrepiece of the emblem design along with illustrations of union benefits. Members would proudly display such emblems in their cottage living rooms.

at Ascott on 20 June 1873, the women wore blue silk dresses provided by the Union and Arch presented them with £5 each, similar to the patronage they might have received from the gentry in different circumstances.[12] Christopher Holloway made a further speech on extending the franchise at a demonstration in Chipping Norton the following July 1873. By November 1873, George Otto Trevelyan, Liberal front bench MP, mentioned lack of representation by the rural poor of Ascott in a parliamentary speech advocating reform concluding: 'Those sorts of things are not done to people who have votes on the eve of a general election.'[13]

The Ascott strike occurred when the NALU was at its zenith. Regrettably for the union, Britain began to be affected by an agricultural depression which was to last for two decades. It was caused by the dramatic fall in grain prices that followed the opening up of the American prairies to cultivation in the 1870s, which undercut British farm prices. From the spring of 1874 a determined farmers' counterattack (supported by the Conservatives) resulted in a large-scale lockout of Union members in eastern England. Strike payments for members effectively bankrupted the Union, which ordered its members to return to work by August. Arch's actions were bitterly criticised and many left the NALU, often joining the independent 'federal' unions which had developed in some counties, exasperated by Arch's domineering and quarrelsome nature. Arch's attempt to stabilise the Union through offering accident, sickness and funeral benefits to its members turned out to be an actuarial disaster for a union with modest contributions, and hastened its downfall. Though subject to periodical revivals by tireless and courageous activists, the Union declined more quickly than it rose and was disbanded in the early 1890s (see graph in essay 2, page 57).

The 1884–1885 Reform Acts

Many miners in coalfield areas were enfranchised under the 1867 Act and their unions allied with Liberal Associations to elect miners' leaders as MPs. These 'Lib–Lab' MPs were at the forefront of more agitation to extend the right to vote. After Gladstone's election victory of 1880 demonstrations were held nationwide, though Conservative opposition, particularly in the House of Lords, delayed the new Reform Act until 1884. The 1867 settlement was extended to all areas, creating nearly two million new voters, although 40 per cent of men and all women were still excluded.[14]

In 1885 the Redistribution of Seats Act abolished the old multi-member county seats in favour of single member rural constituencies, enabling MPs to develop more meaningful links with the electorate. The 1884–1885 acts at last gave voting rights to most of the former Ascott strikers, though not of course the Ascott Martyrs, who were women. Ascott was attached to the new Banbury constituency (now with 8,478 electors), which combined that old borough's radical tradition with the potential of the newly enfranchised farmworkers who could now cast their vote in secret. Ascott's own electorate grew from 16 in 1873 to 61 men by 1895.[15]

Thereafter, aside from two brief intervals, the constituency returned a Liberal until 1922, largely on the strength of farmworkers voting for the party. In the former farmworkers' union stronghold of North West Norfolk Joseph Arch was elected MP for 1885-6 and 1892–1900.

Although active as an additional 'Lib–Lab' MP, it is fair to say that his impact was not great, and no other former NALU leaders were elected, including in Oxfordshire.

Local government

With the spirit of reform embracing both parties, rural local government was improved with the formation of county councils in 1888 and parish councils in 1894. Property qualifications for standing were also abolished, enabling farmworkers' leaders to be elected and allowing some women to vote in local elections. In 1888 Arch was returned as county councillor in Wellesbourne, Warwickshire, where the NALU was first founded. In Norfolk George Edwards, farmworker, Liberal and former NALU activist was elected as a parish councillor and Poor Law guardian along with his wife Charlotte Edwards. (Later he became a county councillor.) This did not prevent him being sacked by a Tory employer for speaking at Liberal meetings in 1895. However, it gave Edwards the political and organisational skills to develop the farmworkers' union in the next generation when he re-founded it in Norfolk in 1906.[16]

In Ascott, 74 people qualified for county and parish council votes in 1895 including seven women for the first time. This made local government more accountable and in the village the vicar and church wardens were questioned about the management of parish charities.[17]

The revival of rural trades unionism and electoral reform

Additional female employment in the area had increased with the opening of a tweed mill by William Bliss in

Chipping Norton in 1872. After the disturbances in the town, when the convicted Ascott women were transferred to Oxford Gaol in May 1873, William Bliss issued a statement claiming that his workers were not involved. The mill provided better paid employment than erratic fieldwork or outdated glove-making for the next generation. In the Edwardian period, the factory was part of the growth of a lively general unionism in Oxfordshire led by the Workers' Union, which also organised farmworkers. Over 200 women and men took part in an unsuccessful strike at Bliss's Tweed Mill between December 1913 and June 1914, over union recognition and higher wages.[18]

As outlined earlier, in 1906 George Edwards revived the farmworkers' union in Norfolk. This was as a direct response to the massive Conservative intimidation and evictions by employers of farmworkers who were suspected of voting Liberal in the 1906 general election landslide. The new union campaigned from the beginning for universal manhood suffrage and representation of farmworkers in Parliament. Initially, the union was still small and regional and wages were still low. The First World War transformed the situation. Nationally 200,000 young farmworkers volunteered for Kitchener's appeal, finding themselves and their families much better off financially in the army. Farmworkers volunteered in disproportionally high numbers compared to other parts of rural society. This created a shortage of labour and the older farmworkers left at home demanded wage increases in a time of massive inflation. Edwards' union, the National Union of Agricultural and Allied Workers, successfully exploited the situation. It raised wages and quickly become larger than the unions of the 1870s, establishing itself permanently.

However, the war brought loss and misery in the villages. In Ascott 13 young villagers died in the conflict. In recognition of the wartime sacrifices, Prime Minister David Lloyd George passed the Representation of the People Act in 1918, which brought in votes for all men and for the first time included women over 30. The size of the electorate was tripled at a stroke. Fanny Rathband, the youngest of the Martyrs, was now on parliamentary and local government electoral rolls at nearby Milton-under-Wychwood.[19]

In 1918, the newly formed Labour Party began to make an impact in rural areas. Building on the former Bliss Mill strikers, a branch was formed in Chipping Norton. The farmworkers' union dissolved its link with the Liberals and George Edwards was elected as a Labour MP for South Norfolk in 1922. Thereafter, however, politics in Oxfordshire (outside the county town) would be dominated by the Conservatives, based on firm handling from local employers and the continuing paternalism of the landed estates. Even in the later general election landslide of 1945, which produced scores of rural Labour MPs, notably in East Anglia, none was returned for Oxfordshire. So, it could be argued that the long-term impact of Joseph Arch's 'Great Momentous Time' was lost and the sacrifices of the Ascott women were in vain.[20]

Conclusion

KEITH LAYBOURN

W hat emerges from this collection of essays is that the Oxfordshire countryside was in turmoil in the 1870s, as a result of both the precarious existence of the agricultural and rural workers and the importation of cheap American grain which was affecting cereal producers throughout Britain. The established authorities – the landed elite, tenant farmers, the Church of England and the clerical magistracy – were thus already under stress even before Joseph Arch organised agricultural labourers into a trade union to threaten strike actions for higher wages. This stress and the new pressures from the Union led to a bitter clash between the rural establishment and the agricultural and rural labourers. It was an unequal struggle where, in order to preserve the existing social and economic relationships of landowners, tenant farmers and agricultural labourers (with all the nuanced relationships in between) and the established level of wages, the rural establishment used the full weight of the law and their power to stifle the resistance of the agricultural labourers.

In normal circumstances this would have meant the possible imprisonment of male agricultural workers for not giving seven days' notice of a strike, but the National Agricultural Labourers' Union, and Joseph Arch, were mindful to avoid such dangers. Their supporters were not so careful. In the end, the case of the 16 women, the Ascott Martyrs, was possibly a result of their action in operating the local community 'rough justice' against those cutting across the moral code of the countryside and this being turned into the molestation of workers under the Criminal Law Amendment Act, provoking a national furore in the press and Parliament. It was possible that the Ascott Martyrs might not have been sentenced and imprisoned, for one clerical magistrate asked Hambidge to drop his charges against them. He did not do so, and so they were imprisoned, although the 'hard labour' element of the sentence was remitted (for those released after seven days, though it is not clear whether this was applied for those released after ten days) by a conditional pardon signed by Queen Victoria, although not an unconditional pardon denoting their wrongful imprisonment. Given that there was considerable protest at the time against their imprisonment it is likely that their release was more to do with the actions of the Home Secretary than a reflection of the interest of Queen Victoria in the affair.

The case of the Ascott Martyrs is one which throws into sharp relief both the poverty and immiseration of rural and agricultural workers and the misogynist nature of British society in the 19th century. It made them unlikely and unwilling secular martyrs because of their railing against the unjust system in which they operated. Yet their fame was fleeting.

Indeed, the impact of their secular martyrdom was short lived. The rural establishment endorsed the vertical paternalistic nature of their rule, the National Agricultural Labourers' Union organised emigration for the impoverished families of rural Oxfordshire, including some of the Ascott Martyrs, and the political and religious dissent that might have led to radical change was never to flicker much in the countryside after the emigration of agricultural labourers, many of whom were Nonconformists in religion. Not surprisingly, the Labour Party was not able to win significant support for democratic change and liberty in rural Oxfordshire.

This is not to say that the sacrifices of these women were in vain, for it represented one aspect of the challenge against the British establishment that was to see the widening of citizenship in Britain and the vote to all adults. They were unjustly imprisoned, accepted as secular martyrs for a short time, but with the revival of interest in them in the last 50 years there has been increasing commemoration of their fate and suffering. Their martyrdom was just as significant and important as that of the Tolpuddle Martyrs and that of Emily Davison in the demand for democratic rights and liberty that were won in the 20th century. It was an early and important part of the slow process which has brought us to the establishment of mass democracy and to women's rights, even if there remains a long way to go.

Appendices

A. LETTERS TO *THE TIMES* AND TO THE *OXFORDSHIRE WEEKLY NEWS*

Researched by Harvey Warner member of Ascott Martyrs Educational Trust study group.

In the days and weeks following the Ascott Martyrs' case going to trial, there were several letters published in national and local newspapers where people exchanged views of the case itself and, in one case, the living conditions of the 'poor' in Ascott-under-Wychwood. Several of these letters were addressed to the editor of *The Times*, the leading national newspaper of the time. These are produced below with the spellings and most of the punctuations as they were published at the time.

THE UNION LETTER – 21 MAY 1873

The first letter of any significance was from a Christopher Holloway, a local union official.

Sir, – Please use the following facts by way of publication in your valuable paper.

I am chairman of the Oxford district of the National Agricultural Labourers Union, and at Ascott, Oxfordshire, in my district, there has been for more than three weeks a lock-out of the farm labourers, and considerable excitement has prevailed in consequence.

Mr. Hambidge, a farmer there, has brought some

workmen from other villages to do the work of his former men, and several of the women of the parish, whose husbands are out of work, assembled on the 12th inst., and meeting Mr. Hambidge's men as there were going to work, tried to induce them to leave his employ. Mr. Hambidge took the matter up and caused 17 of the women to appear to-day before the magistrates at Chipping Norton, in this county, and the magistrates have sent 16 of these poor women to prison, seven of them for ten days' hard labour and nine for seven days' hard labour.

The witnesses swore that some of the women had sticks in their hands, and said that the men would not be allowed to go to work. The women denied this altogether. Anyhow, it was not attempted to be proved that any physical force was made use of. The women are very respectable in the class to which they belong, and there was great excitement in the town of Chipping Norton on the decision of the magistrates being made known, and a crowd soon assembled, and I had considerable difficulty in restraining their anger. I fear that if I had not been present some violence would have been committed.

The people were astonished and bewildered at the sentences passed on such a number of poor women for what appeared to them no offence whatever. The women themselves had no idea that such a law existed as was now brought to bear on them with such terrible force.

I attended the magistrates meeting in the capacity I hold to watch the case and never in my life was I more shocked than to see these 16 poor women dragged off to prison, and some with infants at their breast.

C. HOLLOWAY. Woodstock, May 21.

THE FARMERS' LETTER – 30 MAY 1873

This letter that was signed by seven farmers from Ascott-under-Wychwood.

Sir, – We, the undersigned parochial officers and tenant farmers of the parish of Ascott-under-Whychwood [*sic*], in the county of Oxford will feel greatly obliged if you will allow space in your widely-circulated paper for the correction by us of the misrepresentation and false colouring of the disgraceful conduct of molestation, intimidation and assault and subsequent riot by upwards of 20 women, wives and daughters of our agricultural labourers (Unionists).

The parish of Ascott-under-Whychwood consists of an area of 1,769a. 1r. 5p. of cultivated land, principally arable, and a population, according to the last Census, of 462, two-thirds of which are agricultural labourers and their families.

There is not one distressed family in the village; with two exceptions, the cottages and gardens are good, the rents low, and the allotments close to the village, and the general condition of the labouring poor above the average of that class.

The Agricultural Labourers' Society came to this village last year, since which time the quiet and well-being of this hitherto peaceful and orderly place have been disturbed by the disrespectful, vexatious, and riotous conduct of the employed to their employers.

Mr. Hambidge, the parish churchwarden, occupies a government farm of 400 acres. He settled with his farm labourers on Saturday evening, the 12th of April, apparently on good and friendly terms. The men subsequently attended a Union meeting, and when they presented themselves on the following Monday morning for work, they informed Mr. Hambidge that unless he gave them all an advance of 2s. a week they should leave him. He refused to raise the wages for all, but unhesitatingly advanced his efficient labourers, and observed that the others, from age or infirmity, must for the present remain at 12s, per week, but there was and would be plenty of piecework for them. These offers were refused; they were unanimous that unless all received an advance of 2s. per week, not one would continue to work for him. In a most friendly manner he advised them to consider what course would conduce most to their future well-being, and that if they felt disposed to work on the old terms for the present, he should be glad of their services, as the operations of his farm would be stopped without them, but he could not submit to dictation. They all left. The carters had fed and harnessed the horses and were going into the fields to drill barley. They returned, unharnessed the horses, shut the stable door and left the work.

Mr. Hambidge was left in the middle of a backward barley sowing, with 12 agricultural horses, four working bullocks, a superior flock of 500 sheep at turnips, milking cows, bullocks, and young stock, with only a head shepherd and a youth (yearly servants).

A parish meeting was immediately convened; it was desired to act in unison with neighbouring parishes, where the large, landed proprietors had met their tenants, and considered that 12s. per week for day labourers was a fair price, as there was, and would be continuous piece work at a higher rate than last year.

The following Monday morning, April 21, all the labourers belonging to the Union left the different farms in the village, refused to any kind of work for their former employers, and received 9s. per week from their society to be idle and offensive. After a lapse of a fortnight work was found for them in felling and barking timber five miles distant, whither upwards of 20 left the village, starting at 5 in the morning and returning at 7 in the evening. After walking ten miles and doing a hard day's work, they received 2s. 6d., at the same time they might have worked with their wives in the fields hoeing close to their homes at piece work, and earned more than double that sum. Under these circumstances, we the occupiers of the land had no alternative but to seek non-Union labourers where we could find them. Hence arose the outrageous conduct of upwards of 20 women, first in the public thoroughfare, and subsequently a riot in the village without a check, until a private individual sent for the neighbouring policeman. On his arrival he conducted the two labourers to their work in the fields followed by the women, who with some difficulty were persuaded to return to their homes. All the farmers had left the village at an early hour to attend a large annual horse fair at Stow, on the Wold, Glocestershire, distant 11 miles. The ringleaders left the village at half-past 6, and waited in the turnpike road for the arrival of all labourers coming to Ascott.

Mr. Hambidge's men were not the first molested. A determined non-Union labourer put on a bold front; being a native of the village and his relations living there he was allowed to pass, with a threat that he would be sent back on the morrow if he came. Mr. Hambidge's two men soon followed. Their evidence before the magistrates was, – In proceeding to their work (bean hoeing) they were met on the public road near a gate leading into a field where they were working. All the women, more particularly those with sticks, opposed their going to work, and insisted on their return home.

The men resolutely pushed their way to the field gate, when the assault commenced, and after some rough treatment from the women, whose numbers had increased, they were forcibly bundled or thrown over the gate into the field, again jostled and pelted with stones. Finding it impossible and dangerous to attempt working, they quickly went to the farmhouse, followed by the women, and the police found them there, and the women.

The peaceful and orderly condition of the village had been long disturbed by the Unionists, and it had so seriously increased, that no one from the highest to the lowest, could appear in the village unfavourable to Union principles without being annoyed and assailed with 'Ba, Ba, Blacklegs; old blacklegs, Ba, Ba, Ba.' It was, therefore, considered imperative to appeal to the law for public and private protection, more particularly as the law had been so grievously broken by the unseemly and outrageous conduct of the women, the wives and daughters of the Union labourers, the major part being the exceptional females of the place.

The charge was fully proved against sixteen, the Act of Parliament was read aloud to the whole Court, 'Three months' imprisonment with hard labour.' We, the undersigned, sufferers by this outrage and riot, cannot understand upon what principle of justice the two magistrates can be censured for passing too severe a sentence, when three months are reduced to ten days for the ringleaders and seven days for the remaining nine disorderly women, who, without the least provocation, premeditatingly, and with malice intent, left the village at an early hour with sticks, to break the peace and be injurious to those whose occupation was instrumental in providing for them in sickness and old age.

Mr. Hambidge is a thorough practical farmer, unwearied in the supervision of his farm, and knows the merits of his servants. He has been in the parish seven years, during which time no labourer left his service, until the enemies of social order entered the village. No doubt he was selected as the first victim to Union principals because his staff was the greatest, and all Unionists. He has been brought before the public in a very unfavourable light, and we, one and all, desire to bear our public testimony to the undeniable fact that Mr. Hambidge and his labourers were always well agreed and mutually satisfied, nor do the men, who so abruptly and ungratefully left a good master at so critical a period of agricultural operations, speak unfavourably of him as a master, or of Mrs. Hambidge as a kind and sympathizing friend in the time of sorrow, sickness and need.

After the lapse of a fortnight two of Mr. Hambidge's labourers returned to their work, and it is beyond contradiction that there are at this moment some, and perhaps all who are desirous to return, but they have not the moral courage to do so. One man observed 'that they would kill him if he did.'

These are the unvarnished facts, but the spirit and

temper of the Unionist labourers, and the disruption of social order and kindly feeling between the classes, must be seen and felt to be known. The mischief is originated by a class of men who live by the dissemination of principles which sap the foundation of all social order, peace and good will among men.

Allow us still further to observe that 12s., 14s., and 16s. a week do not represent the full weekly income of the agricultural labourer. There are various sources, independently of Saturday night, that make one pound a more correct calculation. The interior and exterior of their cottages, and the smartness and finery on all occasions, indicate ease and comfort. The dwellings of the idle, improvident, and the intemperate are the exceptions, not the rule.

Apologizing for trespassing so much on your space, we remain,

Your obliged and humble servants,

WILLIAM LARDNER, Churchwarden. ROBERT HAMBIDGE, Churchwarden

EDWIN TOWNSEND, Guardian. JOHN CHAUNDY, Waywarden.

HENRY HOPKINS, Overseer. JOHN GOMM.

JOHN VENNILLE. [*Misspelt – should be Venville*]

THE WOMEN'S LETTER – 2 JUNE 1873

This was signed by a William Mackenzie, from Knightsbridge, London, and was a transcription of statements made by Mary and Elizabeth Pratley on their release from prison to him shortly after their release.

-

The following statements were made by two women Elizabeth and Mary Pratley, who were imprisoned at Oxford, in pursuance of the sentence of the Chipping Norton Justices. I think you will agree with me that it is incumbent upon the Home Secretary to institute an inquiry into the truth of this charge of gross inhumanity perpetrated by the authorities of the prison upon these two mothers and their infants, one ten weeks and the other seven months old. I shall only add that I took down the statements from their own lips in their own cottages yesterday morning. The women, though very poor, and living in miserable habitations, had every appearance of being respectable and trustworthy persons:—

Statement of Mary Pratley.

'I was nursing my baby from the breast, the child was only 10 weeks old; I had as good a breast of milk as any woman in England when I went into prison, but while there had scarcely any, owing to my not having proper food. I had nothing but bread and skilly; I felt the need of a little tea very much. I got rheumatism in my shoulders and limbs very bad, chiefly, I think, owing to the night drive, which was both cold and wet. The doctor came each morning; he looked at my hands the first day. He made no inquiry either about my state or that of the baby. My baby was taken away undressed from the Chipping Norton police-station in the middle of the night. I begged

Superintendent Lakin to give me time to put the child's clothes on, but he refused, saying 'you must come at once, there is no time to mess about.' We were placed in the open van. I wrapped up the child as best way I could in its clothes. The child took a very bad cough, and coughed till it was black in the face on the Sunday when we were in the prison, and the matron saw it. My baby was accustomed to have a little sop, with sugar. I told the matron the child would not take the sop without sugar. She said no sugar was allowed. I was allowed only half a pint of milk morning and evening for the child. Neither the governor, nor the chaplain, nor the doctor, nor the visiting magistrates ever asked if I had food enough for the child or myself, or whether I was suckling the baby. 'Mary Pratley. + Her mark.' June 1.

Statement of Elizabeth Pratley.

'I had while in prison nothing but bread and skilly, no milk, beer, or meat, or broth. My baby, seven months old, was with me. I received for it what they called a pint, but it was not more than three-quarters of a pint of milk, twice a day, not near enough for the child. No milk was allowed for the child during the night-time; only a very little sugar once a day for the child's sop at dinner time. At home it always had plenty of sugar both with its milk and its sop, and always some milk in the night. The child suffered very much from want of proper nourishment and from there being no fire in the cell. I also suffered from want of better food and from cold. I could hardly sleep at nights. I hardly got an hour's sleep any night. The child could not sleep at night, it was so hungry. The doctor saw me twice, but made no inquiry about the baby, nor even looked at it. The child caught cold and coughed so much the night before last (Friday night) I thought it would have died. The child was not unhealthy, but was never strong, and has been a great deal worse since. I got a very bad cold from travelling at night, and from the dampness of the prison cell, I could hardly speak the day after I came home, my throat and chest were so bad and my limbs ached so.'

Elizabeth Pratley. + Her mark. 'June 1' WILLIAM MACKENZIE. Knightsbridge, 2 June.

UNION RESPONSE LETTER – 5 JUNE 1873

Sir. – In *The Times* of the 2d June there is a letter signed by seven farmers of Ascott-under-Whychwood, professing to give a correct statement of the late events in that parish concerning the women who were sent to prison by the Chipping Norton magistrates.

Having read that letter and feeling convinced by my previous knowledge of that village that the statements therein are not founded on fact, I have made it my business (in conjunction with a member of our consulting committee) to visit that village and thoroughly investigate its condition, and every circumstance connected with the event out of which arose the charges against the women.

I am in a condition to prove, by undoubted evidence, of the most respectable character, that the allegation of 'disgraceful conduct, molestation, intimidation, assault, and subsequent riot' is utterly untrue. I was present in the Court at the trial. I heard the evidence of the two young men, and their contradictory replies required all the skill and ability of a practiced advocate to enable the magistrates to convict.

One witness was produced by the women (who could not afford legal assistance), and her evidence was to the affect that no sticks were used, no violence offered, no attempt made to prevent the men going into the field. This evidence, which was ignored by the magistrates, I am in a position to say, is entirely corroborated by numbers of people in the village whom I have seen today.

I have also personally and separately questioned every one of the sixteen women (save one who was away from home) as to their carrying sticks or any other offensive weapon, and they each and all declare that they had no such thing in their hands or in their possession. This is entirely confirmed by those who saw them go and return, and by others, who as on lookers, saw the whole transaction. I have also further proof that the young men themselves declared to several of the women that they never had any fear of being injured, were not hurt, nor subjected to any ill treatment whatsoever, and that of their own will they would never appear against them; and if they were compelled to appear in court, they could not say anything which could do them harm. I, therefore, can only come to the conclusion, that their conduct in court, taken in connexion with their subsequent disappearance from the neighbourhood, can only be accounted for by the supposition that they were improperly influenced.

I also find the statement as to 'the condition of the houses – the rate of wages, the prerequisites, the satisfaction of the people with the existing state of things – that the labourers were contented before the agitators came among them,' each and all to be simply untrue.

About 20 labourers of all ages, from 20 to 80, declare that previous to the Union, the rate of wages was 9s in winter, 10s in summer, 2s per week extra for four weeks' hay time, five weeks' harvest, and about four weeks' piece work, and during those 13 or 14 weeks their time was 12 to 16 hours per day; and astounding as it may appear, those men who were not engaged with horses or cattle usually lost their time and wages on wet days. Since the Union, their wages have been raised 2s per week, and are now 12s. Any money-pay for overtime is quite unknown except that the men who have charge of the cattle receive 1s for their Sunday work. As to the prerequisites, we have quite failed to find a trace of them. Each labourer has to pay rent for his house, and his allotment, which is charged to him, 45s per acre, while the rent to farmers is from 24s to 32s.

As to the condition of the cottages, I can only say that while I admit that some few are in good condition, occupied by railway men and mechanics, yet the condition of the cottages held by farm labourers is very bad indeed, and in many instances is simply horrible and a disgrace to a Christian country. It would require the pen of a Dickens properly to describe three I saw to-day. Imagine a narrow place, like a coal cellar, down which you go two or three steps, no flooring except broken stones, no ceiling, no grate, rough walls, a bare ladder leading to one narrow bedroom about 6ft. wide, containing two bedsteads for a man, his wife and three young children, the whole place as wretchedly bad and miserable as imagination can conceive, and only divided by a rough wooden partition not reaching to the roof, but over which you may look into the bedroom of the next adjoining house, equally wretched and miserable, and with the additional evil that the only way to the bedroom of a third house is through the bedroom of No. 2 house, and that in No. 2 live a man, his wife and six children, and till recently the third house (one room down, one up) was occupied by a man, his wife, and also six children, whose only way to bed was through the bedroom of No. 2, as No. 3 had no staircase or ladder or any other way of access to the bedroom.

Words will utterly fail to give your readers any adequate idea of the abject poverty-stricken appearance of these holes, and it is a matter of extreme astonishment that such quiet and respectably conducted people can live and preserve the commonest decencies of life in such wretched places.

Another house we visited contained one room on the ground floor and one bedroom upstairs, in which the father, mother, one son 10 years old, three daughters, aged respectively 3, 17 and 22 years, all sleep with no other accommodation. I do not want to go into any question as to the personal character of Mr. and Mrs. Hambidge, or any other persons, as my desire is not to be personal; but I must reply to the insulting expression 'that these women were for the most part of exceptional character.' Exceptional they certainly are, but not in the immoral sense implied by the writer, but exceptional in that their character and moral conduct will bear the strictest investigation.

As one of those so-called agitators and disturbers of the piece and quietness of agricultural villages, I may be permitted to direct attention to one paragraph of the letter. 'The farmers of the village deemed it right to act in union with other farmers in the neighbourhood, and the large landed proprietors as to the rate of wages they should pay their labourers.'

What! Farmers Unionists? Then why not labourers? If one is wrong, surely the other is equally so, or shall I say –

quoting our national poet – 'What in the captain is but a choleric word, is in the soldier downright blasphemy.'

Not wishing to occupy too much of your valuable space, I would conclude by thanking you in anticipation of inserting this letter, and to say that I am prepared with facts, places, and persons to justify every statement I have made.

I am, Sir, your obedient servant,

C. HOLLOWAY, Chairman of the Oxford District. Woodstock. June 5.

THE HAMBIDGE LETTER – 5 JUNE 1873

Crown Farm Manager Robert Hambidge replies to statements made at the Agricultural Labourers Conference in Leamington Spa, by a Mr. Banbury from Woodstock on 28th May 1873.

Sir, – I shall feel greatly obliged if you will allow me space in *The Times* to contradict the statements made by Mr. Banbury (Woodstock) at the Agricultural Labourers Conference, at Leamington, on Wednesday, May 28, 1873.

I will reply to the remarks as they stand in the report of the Conference, published in the London papers.

Mr. Banbury stated that 1. 'The farmer named Hambidge had been a bitter opponent of the Union since the commencement. At the first meeting held in the district, he went and took down the names of the men who joined the Union, and threatened them with the loss of work and dismissal from the cottages they occupied of which he was the trustee.'

Answer. – Until the first meeting of the delegates on our village green I in no way interested myself in the

Labourers Union. Wishing to know the names of the labourers favourable to the Union I went to the green and put some names down, but I emphatically deny that either then or at any other subsequent period I have threatened a labourer with dismissal either from work or from a cottage. I am no trustee of feoffee of the village charity, nor can I in any way interfere with the letting of the property.

2. 'He tried his best to destroy the Union, but was obliged to take back the men he had discharged.'

Answer. – I repudiate the assertion of attempting to destroy the Union or in any way interfering with it or its members either in word or deed. During my seven years in the parish, I never dismissed a labourer, nor did any labourers leave my service until Union principles were afloat, consequently there could be no taking back.

3. 'He had been paying them 9s. a week, and after he took them back, he gave them 10s., and within the last few months had had given them 12s.'

Answer. – In this and the surrounding villages 9s per week for day labourers has ceased upwards of 2 years 10s. was subsequently given; and when these enemies of social order presented themselves in this peaceful village, I had been, and was, giving my day men 12s. a week, 2 bushels of malt, and one and a half pound of hops for one month's hay-making. This was 12 months since and so it has continued without variation to the present time.

4. 'In the case they were considering, the men sent in a respectful request for an increase in wages, and at the end of the week, instead of giving them what they asked, he locked them out.'

Answer. – I settled with my labourers on our usual

good and friendly terms on Saturday, after which they attended one of their meetings. On Monday morning, when my labourers came, they informed me that they must all have an advance of 2s. or they should leave. In a friendly manner I advised them to consider what course would conduce most to their future wellbeing. I raised the wages of all my efficient labourers, but those who from age or infirmity could not do equal to the others must for the present remain at 12s. per week, but that there was and would be plenty of piece work. They were unanimous and decided that unless all had the rise not one should continue to work for me. Discussion was useless, and I told them I could not yield to dictation. They all left in the middle of backward barley sowing. These are facts; consequently, I did not lock out my agricultural labourers, but offered them their own terms (the efficient labourers). Mutual obligations and relative duties were forgotten, and I was left at a critical period of agricultural operations with 12 working horses, four working oxen, a superior flock of 500 sheep at turnips, milking cows, bullocks, and young stock, with only a head shepherd and a youth, both yearly servants.

5. 'That man had been in the habit of giving men 2s. per day for working in the harvest time until 11 o'clock at night'.

Answer. – My labourers were never in the harvest field at 11 o'clock at night. I always have a good staff, plenty of horse strength, and personally direct the whole machinery to the last. It is a very rare occurrence for me to be late; when it happens, I square it with interest and perfect satisfaction to my workpeople, if there is any meaning in a cheerful, contented countenance and the hearty 'Goodnight master; thank you kindly.'

6. 'When he locked out the men one of his yearly servants left work, feeling so much annoyed at his conduct. That man was summoned before the magistrates, and made to pay 4l. 12s. 6d. for leaving work. (Shame).'

Answer. – My carter was a weekly, not yearly tenant. From Michaelmas I had given him 14s. per week, and when I was asked on Monday morning to give 2s. additional to all, I repeatedly offered him 16s. a week, which he refused unless all had the advance. He left with my other labourers. His conduct is the more reprehensible from the circumstance that all my agricultural horses were on their way into the fields to drill barley. He brought them back, put them into the stables, shut the doors and went away. The arm of the law alone can deal with such conduct provoked by Union principles.

On public as well as on private grounds it was imperative to appeal to the law. The charge was fully proved, he was fined; the Union delegate was there and paid the fine, and thus is fostered the vexatious conduct of the agricultural labourers by a class of men who live by the dissemination of principles that sap the foundation of social order, peace, and good-will among men.

7. 'They all knew the circumstances attending the committal of the women to prison. *The Times* sent down a special correspondent, and the matter was put in the paper under the heading 'Impossible.'

Answer. – Mr. Holloway of Woodstock sent the letter to *The Times* so headed, not *The Times* correspondent. Mr. Holloway attended the magistrates meeting at Chipping

Norton, he says in that letter, – 'I am secretary to the Labourers Union, and attended at Chipping Norton in that capacity to watch the case.' An answer appeared in *The Times* on Monday, June 2; it is a faithful and unvarnished statement of the whole affair, signed by every occupier of land in the parish, to testify to its truthfulness.

8. 'The men did not strike; they were locked out.'

Answer. – My labourers voluntarily left my service because I would not raise the wages of all. Therefore, I prove to demonstration that I did not lock out my labourers.

These facts prove the groundlessness of the unmanly made upon my character at a public meeting by Mr. Banbury, who is a perfect stranger to me, to my agricultural labourers, and the social condition of Ascott-under-Whychwood.

Apologizing for the trespass on your space, I remain yours greatly obliged,

ROBERT HAMBIDGE   Ascott-under-Whychwood, June 5.

THE BANBURY UNION LETTER – 11 JUNE 1873

This letter was published in The Times *on 14 June 1873. It was signed by Mr. John Banbury, a delegate of the National Union of Agricultural Labourers and was a direct reply to the letter from Robert Hambidge, published in* The Times *on 5 June, which criticized Mr. Banbury's speech to the Union Conference held on 28 May.*

THE CHIPPING NORTON CASE

Sir, – Mr. Hambidge's reply to my speech at Leamington is no refutation of any important statement I made. I assert that he attended the first meeting the Unionists held at Ascott, and tried to take down the names of all the labourers who joined. Those who joined were discharged. That the wages had been 9s. per week until the Union began to be talked about. That his labourers during haymaking and harvest received only 2s. Per day, working early and late. That when, this Spring, his men applied for an advance he discharged them at once.

And all these statements I adhere to.

Mr. Hambidge admits that up to a recent date 9s. per week was the standard wages paid at Ascott, and I beg to add that out of this miserable pittance pay for wet time was stopped.

Mr. Hambidge admits, without thinking it necessary to justify the act, that he has united with other farmers to regulate the price of labour, yet he objects for his labourers to follow the example he has set them

Sir, what further justification do we need for our efforts, what more is necessary to prove the need for a Labourers' Union? I beg to say I made no attack on Mr. Hambidge's private character; but when Mr. Hambidge takes public action against a public Association he must expect public criticism.

I am, yours very sincerely.

JOHN BANBURY, Hill House, Woodstock, June 11.

THE ASCOTT FEOFFEES' LETTER – 13 JUNE 1873

This letter was dated 13 June 1873 and sent to the editor of The Oxfordshire Weekly News, *which was a local weekly newspaper, but the letter was not published until Wednesday 2 July 1873. It was intended to be a direct reply to a letter written by Christopher Holloway that was published in* The Times *on 5 June 1873, where Mr Holloway was critical of the condition of several of the houses that agricultural labourers were living in at Ascott. The Ascott feoffees were thought to be the trustees of a number of cottages built by a charity in Ascott to house the poor.*

THE ASCOTT SCANDAL
TO THE EDITOR OF THE *OXFORDSHIRE WEEKLY NEWS*

Sir, – We shall feel greatly obliged if you will allow us a small space to rebut the unwarrantable statements of Mr. Holloway, the Unionist, contained in a letter in your paper, reprinted from *The Times* in reference to Ascott-under-Wychwood:—

'We, the undersigned Feoffees of the village charity, which consists chiefly of cottages assert that, with the exception of two homes, the cottages and gardens are good, the rents low, and the general condition of the labouring poor above the average for that class. The dwellings described as cottages by Mr. Holloway as 'horrible and a disgrace to a Christian country,' are not cottages, and never were, but a large old building erected in the time of Queen Elizabeth for a village workhouse, and so used until the time of the establishment of the Union Workhouses.

The Workhouse, for it still retains the name, has become a lodging-house for two classes of the labouring poor, viz., those who will not pay more than 6d. or 1s. per week for rent, and those who are so objectionable as tenants that owners of cottages refuse to receive them. The two women who were sent to prison for ten days, with the infants, have rooms in this house. The two room communicate and are generally occupied by the same family, who have also the use of a large attic over the whole. As is the case with many old buildings, there is one step down on entering, but neither of the rooms resemble a coal cellar, as stated by Mr. Holloway, as they are neither dark nor underground. It may be mentioned that when there is a change of tenants in this lodging house, the rooms are restored and whitewashed. Mr. Holloway remarks on a cottage with one room down and the same up, occupied by a man, his wife, a son aged 10, and three girls of the ages of, 3, 17, and 22. This cottage is *not* occupied by an agricultural labourer, and belongs to an individual at a distance. The occupier does not require anything of the parish, could arrange very differently for his family if he thought well to do so, and would not yield to dictation in the matter, or advice from Feoffees or parish officers. The case, which is an isolated one, has no bearing on the recent circumstances, except that the girl of 17 was one of those sent to prison for ten days.'

This will suffice to show the temper and spirit in which Mr. Holloway writes, and the mode of warfare now being waged against the farmers by the professional agitators representing the Agricultural Labourers Union.

Thanking you for granting us space for our reply, We remain your obedient servants,

WILLIAM LARDNER, RICHARD HYATT, EDWIN TOWNSEND, EDWARD GOMM,

JOHN CHAUNDY and JOHN VENVILLE.

Feoffees of the Ascott Charity, Ascott-under-Wychwood, June 13, 1873

B. Extracts courtesy of the *Spectator* archive

THE CHIPPING NORTON MAGISTRATES
31 MAY 1873

The women appeared at the Petty Sessions in the neighbouring town of Chipping Norton; they were undefended; they met the evidence of the farmer's two witnesses with a general denial, but had prepared no testimony on their own behalf. Of the law, it is certain, they knew nothing, for they had made preparations for the payment of the fine they expected to be imposed on them, —an alternative punishment not provided for in the Act. But two country clergymen, the Rev. T. Harris and the Rev. W. E. D. Carter, were the presiding justices on this occasion, and more jealous for the farmers' right to grind down his labourers than the farmers themselves, they refused to release the women on that own recognisances with a warning,—evidently the proper course, where intemperate language only was charged,— or even to accept sureties, but passed a sentence of a week's imprisonment with hard labour on nine of the defendants, and of ten days' on the remainder. All the women thus unexpectedly condemned to a sojourn in Oxford Gaol bore an excellent character, and the punishment meted out to them for the too free use of the tongue, of which they were at the worst accused, fell as severely on them as it would have fallen on the wife of any decent workman in a manufacturing town.

It is too late to redress the wrong done to these poor women, for wrong it unquestionably is, when the penalty is so far disproportioned to the offence; but it is not too late to take notice of the conduct of the clerical justices who presided at the Chipping Norton petty sessions. It may be said that they were guilty of nothing worse than an error in judgment, but such errors in judgment., if passed over in silence, would quickly break down that respect for law which is the surest guarantee for order in this country, and which makes political progress possible without risk to the framework of our institutions. The Lord Chancellor has the power to remove magistrates who have shown themselves unfit to exercise authority from the commission of the peace, and in the present instance this power ought certainly to be used. We do not see much reason to hope for an improvement in the Criminal Law Amendment Act that will make such acts of injustice impossible for the future. It would be difficult to abolish 'intimidation' as an offence altogether, and yet if the offence remain, its definition must to a great extent be left to those who have to decide on the facts. Technically, the women tried at Chipping Norton were probably guilty of 'intimidation,' but the degrees of guilt in this offence are infinitely various, and if the magistrates had not been influenced by a partisan spirit to 'make an example' of the offenders, a sharp rebuke, or even a light penalty, would have been tolerated by public opinion. The worst of it is, that the labourers are beginning to feel that they cannot count on an impartial trial by magistrates of the temper of the clerical Shallows of Chipping Norton, and a deep distrust of those who administer the law is growing among them. The time is coming when there will be a cry to which the Legislature cannot turn a deaf ear for the reorganisation of the Magistracy, and the squires, with their clerical allies, have themselves to thank for the revolution that will eject them from the last stronghold of their power.

7 JUNE 1873

The women so unfairly and unwisely committed to prison by the Chipping Norton magistrates have been released on the expiration of their sentence, and have of course been received with eager popular demonstrations by the agricultural labourers of their neighbourhood. Indeed, two of the women, who had babies at their breast, seem to have been treated with needless rigour, and to have been refused the proper food for their infants,—and this statement, whether true or false, has more than ever made them into martyrs. On the other hand, the friends of the Chipping Norton magistrates have put out a 'defence of their conduct,' which comes to very little, except that it is asserted that Mr. Hambidge, the employer of the non-Union men who were dissuaded by the women from going to work, was a very good and popular employer; that it was a strike for wages, and not a lock-out, which deprived him of labourers; that he was willing to advance the wages of the efficient labourers, though not of the inefficient ones ; and that the women were really armed with sticks, used them in a threatening manner, and called 'Ba, ba! black sheep!' after the non-Union men. For the rest, even if all these allegations be strictly accurate,—which is much disputed on the other side,—Mr. Hambidge's friends do not maintain that the women actually did any violence to the non-Union men, and it remains just as plain as ever that to have discharged the women on their own recognisances would have been the proper and only humane course. Mr. Hambidge's friends are evidently possessed with a deep feeling of the ingratitude of the strike,—if strike it was,—and it does not occur to them that Mr. Hambidge probably owes rather more gratitude to those who have worked for him so long, than they owe, however kind he may have been, to Mr. Hambidge. The gratitude of society is always expected to have an upward gaze, but an immense balance of the article is really due in the other direction.

8 AUGUST 1873

The Lord Chancellor has, it appears, asked the Lord-Lieutenant of Oxfordshire for an explanation of the magistrates' severity in the Chipping Norton case, when sixteen women were sent to prison on a charge of deterring labourers from work. Lord Selborne considered that while punishment might have been necessary, the severe and indiscriminate punishment of such large numbers, many of whom might have been led away, created sympathy with the law-breakers and weakened the law. The Duke of Marlborough replied that he thought the magistrates had acted 'not unwisely,' that the fact of the assailants being women did not exempt them from the law—which implies that in a street riot women ought to be shot like men—that he does not like clerical magistrates, but that laymen would have done just the same, which may be true if they were also Oxford squires, but is opposed to experience. The Lord Chancellor, in reply, states his opinion that the magistrates had made a mistake, requests that his Grace will communicate his remarks to the justices, and trusts that the views 'he had submitted would, on any other occasion, receive more consideration than appears to have been given them on this.' That is satisfactory enough to the public, but the two clerical magistrates, with their local duke at their back, will think no more of Lord Selborne than of their Testaments.

C. Lawyer's letter to *The Times*, 2 June 1873

This letter was published in The Times *on 2 June 1873. It was signed by Frederic Harrison, who was a British jurist and historian. While studying at Oxford, he became involved with positivist philosophy and was president of the English Positivist Committee from 1880 to 1905. Spellings and punctuations are as they were printed in the paper.*

'THE CHIPPING NORTON CASE.'
TO THE EDITOR OF THE TIMES.

Sir,

Masters and men alike have to thank you for your powerful criticism on the recent sentence at Chipping Norton. But I wish to point out that this gross miscarriage of justice is no solitary case, since the Act is responsible for constant cases of similar harshness, and gives permanent cause for the same indignation. The two magistrates whom you rebuke may have brought the Act into discredit; but it is the Act which led the two magistrates into their blunder. They simply did what has been done 20 times before under its provisions, though the employing world heard nothing about it, till you drew public attention to the recent case. I have now before me reports (from local newspapers) of nearly all the cases decided under the Act; and whatever may be the merits of its clauses as it stands on the Statute Book, its practical working would leave one to think it was specially designed to exasperate the working classes with the administration of justice. Politicians are not wont to be satisfied with a Statute, which lawyers may approve, if its administration in practice results in a permanent scandal. Now, what is the operation of this Act as we read its doings in the files of local newspapers? Ostensibly, and in terms, it is an ordinary part of the criminal law. In reality we find it a legal instrument which one party in a trade dispute uses to cripple the other, the party using it being in possession of the whole judicial power, and indirectly able to dispose of the police. The Act is rarely put in force, except during a hard-fought trade dispute. Then what occurs is this:- The charge ceases to be an ordinary matter of police law; it assumes the character of a party manoeuvre. The most trumpery cases are preferred, and often abandoned after the charge has had its intimidating effect. The local police busy themselves with manufacturing cases, and unseemly altercations ensue as to the party interest of the sitting magistrates. In the excited opinion of the district every prisoner sentenced, and even every prisoner arrested, becomes a victim; every official witness is accused of perjury; and every magistrate of prejudice. Now, even supposing the Act to be just in its language, does it in practice give any guarantees for order, that all are at tanti – that it will outweigh the hatred it scatters on the common administration of justice? I have not so bad an opinion of the working-classes as a body as to think that all this animosity could be possibly awakened by an Act that was honestly employed to put down outrage. I believe they have only too much ground for their belief that the Act in its actual working is little but a class instrument, and is constantly resulting in scandalous abuses of criminal law. I turn to some of the decided cases. Not long after the Act was passed, the struggle of the engineers for the nine hours began in the North. The dispute was singularly clear of anything like real outrage, but a number of cases were brought before the magistrates, which were anything but credible to our judicial system. I give one as a specimen. A man singly addresses a workman in the highway, receives a curt reply, and walks off; a policeman is watching them; without hearing the words that pass, he comes up to the workman addressed, asks him what the man had said to him, and then goes off and arrests the man. The man, for spoken words that the policeman had extracted by questioning the other, is arrested, bail is refused, and he is imprisoned for five days. The Bench, on hearing the charge, dismissed it altogether, after an unseemly wrangle as to one of the sitting Justices being a party interested, and disqualified under the Act from hearing the case. Here we have the local police employing themselves in extracting conversations on the strength of this report of spoken words alone, and a respectable man imprisoned for five days on a frivolous charge. In another case the police seize a bundle of hand bills, which were found to be quite unobjectionable, and arrest a man who was distributing them in the street. Here again, the charge was dismissed, as there was no sort of offence committed; but the police evidently conceived that the Act put them in the position enjoyed by the gendarmes of the late French Empire, and entitled them to arrest persons and seize private property in defence of 'order' in general. In another case, a man gets intoxicated, goes down to a neighbour's door and shouts, calling him 'blackleg', and challenges him to fight, and ends by asking him to take a glass of beer. There was no evidence of concerted disorder, none of any injury intended, or feared.

It was a mere case of 'drunk and disorderly'; but there happened to be a strike, and so the man was imprisoned for one month. In several other cases, men shouting out 'blackleg', and not proved to be drunk, were imprisoned for two months. A lad throws a stone and is imprisoned for a fortnight; two men throwing a piece of coal are imprisoned for a month; in each of these cases there was a violent conflict of testimony. I have no wish to justify these acts. I object as any man to people who are drunk and disorderly, boys who throw stones, and to men and women who use bad language. If laws are needed honestly to protect workmen from the violence of their fellow workmen, it is idle to suggest that any of us would obstruct them. But I ask if it is wise to make trumpery matters of bad language affairs of State, and if the rich can find it worthwhile to let the poor think the administration of justice can be perverted into an instrument of class oppression, and if the Liberal Government and party are content to see laws affecting industry covered with the suspicion, the irritation, and the undoubted malpractice which deeply discredit the working of the Game Laws? The practical operation of the Act teems with scandals. In one case before me, the employer, the real prosecutor, sends off the nominal prosecutor, a lad who asserted that he had been roughly addressed, and keeps him for a week at an hotel at the seaside, of course it was said to keep him out of harm's way; and of course it was replied, virtually to bribe him. In all these cases there is this objectionable feature. The person who is alleged to be injured or threatened is never the real prosecutor, who is some powerful employer or association of employers. The lawyers in the case in the most natural way inform the Court that they are instructed by Messers. — — to prosecute; that this most eminent firm must ask for a heavy penalty, as their works have been inconvenienced by the strike, and that Messers. — — will be satisfied with a month's imprisonment &c. All the while the 'prosecutor', the man supposed to be injured is no more considered than if he were an unimportant witness. If they can get him to give some colour to the case, that is enough. The whole thing is arranged between the eminent firm of Messers. — —, their neighbours on the Bench, and the efficient officer at the head of the constabulary. It will hardly be wondered at if after this the whole district believes the case is trumped up, that the policemen give evidence with more zeal than care, that the prosecutor is a tool, and the Bench prejudiced. Where the crime consists in stealing property, or injuring the person, a Bench of Justices may safely be trusted to decide reasonably; but they will often decide unreasonably, where the crime is the speaking of words or the offering a passerby a handbill. This latter is a real not imaginary case. In 'Turk's case', the prisoner was charged by his employer with 'molesting' him by distributing, to workmen passing by in the street, handbills which quietly requested workmen not to interfere with the strike. There was no evidence of the slightest annoyance to the employer, who did not even see the man with the handbills, and no evidence of any sort of 'coercion', other than the attempt peaceably to persuade workmen to work for him only on certain terms. A metropolitan police magistrate, however, held that the employer had been 'molested' within the Act, and he ordered the prisoner to be imprisoned for two months. The case was appealed, and no one appeared to prosecute, and the man was subsequently bailed. But for three days he had endured the life of a common prisoner and the end of the employer was obtained. In another case (afterwards reversed) a man was arrested and sentenced to two months imprisonment for asking a fellow-workman to pay a fine due to the club, and this a bench of magistrates considered was 'besetting' the man within the Act. Nor is it singular that these constrictions are put on the Statute, for the clause in question consists of what is practically a single sentence of no less than 40 lines in the Queen's printer's copy, and it employs several ambiguous words such as 'coerce' and 'beset' which are unexplained and are new in law. I am not about to enter into any detailed analysis of this complicated clause, It would be profitably done only in a legal treatise, and my complaint is that the Statute is far too ambiguous and intricate to be left to petty sessions to determine its effect. Nor am I about to argue that the acts of violence against which the Statute is aimed should go unpunished. The Act punishes three offences. The first, as to assaults, is amply punishable by the existing law of assault; the second, as to the threats, is also within the reach of the existing law, so far as it is safe to visit spoken words with punishment at all; the third offence in the Act is so ambiguous and so easily abused in practice I would never consent to its remaining law, with this notable exception, which I am about to state. I am not only willing, but I desire (as do workmen themselves) that 'rattening' or removing tools, should be made a crime, and the proper way to do this is by adding a few words to the existing laws relating to malicious injury to property This is the sole feature in the Act which is really needed, and this end can be much better attained without it. It is not now for the first time that this Act has discredited justice and shaken the magisterial system. It will continue to do this until it is repealed. It is not the first time that women have been sent to prison for noisy behaviour, and decent men and women sentenced under the disputed evidence of policemen and informers. It is a matter of continual occurrence throughout the country that batches of women are sent to gaol for longer periods than these women at Chipping Norton. It has often happened that a whole district has been roused to indignation by sentences far more severe and disproportionated, and that far better grounds existed for believing the case to have been judged with prejudice. These scandals and evils will continue as long as the Act. The only difference in this case is, that your powerful influence has turned the light of publicity upon it.

I am &c,,

FREDERIC HARRISON. Lincoln's-inn'.

Acknowledgements

Personal acknowledgement from publisher Paul Jackson Founder of the Ascott Martyrs Educational Trust (www. ascottmartyrs.co.uk):

Where do you start at the beginning of a 11-year marathon? My first stops were Ascott resident and local historian Wendy Pearse (provider of the front cover drawing) and Ralph Mann (history master at the local Kingham Hill School), who encouraged me to dig deeper, then on to Unite, the union where senior officials Mark Pryor and Diana Holland expressed total ignorance but again actively encouraged me with some seed money and much-needed personal support.

I will always be grateful for help in setting up the Ascott Martyrs Educational Trust, particularly the support of local residents descendent Marilyn Baker (née Moss), Carol Anderson, who at the time was Director of Oxfordshire Museum and is now the chair of the Trust, plus Kester Harvey (who became a trustee), local resident and son of Chris Harvey who encouraged me to dig deeper, and then enabled support from his employer The Rooflight Company.

Along the way The Cotswolds National Landscape (AONB), West Oxfordshire Council and Midlands Cooperative all gave generously, enabling us to upgrade the information on the memorial seats on the village green, fund the commemorative textile hanging with the WEA and achieve national recognition and support.

The culmination of the above led to the creation of this book to coincide with the 150th anniversary of the women's imprisonment for 2023.

Top of the list to thank for his contribution is the editor, Keith Laybourn, an extraordinarily committed man to whatever he takes on. Editing a group of academics and a bunch of local historians (including myself) has been a herculean task. Thank you, Keith.

A big thank you also goes to all the various authors who have risen to the challenge of writing an unusual book focusing on their specialist subjects yet linked as one in wanting to highlight a forgotten part of our history. Andrew Chapman of www.preparetopublish.com has been a real hero providing his time, guidance and the cover on a complimentary basis. Thank you all, a great team effort.

Almost finally I would like to thank Alice Prochaska, who provided a link to the academic world and a much-needed mentoring role to me personally.

I shouldn't close here without thanking my wife Pauline who has for 11 years lived with my obsession with the Ascott Martyrs; I couldn't have got to first base without her patience and understanding.

General acknowledgements

The generosity of others is vital to the preparation and publication of any book, and this collection of essays in no exception. Central to this has been the Ascott Martyrs Educational Trust, particularly chair Carol Anderson for her essay, Andrew Weaver for research in the newspapers of the period and researcher Harvey Warner for his industry and persistence, and Paul Jackson, who has been the driving force behind this publication.

The work of Beverley McCombs has also been acknowledged many times in these essays and Martin Greenwood particularly thanks her for the use of some of the illustrations in his essay. He also thanks her for drawing his attention to Rollo Arnold's book *The Farthest Promised Land* (fully cited in his essay) and the Tackley Local History Society for the image of their memorial to the *Cataraqui* disaster, and Alan Vickers for the image of the Shipton memorial to the *Cospatrick* disaster. Martin is grateful to the National Maritime Museum for allowing the image of the *Cospatrick*. He would also like to thank Julie Barrett for drawing the excellent map of New Zealand.

We would also like to thank Richard Fairhurst for the maps of England and the local villages. Many other individuals and institutions have given their permission for the use of their material, which are either listed below, in the text or in the footnotes. Ben Jackson, Christine Elliott, Martha Smith and Ellen Beauchamp have made their contributions. The National Portrait Gallery, the People's History Museum, the Museum of English Rural Life, Chipping Norton Museum, the Churchill and Sarsden Village Archives, Englesea Branch (National Methodist) Museum, the Oxfordshire History Centre, the Warden and Fellows of Nuffield College, University of Oxford, and the Wychwood Local History Society all helped with grace and enthusiasm.

Last, but not least, we must thank the numerous newspapers that have provided written evidence of what happened, even though some no longer exist. In particular, we must thank *The Spectator* (for the use of their material) and *The Times* newspaper for giving permission for us to use letters and correspondence.

Every effort has been made to avoid any infringement of copyright. However, we apologise unreservedly to any copyright owners whose permission has inadvertently been overlooked.

About the contributors

Carol Anderson BA PGCE FSA AMA was formerly Museums Service Manager for Oxfordshire County Council/Director of Oxfordshire Museum. She is currently chair of Ascott Martyrs Educational Trust.

John Bennett MA (BA Hons) is secretary of Wychwood Local History Society.

Brian Cox MA FRSA is a descendent of the Moss family in Ascott-under-Wychwood.

Keith D. Ewing is Professor of Law at King's College, London, and is recognised as a leading scholar in public law, constitutional law, law of democracy, labour law and human rights. He has published over 60 articles and 14 books.

Christine Gowing MA PhD is a local and medical historian and secretary of the Churchill and Sarsden Heritage Centre.

Martin Greenwood MA is a local author of many historical books focusing on Oxfordshire, who has recently published a book on rural emigration in the 19th century.

Paul Jackson is the founder of the Ascott Martyrs Educational Trust (although he is no longer a trustee) and promoter and publisher of this book.

Keith Laybourn BSc MA PhD FRHistS FHA is editor and Diamond Jubilee Professor Emeritus at the University of Huddersfield. He focuses upon British labour history and has published 50 books and about 100 articles.

Les Kennedy BEd was a history teacher and is now organiser of the Tolpuddle Radical History Group.

Nick Mansfield BA (Hons) BPhil AMA PhD is Professor of History at the University of Central Lancashire. He is a labour historian who researches 19th and 20th century British working-class history, including rural history.

John Martin FRSA is Visiting Professor of Agrarian History at the Museum of English Rural Life, Reading University. He is also a member of the British National Life Stories Advisory Committee for 'An Oral History of Farming, Land, Management and Conservation in Post-war Britain' funded by the Arcadia Foundation.

Alice Prochaska BA DPhil FRHistS is an adviser on the project; she is a former archivist and senior librarian, who served as Pro-Vice-Chancellor of the University of Oxford and Principal of Somerville College, Oxford from 2010 to 2017.

Nicola Verdon BA MA PhD is Professor of History at Sheffield Hallam University and has written extensively on life and labour in 19th century England. She is author of *Rural Women Workers in 19th Century England* (Boydell, 2002) and *Working and Land: A History of the Farmworkers in England from 1850 to the Present Day* (Palgrave, 2017).

Harvey Warner is a local researcher and member of the Ascott Martyrs Educational Trust Study Group. He is the son of Dorothy Warner who pioneered research into the Ascott Martyrs, and was responsible for the commemorative tree planted at the centenary celebration on the village green in 1973.

Illustration credits

Front cover
Illustration of the Ascott Martyrs.
Wendy Pearse.

Front matter
Maps.
Richard Fairhurst, www.systemed.net

Dedication plaque on bench, Ascott-under-Wychwood.
Photo: Alan Vickers, photo editor of the Wychwood Local History Society

Preface
Seats in Ascott-under-Wychwood.
1953. Doris Warner, local historian, with husband Ivor, planting the Martyrs' tree. They also gave the original seats to the village (1973). Unveiled by Reg Bottini (left), General Secretary of the National Union of Agricultural Workers and Florentia Tait, chair of Parish Council.
Reproduced with the kind permission of John Mann
October 2019. Ivor Townsend (second left), grandson of Martyr, Fanny Honeybone, unveiling the full explanation of the Ascott Martyrs' story, following a long campaign.
Reproduced with kind permission of Ascott Martyrs Educational Trust.

Commemorative textile hanging. Stitched by descendants and members of the local community, guided by a WEA tutor. Completed in June 2018, now in village church.
Reproduced with the kind permission of The Ascott Martyrs Educational Trust

Introduction
Christopher Holloway, n.d. Small Collection, N1/1/18.
Reproduced with the kind permission of the Warden and Fellows of Nuffield College, University of Oxford.

Essay 1
Crown Farm, Ascott-under-Wychwood, the labourers of which were the first to strike in Ascott-under-Wychwood.
Photo: Carol Anderson.

Chipping Norton Police Station.
Photo: Carol Anderson.

Warrants of commitment, Oxfordshire History Centre, ref. CPZ 16/2.
Reproduced with the kind permission of the Oxfordshire County Council.

Fanny Honeybone
Reproduced with the kind permission of Ivor Townsend, grandson.

Rebecca Smith
Reproduced with the kind permission of The People's Museum, Manchester.

Cartoon 'Farmer in his fields'.
Infants Magazine 1868.

Essay 2
Poster 'Guilty of Felony'.
© Trades Union Congress. Reproduced with permission.

Joseph Arch (1826-1919).
From Notables of Britain, 1897, at Internet Archive.

Warwickshire farm labourers' strike meeting, 1872, at Whitnash.
Historical Images Archive / Alamy stock photo.

NALU membership decline.
Created by Ben Jackson from research by Les Kennedy.

Essay 3
Women haymaking.
Reproduced with the kind permission of the Museum of English Rural Life.

West Oxfordshire gloving industry, 1871. 1,103 outworkers including 60 in the Wychwoods.
Source: 1871 Census, researched by Harvey Warner. Created by Ben Jackson.

Mrs Brackenborough, a gloveress, sitting outside her home in Woodstock.
Oxfordshire History Centre D260610a. Reproduced with the kind permission of the Oxfordshire County Council.

Essay 4
Farming in the field; a typical agricultural scene.
Reproduced with the kind permission of the Chipping Norton Museum.

Ascott-under-Wychwood panorama, showing the position of Crown Farm Land
Photo: Alan Vickers.

Crown Farm advertisement, *Jacksons Oxford Journal.*
Newspaper image © The British Library Board, with thanks to the British Newspaper Archive.

Essay 5
Shipton-under-Wychwood.
Reproduced with the kind permission of the Wychwoods Local History Society.

Holy Trinity, Ascott-under-Wychwood. Robert Hambidge was buried here and several Martyrs christened here.
Reproduced with the kind permission of the Wychwoods Local History Society.

James Haughton Langston.
Reproduced with the kind permission of Chipping Norton Town Council.

Church of SS Simon and Jude, Milton-under-Wychwood.
Photo: John Bennett.

Baptist Chapel Milton-under-Wychwood.
Photo: Alan Vickers.

Interior of the Zoar Baptist Chapel, Milton-under-Wychwood
Reproduced with the kind permission of the Wychwoods Local History Society.

Ascott-under-Wychwood Baptist Chapel, now a private residence.
Photograph by permission of Marilyn Baker (née Moss), a Martyr's descendent.

A Groves family wedding group, Milton-under-Wychwood Baptist Chapel.
Reproduced with the kind permission of the Wychwoods Local History Society.

Rev Charles Haddon Spurgeon.
Creative Commons: https://commons.wikipedia.org/wiki/File:Portret_van_Charles_Spurgeon_Rev._C.H._Spurgeon_ (title_op_object),_RP-F-2001-7-235D-15.jpg

Former Primitive Methodist Chapel Milton-under-Wychwood.
Photo: John Bennett.

Miss Annie Arch, Small collection N.1/1/14.
Reproduced with the kind permission of the Warden and Fellows of Nuffield College, University of Oxford.

Essay 6
Evicted cottagers.
Small collection N.1/1/23. Reproduced with the kind permission of the Warden and Fellows of Nuffield College, University of Oxford.

Songs for singing at Agricultural Labourers' Meetings by Howard Evans, n.d.

Small Collection N.1/1/10. Reproduced with the kind permission of the Warden and Fellows of Nuffield College, University of Oxford.

The Chipping Norton Union Workhouse 1836–1929.
Fanny Honeybone became an inmate here.
Reproduced with the kind permission of Chipping Norton Museum.

Ascott-under-Wychwood school, 1873.
Reproduced with the kind permission of Wychwood Local History Society.

Essay 7

Henry Austin Bruce, 1st Baron Aberdare. Home Secretary. By John Watkins. Albumen print, 1870 or before.
National Portrait Gallery, Ax21859, by licenced permission.

1st Earl of Selborne Roundell Palmer, Lord Chancellor. By Alexander Bassano. Albumen *carte de visite*, 1883.
National Portrait Gallery by licenced permission.

Essay 8

Rev William Edward Dickson Carter JP, Rector of Sarsden.
Reproduced with the kind permission of the Churchill and Sarsden village archives.

Committal document, Warrants of commitment.
Oxfordshire History Centre, CPZ 16/1 and CPZ 16/2. Reproduced with the kind permission of Oxfordshire County Council.

Telegram to Oxford Prison from the Home Secretary.
Oxfordshire History Centre, CPZ 16/6. Reproduced with the kind permission of the Oxfordshire County Council.

The 7th Duke of Marlborough (1822-1883).
National Portrait Gallery by licenced permission.

Justice of the Peace oath of Rev Thomas Harris JP (1852).
Oxfordshire History Centre. Reproduced with the kind permission of Oxfordshire County Council.

Essay 9

Tackley memorial to the *Cataraqui* disaster.
Reproduced with the kind permission of the Tackley Local History Group.

The *Cospatrick* at Gravesend, 1856.
Reproduced with the kind permission of the National Maritime Museum, Greenwich.

Shipton-under-Wychwood memorial to the *Cospatrick* disaster. The appalling tragedy (the loss of 441 lives) shocked the nation. The Board of Trade enquiry later concluding that the fire probably started as a result of someone attempting to raid the liquor store. It was one of the worst maritime disasters of the century and probably contributed to the waning of interest in emigration thereafter. In 1877 a committee in Shipton-under-Wychwood raised £70 towards a memorial to the local victims of the disaster and the fountain was erected on the green a year later. (Wychwood Local History Society).
Photo: Alan Vickers.

New Zealand map.
Julie Barrett.

Eli and Jane Prattley and their children.
Reproduced with the kind permission of Beverley McCombs, a descendent of the family.

Essay 10

Membership emblem of the National Agricultural Labourers' Union, 1872. The emblem is 60.4 x 45 cm.
Reproduced with the kind permission of The People's History Museum, Manchester.

Back cover

Imagined court scene.
Photo: Pauline Jackson, taken during filming. See: www.ascottmartyrs. co.uk/martyrs-in-film-song

Endnotes

Introduction

1   Beverley McCombs, *The Ascott Martyrs: Sixteen women from Ascott-under-Wychwood who were sent over the hills to glory*, Wellington, New Zealand: Writes Hill Press, 2016, second edition 2017.
2   Mark Curthoys, 'Oxfordshire's Tolpuddle: The case of the Ascott Martyrs' appeared in *Oxoniensia*, vol. 86, 2021, 159–178.
3   For more detail on the nuances and for calculators, see the website measuringworth.com.

Essay 1

1   *The Times*, 2 June 1873.
2   Ibid., 1 June 1873.
3   Ibid., 2 June 1873.
4   *The Daily News*, 27 May 1873.
5   Ibid.
6   Ibid.
7   *The Daily News*, 29 May 1873.
8   *Buckinghamshire Advertiser*, 31 May 1873.
9   Warrants of commitment on conviction OHC CPZ 16.
10 *The Daily News*, 27 May 1873.
11 Letter from Lord Selborne to the Lord Lieutenant of Oxfordshire OHC CPT 16.9.
12 Telegram from the Home Secretary to the governor of Oxford Prison OHC CPZ 16.6.
13 *The Times*, 29 May 1873.
14 Ibid., 9 June 1873.
15 *Jackson's Oxford Journal*, 21 June 1873.
16 Letter from the Lord Chancellor to the Lord Lieutenant OHC CPZ 16.9.
17 From 'The Two Curates' published in *The Scottish Magazine*, 1852.
18 *The Times*, 7 June 1873.
19 *Banbury Advertiser*, 6 June 1873.
20 *Oxford Chronicle and Berks & Bucks Gazette*, 7 June 1873.

21 *The Daily News*, 27 May 1873.

22 *The Times*, 3 June 1873.

23 Secretary of State to Visiting Justices for Oxford Gaol OHC CPZ 16.10.

24 *Oxford Weekly News*, 25 June 1873.

25 Pamela Horn, *Joseph Arch (1826-1919): The Farm Worker's Leader,* Kineton: The Roundwood Press, 1971, p. 88,

26 Beverley McCombs, *The Ascott Martyrs*, Wellington, New Zealand: Writes Hall Press, 2016, pp. 82–84.

27 The context of these events is also provided by the following: Joseph Arch, *Joseph Arch: The Story of His Life*, London: Hutchinson 7 Co., 1898; Carl Boardman, *Foul Deeds and Suspicious Deaths around Oxfordshire*, Barnsley: Pen & Sword, 2004; Mark Curthoys, 'Oxfordshire's Tolpuddle: The Case of the Ascott's Martyrs', *Oxoniensia*, vol. 86, 2021; J. R. Hodgkins, *Over the Hills to Glory: Radicals in Banburyshire 1832-1945*, Southend: Clifton Press, 1978; Eric Moss, *'Walk Humble My Son': including My Personal Memories by Doris Warner*, Charlbury: Wychwood Press, 1991; W. Pearce, *Defiant Women – The Ascott Martyrs*. Wychwood History 23 (2008), pp. 3-16.

Essay 2

1 G. Bernard Shaw, 'A Shavian Commentary on Martyrs' in Trades Union Congress (TUC), *The Book of the Martyrs of Tolpuddle.1834–1934: The story of the Dorsetshire Labourers Who Were Convicted and Sentenced to Seven Years' Transportation for Forming a Trade Union,* London: Trades Union Congress, 1934, p. ix.

2 Ibid., p. 5.

3 Ibid.

4 Ibid., p. 8.

5 Ibid., p. 13.

6 Ibid., p. 9.

7 Ibid., p. 13.

8 Ibid., p. 63.

9 https://research-information.bris.ac.uk/en/publications/hornby-v-close-1867

10 Arthur Clayden *The Revolt of the Field*, London: Hodder and

Stoughton, 1874, reissued and replicated by Book on Demand, 2015, p. 6.

11 Ibid., p. 53.
12 Pamela Horn, *Joseph Arch*, Kineton, Warwick: The Roundwood Press, 1971, p. 98.
13 Clayden, *Revolt of the Field*, p. 24.
14 Ibid., p. 43.
15 Ibid., p. 44.
16 Ibid., p. 47.
17 Ibid., p. 49.
18 Ibid., p. 145.
19 Ibid., p. 150.
20 Ibid., p. 150.
21 Horn *Joseph Arch*, p. 109.
22 Graph based upon details gathered from Horn's book on *Joseph Arch* and many other sources.
23 Horn, *Joseph Arch*, Appendix 1, p. 222.
24 P. Horn, 'Christopher Holloway: An Oxfordshire Trade union Leader', *Oxoniensia*, 33 (1968), p. 126.
25 *Jackson's Oxford Journal*, 10 August 1872.
26 Minute Book Local Preachers Meetings, meeting 26th June 1872. E6 Bodleian Library.
27 P. Horn, 'Christopher Holloway', p. 130.
28 Ibid., p. 131.
29 Ibid., p.133.
30 Mark Curthoys, 'Oxfordshire's Tolpuddle? The Case of the Ascott Martyrs', *Oxoniensia* vol. 86, 2021, p. 178.

Essay 3

1 Records in the 1871 Census for Combe suggest this was Mary Huckin, aged 23.
2 British Parliamentary Papers (B.P.P), 1868-9, XIII, Royal Commission on the Employment of Children, Young Persons and Women in Agriculture, Evidence to Mr Culley's report, p. 341.
3 For an overview see Nicola Verdon, *Rural Women Workers in Nineteenth-Century England: Gender, Work and Wages*, Woodbridge: Boydell, 2002.
4 Nicola Verdon, *Working the Land: A History of the Farmworker in*

England from 1850 to the Present Day, Basingstoke: Palgrave, 2017, chapter 3.

5   B.P.P., 1868-9, XIII, Report by Mr Culley, p. 79.
6   Nicola Verdon, 'The employment of women and children in agriculture: A reassessment of agricultural gangs in nineteenth-century Norfolk', *Agricultural History Review*, 49 (2001), 41–55.
7   B.P.P., 1868-9, XIII, Report by Mr Culley, p. 83.
8   Edward Higgs, 'Occupational censuses and the agricultural workforce in Victorian England and Wales', *Economic History Review*, XLVIII (1995), 700–716.
9   Joyce Burnette, 'The wages and employment of female day labourers in agriculture, 1740–1850', *Economic History Review*, 57, 4 (2004), 664–690.
10   Verdon, *Working the Land*, p. 91.
11   Pamela Horn, *Victorian Countrywomen*, Oxford: Wiley-Blackwell, 1991, pp. 166–7.
12   N. L. Leyland and J. E Troughton, *Glovemaking in West Oxfordshire*, Oxford City and County Museum, 1974. See also Melanie Dubber, 'Making ends meet: Working-class women's strategies against poverty in West Oxfordshire, c. 1850 – 1900'. Unpublished PhD thesis, Oxford Brookes University, 1997.
13   B.P.P., 1868-9, XIII, Evidence to Mr Culley's report, p. 344.
14   Ibid.
15   B.P.P., 1868-9, XIII, Evidence to Mr Culley's report, p. 344.
16   B.P.P., 1868-9, XIII, Report by Mr Culley, p. 80 and Evidence to Mr Culley's report, p. 345.
17   B.P.P., 1868-9, XIII, Report by Mr Culley, p. 84.
18   Ibid., p. 344.
19   B.P.P., 1868-9, XIIIth, Evidence to Mr Culley's report, pp. 331–332; Mr Culley's report, p. 84.
20   Karen Sayer, *Women of the Fields: Representations of Rural Women in the Nineteenth Century*, Manchester: Manchester University Press. 1995, p. 128.
21   Joseph Arch, *From Ploughtail to Parliament: An Autobiography*, London: Ebury Press, 1986 edn, p. 250.
22   Karen Sayer, 'Field-faring women: the resistance of women who worked in the fields in nineteenth-century England,' *Women's History Review*, 2, 2 (1993), 185–198.

Essay 4

1   Lord Ernle, *English Farming Past and Present*, London: Longmans and Co, 1922, p. 374.

2   Gordon E. Mingay, *Rural Life in Victorian England*, London: Heinemann, 1852, p. 52.

3   Richard Hoyle, *The Farmer in England 1650-1980*, Farnham, Ashgate, 2007, p. 1.

4   James Caird English *Agriculture in 1850-1*, London: 1852, pp. 24–6

5   F.M. L. Thompson, 'The second Agricultural Revolution 1815–1880', *The Economic History Review*, Second Series, 1968, 62.

6   James Caird, *High Farming as the best Substitute for Protection*, London, Longman, 1849.

7   Lord Ernle, *English Farming Past and Present*, London: Longmans and Co., 1922, p. 374.

8   Michael Winstanley, 'Agriculture and Rural Society, c.1800-1914', in C. Williams (ed.), *A Companion to Nineteenth Century Britain*, *Oxford: Oxford University Press, 2004, pp. 211–218.*

9   J. Caird, section on 'The Fen Country,' in *English Agriculture in 1850-51,* Cambridge Library Collection – British and Irish History, 19th Century, Cambridge: Cambridge University Press, 1770184, doi: 10: 1017/CB09780511791642022.

10 *Report of the Select Committee on Agricultural Customs and Minutes of Evidence*, Parliamentary Papers (PP) 1947–8, vol. 7.

11 L. Dudley Stamp (ed.), *The Land of Britain: The Report of the Land Utilisation Survey of Britain. Part 56 Oxfordshire*, London: Mary Marshal Geographical Publications, 1943, p. 218.

12 John Kibble , *Historical and Other Notes on Wychwood Forest and Many of its Border places*, Oxford: The Oxford Chronicle, 1928, p. 52. For a more detailed account of the decline of customary rights see Robert Colls, *This Sporting Life: Sports & Liberty in England, 1760–1960*, Oxford: Oxford University Press, 2020, pp. 101–133.

13 *Jackson's Oxford Journal*, Saturday 9 January 1892.

14 Thompson, 'The second Agricultural Revolution', 201–202.

15 Howard Newby, *The Deferential Worker*, London: Allen Lane, 1977, p. 47.

16 Celia Miller (ed.), *Rain and Ruin: The Diary of an Oxfordshire Farmer John Simpson Calvertt 1875–1900*, Stroud: Alan Sutton, 1983, pp. 54, 57.

17 Ibid., p. 82.

18 *Report of the Select Committee on Agricultural Customs and Minutes of Evidence*, PP 1947–8 vol,7,Q 1938.

19 T.E. Wilton, *Sports and Pursuits of the English as bearing on their national character,* London: Harison, 1869, p. 224.

20 John Martin, 'The wild rabbit: plague, polices and pestilence in England and Wales, 1931–1955', *Agricultural History Review*, vol. 8, part 2, 2010, 255–258.

21 S. Andrews, *Eighteenth Century Europe:1600 to 1815*, London: Longman, 1965.

22 Pamela Horn, 'The Village in Victorian Oxfordshire,' *Oxfordshire Local Historian*, vol. 1, no. 6, Spring, 109, 1983, 20–22.

23 *The Times*, 2 June 1873.

24 Mark Curthoys, 'Oxfordshire's Tolpuddle; The case of the Ascot Martyrs', *Oxoniensia*, vol. 86, 2021, 163–164.

25 Alun Howkins, *Reshaping Rural England: A Social History 1850–1925*, Harper Collins, 1991, p. 109.

26 Mark Curthoys, 'Oxfordshire's Tolpuddle', 173.

27 Ibid., 166.

Essay 5

1   Verse from the Anglican hymn 'All Things Bright and Beautiful' by Cecil Frances Alexander, 1848.

2   The quote comes from a report on meeting of agricultural workers in Milton-under-Wychwood, *Jackson's Oxford Journal*, 6 July 1873.

3   Kate Tiller in the introduction of *Church and Chapel in Oxfordshire 1851*, Oxford: Oxford Record Society, vol. 55, 1987, gives a detailed analysis of religious affiliations derived from those census returns, pp. xv passim.

4   On the fluidity of denominational affiliation see Frances Knight, *The Nineteenth Century Church and English Society*, Cambridge, 1995, pp. 24–36.

5   Ascott had achieved some status as an independent ecclesiastical parish by about 1600; see *Victoria County History*, vol. XIX, 2019, p. 83.

6   Recorded as early as 1458 – see *Victoria County History,* vol. XIX, 2019, p. 153.

7   On the Church Building Commission see M. H. Port, *Six Hundred New Churches*, London, 1961.

8   On J. H. Langston see *Chipping Norton Deanery Magazine*, Number 90, June 1888, unpaginated.

9   *The Diocese books of Samuel Wilberforce*, Bishop of Oxford 1845–1869, Oxfordshire Record Society, vol. 66, 2008, p. 11.

10 *Jackson's Oxford Journal*, 16 August 1862, p. 5.

11 Chipping Norton Deanery Magazine, 1888, op. cit.

12 Jackson's Oxford Journal, 4 May 1872, p. 8.

13 *Jackson's Oxford Journal*, 28 January 1871.

14 '... but many people here as elsewhere will attend both church and meeting' – Rev. Thomas Dand's (vicar of Bletchingdon) comment on the 1851 religious census return, quoted in Kate Tiller, 1987, op. cit. p. xx.

15 Frances Knight, 1995, op cit., pp. 61–86.

16 *Oxfordshire Weekly News*, 11 August 1869.

17 See *Victoria County History*, vol. XIX, 2019, p. 120.

18 Pamela Horn, *Joseph Arch*, Kineton: The Roundwood Press, 1971, pp. 26-27

19 On the early history of the Baptists in Milton see G. W. Davidson, *A Brief History of the Baptist Church, Milton, Oxfordshire*, Chipping Norton, n.d. [1889]

20 On the Groves dynasty in Milton see Norman Frost, 'The Groves Family of Milton-under-Wychwood,' *Journal of The Wychwoods Local History Society*, Vol 7 (1992), pp. 10-28; Vol 8 (1993), pp. 27-37; Vol 9 (1994), pp. 48–55.

21 Ibid.

22 Build date of 1812 given in the 1851 census return, see Kate Tiller, 1987, op. cit. p. 4.

23 Ibid, p. 4.

24 VCH, vol. XIX, 2019, p. 120.

25 *The Diocese Books of Samuel Wilberforce, Bishop of Oxford 1845–1869*, The Oxfordshire Record Society, Vol. 66, 2008, p. 106.

26 Ernest Gaskell, *Oxfordshire Leaders, Social and Political*, London: The Queenhithe Printing and Publishing Co Ltd, n.d. [c 1900].

27 *The Oxfordshire Weekly News*, 21 July 1872, p. 5.

28 *The Oxfordshire Weekly News*, 19 June 1872, p. 5.

29 Celia Miller (ed.), *Rain and Ruin. The Diary of an Oxfordshire Farmer John Simpson Calvertt 1875–1900*, Gloucester: Alan Sutton,

1983, p.41. Ringwood is the farm of the Abrahams family, friends of the Calvertts and Mr Abraham being a close acquaintance of C. H. Spurgeon.

30 *The Oxfordshire Weekly News,* 17 April 1872.

31 See Kate Tiller, 1987, op cit. p. 68. This first chapel is no longer extant but was sited in a central location in Milton-under-Wychwood near to the village green.

32 Ibid., p. 68.

33 John Kibble, *Wychwood Forest and its Border Places,* 1928, re-issued by The Wychwood Press, Charlbury, 1999, pp. 79–80. Isaac Castle's coffee house seems to have come later, circa 1891, and is now a residential property at 64 High Street, Milton-under-Wychwood.

34 M. K. Ashby, 1974, op cit. p. 375, mentions camp meetings in Chadlington, Milton, Lyneham and Chilson.

35 For an account of camp meetings in Ascott in the 1920s and 1930s see Eric Moss, *Walk Humble, My Son,* Charlbury, 1999, p. 74.

36 See N. A. D. Scotland, *Methodism and the Revolt of the Field. A study of the Methodist contribution to agricultural trade unionism in East Anglia 1872–96,* Stroud: Alan Sutton, 1981, p. 22.

37 Pamela Horn, 1971, op. cit. p.16.

38 Pamela Horn, *Agricultural Trades Unionism in Oxfordshire 1872-81,* The Oxfordshire Record Society, vol. XLVIII, 1974, p. 27.

39 For further evidence of links between Nonconformist groups, including the Primitive Methodists, see: Nigel Scotland, *op. cit.,* 1981; and Pamela Horn, 1971, op. cit.

40 P. Horn, 1974, op. cit. p. 28.

41 See N. A. D. Scotland, Methodism and the English Labour Movement 1800–1906, *Anvil,* vol. 14/1, 1997, p. 40.

42 A brass band from Lyneham was in attendance at a Union meeting in Milton-under-Wychwood on 1 July 1872; see *Jackson's Oxford Journal,* 6 July 1872.

43 Joseph Arch, *From Ploughtail to Parliament,* London: The Cresset Library, 1986, p. xxiv. For examples of union songs see Pamela Horn, *Joseph Arch,* Kineton: The Roundwood Press, 1971, pp. 244–247.

44 *The Witney Express,* 11 April 1872 reports on presence of women and children at a meeting in Stretton, Warwickshire; and *Jackson's Oxford Journal,* 32 August 1872, p. 8, comments on the number of women present at a meeting in Woodstock.

45 *The Witney Express*, 18 April 1872.
46 Pamela Horn, 1974, op. cit. p. 10.
47 On this correspondence see also Nigel Scotland, 1981, op. cit. p.76.
48 N. A. D. Scotland, Methodism and the English Labour Movement 1800–1906, "*Anvil*" vol. 14/1, 1997, p. 42.

Essay 6

1   Reginald Groves, *Sharpen the Sickle: The History of the Farm Workers' Union*, London: Merlin Press, 1983, p. 33.
2   Pamela Horn, *Joseph Arch*, Kineton: The Roundwood Press, 1971, p. 35.
3   J. V. Beckett, *The Aristocracy in England 1660–1914*, Oxford: Basil Blackwell, 1986, p. 324.
4   Ibid., p. 324.
5   Ibid., p. 161.
6   Pamela Horn, *Joseph Arch*, p. 35.
7   Marjorie Filbee, *Cottage Industries*, Newton Abbot/North Pomfret, VT: David & Charles, 1982.
8   'The Corn Laws' in *The Morning Chronicle*, 18 February 1819.
9   Barry Reay, *The Last Rising of the Agricultural Labourers*, Oxford: Oxford University Press, 2010, p. 18.
10 Pamela Horn, *Agricultural Trade Unionism in Oxfordshire, 1872–81*, Oxford: Oxfordshire Record Society, 1974, XLVIII, p. 121.
11 J. P. D. Dunbabin, 'The 'Revolt of the Field': The Agricultural Labourers' Movement in the 1870s', *Past & Present*, 26, 1963, 68–97, particularly 74.
12 David Kent, 'Containing Disorder in the 'Age of Equipoise': Troops, Trains and the Telegraph,' *Social History*, 38.3 (2013), 308–27, particularly 310..
13 Gordon Mingay, 'The Sources of Productivity in the Agricultural Revolution in England,' *South African Journal of Economic History*, 6.1 (1991), 1–18, particularly 5
14 Horn, *Joseph Arch*, p. 35.
15 Reginald Groves, *Sharpen the Sickle: The History of the Farm Workers' Union*, London: Merlin Press, 1981, p. 33.
16 Nigel Scotland, 'The NALU and the Demand for a Stake in the Soil 1872-1896', in *Citizenship and Community: Liberals, Radicals, and Collective Identities in the British Isles, 1865-1931*, ed. by Eugenio

F. Biagini, Cambridge and New York: Cambridge University Press, 1996, p. 152.

17 Pamela Horn, 'Farmers' Defence Association in Oxfordshire 1872–1874', *History Studies*, 1.1 (1968), 63–70.

18 'Letter from the Duke of Marlborough to His Grace's Tenantry,' *Jackson's Oxford Journal*, 8 March 1872, 8.

19 M. C. Curthoys, *Governments, Labour, and the Law in Mid-Victorian Britain: The Trade Union Legislation of the 1870s*, Oxford: Clarendon Press, 2004, p. 72.

20 George Griffith, 'Letter Regarding Agricultural Labourers' Union,' *Jackson's Oxford Journal*, 9 May 1874.

21 Steven King, *OU Readings for Block 6 – Poverty and Welfare in England 1700-1850*, Manchester: Manchester University Press, 2000, p. 5.

22 Keith D. M. Snell, *Annals of the Labouring Poor: Social Change and Agrarian England, 1660 – 1900*, Cambridge Studies in Population, Economy and Society in Past Time, 2, 1, Cambridge: Cambridge University Press, 1995, p. 116.

23 Robert Hambidge and others, letter, *The Times*, 2 June 1873, p. 8.

24 Snell, *Annals of the Labouring Poor*, p.118.

25 Alun Howkins, *Reshaping Rural England: A Social History, 1850-1925*, London: HarperCollins Academic, 1991, p. 85.

26 A. F. J. Brown, *Meagre Harvest: The Essex Farm Workers' Struggle against Poverty, 1750-1914*, Essex Record Office Publication, no. 106, Chelmsford: Essex, Essex Record Office, 1990, p. 27.

27 Ibid., p. 27.

28 Lynn Hollen Lees, *The Solidarities of Strangers: The English Poor Laws and the People, 1700-1948*, 1st edn, Cambridge, Cambridge University Press, 2006, p. 180.

29 Brown, *Meagre Harvest*, p. 27.

30 Ibid., p. 29.

31 OHC, S9/1 A1/1, 'Ascott-under-Wychwood School Log Book', 1873.

32 Brown, *Meagre Harvest*, p. 32.

33 'Godless Knowledge,' *Reynold's Newspaper*, 23 January 1870, p. 4.

34 OHC, S9/1 A1/1.

35 Eugenio F. Biagini, *Liberty, Retrenchment and Reform Popular Liberalism in the Age of Gladstone, 1860–1880*, Cambridge: Cambridge University Press, 1992, p. 196.

36 Edward Barber, *Oxford Diocesan Inspection – General Report*

for the Year 1880, Radley, Abingdon: Oxford Diocesan Board of
Education, 1881, p. 3.

37 Ibid., p. 3.

38 Ibid., p. 3.

39 Ibid., p. 4.

40 Ibid., p. 4.

41 Kent, 'Containing Disorder', p. 310.

42 Hansard, Millbank, Second Reading (Hansard, 19 April 1871)
Game Laws Abolition Bill, HC Deb 19 April 1871 Vol 205 cc1349-
80, 1871, CCV, 1349–80.

43 Oxford, Nuffield College, Small Collection: P, 'Milton Agricultural
Labourers' Union Minute Book,' 1872. Christopher Holloway,
'Diary of Christopher Holloway', 1874, Nuffield College Library,
MSS Small Collection – P – Box 2.

44 Viscount Cranbourne, *Representation of the People Bill*, HC Deb 27
April 1866 Vol 183 Cc6-156, CLXXXIII, 6–156.

45 *Master and Servant Act*, HC Deb 01 March 1867 Vol 185 Cc1259-62.

Essay 7

1 Karl Marx, *Capital*, vol. 1, 1887 edition, London: Lawrence and
Wishart, 1974, p. 692.

2 Sidney Webb and Beatrice Webb, *The History of Trade Unionism,
1666–1920*, London: Longman, Green, London 1920, chapter 6.

3 See *Second and Final Report of the Royal Commission on the Master
and Servant Act, 1867 and the Criminal Law Amendment Act, 1871*,
C 1157, 1875, Appendix, Notes of Cases. The Royal Commission
Report also includes a Table of Cases with a brief account of the
circumstances of more than 50 prosecutions that had taken place
under the Act, with information about the defendant's conduct
and sentence in each case. See also Mark Curthoys, *Governments,
Labour, and the Law in Mid-Victorian Britain: The Trade Union
Legislation of the 1870s*, Oxford: Oxford University Press, 2004,
chapter 6. See also the powerful and lengthy letter to *The Times*
by Frederic Harrison, 2 June 1873, referred to below, and attached
as appendix C.

4 See especially *R. v Duffield* (1851) 5 Cox CC 404, and *R. v Rowlands*
(1851) 5 Cox CC 436.

5 (1867) LR 2 QB. 153. See J. H. McCunn, '*Hornby v Close (1867)*', in A.

Bogg, A. Davies and J. Prassl (eds), *Landmark Cases in Labour Law*, Oxford: Hart Publishing, 2022, forthcoming.

6   Henry Pelling, *A History of British Trade Unionism*, Harmondsworth: Penguin Books, 1963, p 65. See Royal Commission on the Organisation and Rules of Trades Unions and other Associations, *Report* presented to the Trade Union Commissioners by the Examiners appointed to inquire into Acts of Intimidation, Outrage, or Wrong, alleged to have been Promoted, Encouraged or Connived at by Trade Unions in the Town of Sheffield, London, HMSO, 1867. The Royal Commission also dealt at length with acts of violence associated with trade unionism in Manchester, notably in the building trades: Royal Commission on the Organisation and Rules of Trades Unions and other Associations, *Report* presented to the Trade Union Commissioners by the Examiners appointed to inquire into Acts of Intimidation , Outrage, or Wrong, alleged to have been Promoted, Encouraged or Connived at by Trade Unions in Manchester and its Neighbourhood, London, HMSO, 1867–8, published in 1868.

7   Sir William Erle, 'Memorandum on the Law Relating to Trade Unions', *Eleventh and Final Report of the Royal Commission on the Organisation and Rules of Trades Unions and other Associations*, p. lxv.

8   Ibid., p. lxxxii.

9   *Eleventh and Final Report of the Royal Commission on the Organisation and Rules of Trades Unions and other Associations*, para. 75.

10 *Gibson v Lawson* [1891] 2 QB 545 (Lord Coleridge, CJ) (p. 559).

11 J. V. Orth, *Combination and Conspiracy: A Legal History of Trade Unionism 1721–1906*, Oxford: Oxford University Press, 1991, p. 141. See also Curthoys, *Government, Labour and the Law in Mid-Victorian Britain*, pp. 142–8.

12 Criminal Law Amendment Act 1871, s. 1.

13 In contrast to the 1825 Act where the requirement was that the conduct was designed to 'force' or 'endeavour to force', or 'induce'.

14 (1875) 13 Cox CC 82.

15 Ibid., p. 87. Emphasis added.

16 Ibid.

17 (1867) 10 Cox CC 592; see also Webb, above, pp. 278–279.

18 Webb and Webb, *The History of Trade Unionism*, pp. 276–7.

19 (1875) 13 Cox CC 82.

20 Mark Curthoys, 'Oxford's Tolpuddle? The Case of the Ascott Martyrs' (2021) 86 *Oxoniensia* 159, p. 164.

21 On the position at common law, see *Dimes v Grand Junction Canal Proprietors* (1852) 3 HLC 759.

22 Webb and Webb, *The History of Trade Unionism*, pp. 331–333.

23 See *Second and Final Report of the Royal Commission on the Master and Servant Act, 1867 and the Criminal Law Amendment Act, 1871*, Appendix, Notes of Cases, p 9, where this is referred to as the 'Martha Smith case'. The same account adds remarkably that 'the evidence at the hearing was not taken down in writing' (ibid.).

24 This was not unusual. Curthoys, *Governments, Labour, and the Law in Mid-Victorian Britain: The Trade Union Legislation of the 1870s*, above, refers to claims that only 10 per cent of those convicted under the Act were trade unionists, the rest being 'non-unionised strikers, strikers' wives, and sympathisers' (p. 163).

25 *R. v Rowlands*, above, p. 489 (Lord Campbell, CJ).

26 (1875) 13 Cox CC 82.

27 Ibid., p. 87.

28 Curthoys, 'Oxford's Tolpuddle?', p. 166.

29 HC Debs, 6 June 1873, cols 548-9. Emphasis added.

30 *Gibson v Lawson* [1891] 2 QB 545, reflecting on the 1871 Act in a prosecution on the 1875 Act below. This is because the Act limits 'intimidation' to 'such intimidation as would justify a magistrate in binding over the intimidator to keep the peace towards the person intimidated' (p 559).

31 Further evidence (albeit unreliable) that violence, threats and intimidation were used is provided by Joseph Arch, who records that the women 'mobbed' Hodgkins and Millin, and that while only verbal blows were struck, Arch had 'heard' that some of the women 'carried sticks.' Although 'it was plain enough to any unprejudiced person that no physical injury was attempted,' 'at most there might have been a little hustling.' Having unsuccessfully seduced the men with the offer of a drink, the men 'went to work on Hambridge's (sic) farm under the protection of a police constable' according to Joseph Arch, *The Autobiography of Joseph Arch: Preface by Frances Countess of Warwick*, London, Macgibbon & Kee, Fitzroy edition,1966, pp. 73-74.

32 Ibid., p. 74.

33 HC Debs, 6 June 1873, cols 549–550.

34 Erskine May, *Treatise on the Law, Privileges, Proceedings and Usage of Parliament* , 25th edition, Norwich: HMSO, 2019, para 21.23, f/n 5 (dealing with magistrates).

35 See Curthoys, 'Oxford's Tolpuddle?', p. 171.

36 HC Debs, 4 July 1873, col 1785. When subsequently pulled up for his remarks made in the House of Commons on 6 June 1873, the Home Secretary added that another option was for the 'absolute dismissal of the case' against some or all of the women involved, having been told that 'nothing is more common than to dismiss with a warning from the Bench persons charged with slight offences': HC Debs, 4 July 1873, col 1785.

37 Beverley McCombs, *The Ascott Martyrs*, Wellington NZ: Writes Hill Press, 2nd ed, 2017, pp. 69–70, referring to correspondence between Selborne and the Duke of Marlborough. This is an important book that has done much to revive interest and to inform a wide audience about the Ascott case specifically, and the operation of the 1871 Act more generally. See also Curthoys, *Governments, Labour, and the Law in Mid-Victorian Britain: The Trade Union Legislation of the 1870s*, p. 162.

38 See the discussion in Curthoys, 'Oxford's Tolpuddle?', p. 177.

39 Figures produced by the Royal Commission on Labour in 1874 suggest that by 1873, those who appealed did so with a sporting chance of success: there were 12 appeals from 39 convictions in that year leading to convictions being quashed in eight cases: *Second and Final Report of the Royal Commission on the Master and Servant Act, 1867 and the Criminal Law Amendment Act, 1871*, p. 24.

40 *The Times*, 2 June 1873. See appendix C for the full text of the letter. Harrison was a barrister and adviser to the TUC who had served on the Erle Royal Commission, and co-authored what was to be the influential Minority Report of the Royal Commission. See also *The Spectator*, 31 May 1873; 7 June 1873. The thrust of the former was for reform of the magistracy, not the substantive law; the latter was very critical of the employer and his friends locally. See also the six items of correspondence in *The Times* between 2 May and 14 June 1873 reproduced in the appendix.

41 Trade Union and Labour Relations (Consolidation) Act, ss 241 and 220.

42 It was nevertheless a pyrrhic victory, doing so by extending criminal liability to all rather than remove it from some. Nevertheless, for the trade union leadership, naively 'the work of emancipation [was] full and complete': Roderick Martin, *TUC: The Growth of a Pressure Group 1868–1976*, Oxford: Clarendon Press, 1980, p. 51. For trade union members it did not feel like a victory, with Charles Bradlaugh drawing attention to a motion at the TUC Annual Conference in 1890 demanding the repeal of the CPPA 1875, s. 7 as being 'dangerous to the liberties of the working classes': C. Bradlaugh, *Labour and Law*, London: R. Forder, 1891, p 14. For a discussion of the early cases under the 1875 Act, see C. Grunfeld, *Modern Trade Union Law,* London: Sweet and Maxwell, 1966, ch. 22.

43 Ironic in the sense that while we cannot say that there is a direct link between the Ascott convictions and the CPPA 1875, s. 7, it seems certain nevertheless that they contributed to the agitation for repeal of the 1871 Act, and with it reform of both the substance and procedure of the law relating to strikes and picketing. See Webb and Webb, *The History of Trade Unionism*, p. 333, who claim that 'The public disapproval of the sentence in the Chipping Norton case was used by the Trade Union leaders as a powerful argument for the repeal of the Criminal Law Amendment Act.' See also Curthoys, *Governments, Labour, and the Law in Mid-Victorian Britain*, p. 164. For a possibly more sceptical view of the direct political influence of the convictions, see Curthoys, 'Oxford's Tolpuddle?'.

44 A point also made by Curthoys, 'Oxford's Tolpuddle?'.

45 Conspiracy and Protection of Property Act 1875, s. 7. See subsequently Trade Disputes Act 1906, s. 2, and now Trade Union and Labour Relations (Consolidation) Act, ss 241 and 220.

Essay 8

1 'The cross in one hand the gibbet in the other.' was how Richard Fryer, MP for Wolverhampton in 1832 described the conflict of interest faced by clerical magistrates, quoted in Roger Swift, *English Urban Magistracy*, p.81. Of course, hyperbolic reference to 'the gibbet' is an overstatement of a JP's power in petty sessions.

2 Joseph Arch, *Joseph Arch: the story of his life*, London: Hutchinson, 1898, p. 138.

3   *Daily News*, 27 May 1873.

4   E.g., (1) 'Harris and Carter had sealed the death warrant of clergymen acting as magistrates. Very quickly over the next few years, the number of clergymen on the bench was run down.' Carl Boardman, *Foul Deeds and Suspicious Deaths around Oxfordshire*, Barnsley: Pen & Sword, 2004 and (2) 'This "intimidation case" made the national headlines and brought such heavy criticism of clergy magistrates that the custom of appointing ordained men to the Bench was discontinued.' Neil Bromwich, *A Brief Historical Record of Churchill and Sarsden* (unpublished).

5   As recorded in the Home Secretary's speech following the event.

6   Mark Curthoys, 'Oxfordshire's Tolpuddle? The Case of the Ascott Martyrs', *Oxoniensia*, vol. 86, 2021, pp. 174–175.

7   Included in Carter and Harris's statement to the Lord Chancellor. Parliamentary Papers online.

8   *The Times*, 26 May 1873. 'Two magistrates adopted a course which was extremely harsh, ill-advised and... led to a serious riot.'. A *Times* article the following day called for reforms of the bench and for clerical magistrates to be banned following the 'monstrous act of Messrs. Harris and Carter'.

9   *The Spectator*, 31 May 1873. See appendix B. Nevertheless, *The Spectator* wrote 20 years later that ministers 'often make admirable magistrates; and to deny them their right to fulfil that function, when it does not interfere with their other duties, is either a folly or the outcome of ideas which would in the end change all teachers of Christianity into a secluded and inexperienced priestly caste.' 19 January 1895, p. 81.

10   *The Times*, 2 June 1873. See appendix C.

11   Published as a Parliamentary Paper in 1873.

12   Clive Emsley, 'The English Magistracy, 1700-1850', *IAHCCJ Bulletin*, No. 15, February 1992.

13   Carter to Duke of Marlborough, 14 June 1873. Copy of correspondence between the Lord Chancellor and Lord Lieutenant respecting the sentence passed by the magistrates of the Chipping Norton bench on certain Women lately Convicted of Obstructing some Labourers in the performance of their work. Parliamentary Papers online, accessed 20 June 2022.

14   Duke of Marlborough to Lord Chancellor, Parliamentary Papers online, accessed 20 June 2022.

15 Ibid., 18 June 1873.

16 George C. Brodrick, *English Land and English Landlords. an Enquiry into the Origin and Character of the English Land System, with Proposals for Its Reform*, London: Cassell, Peter, Galpin & Co, 1881, p. 162. Quoted in Brian Cox, 'How far was the rise of agricultural combinations a symptom rather than a cause of the deteriorating relationship between land owners (including farmers) and their agricultural labourers in Oxfordshire between 1871 and 1874?', unpublished MA dissertation, Open University, 2016. Lodged at Oxford History Centre, Ref: PA 1801.

17 Thomas Skyrme, *The Justices of the Peace* vol. 2, Chichester, Barry Rose, 1991, p. 165.

18 F. Witts, *A Diary of a Cotswold Parson*, edited by David Verey, Gloucester: Amberley Publishing, 1991.

19 The 1813 Local Act in Manchester introduced the first paid magistrates, but this was only to be in boroughs and the 1835 Municipal Corporations Act enabled boroughs to request stipendiary magistrates. In 1863, the Stipendiary Magistrates Act became law in urban areas with populations of more than 25,000. Oxford and Oxfordshire did not qualify.

20 Samuel Stone, *The Justices' Manual, or Guide to the Ordinary Duties of a Justice of the Peace' with an appendix of forms and table of punishments*, London: Shaw and Sons, 1867.

21 John W. B. Tomlinson, 'The Decline of the Clerical Magistracy in the Nineteenth-Century English Midlands', *Studies in Church History*, vol. 56: 'The Church and the Law', CUP, June 2020, pp. 419–433.

22 National figures quoted here from Carl H. E. Zangeri, 'The Social Composition of the County Magistracy in England and Wales, 1831–1887', *Journal of British Studies*, 11 (1971), 113–25.

23 E. C. Lubenow, 'Social recruitment and social attitudes: the Buckinghamshire Magistrates 1868-1888', *Huntingdon Library Quarterly* 4 (1977), pp. 247–68.

24 Home Secretary, Henry Bruce *Hansard*, 3rd ser.ccxvi (6 June 1873), col. 550.

25 *Reynold's News*, 1 June 1873.

26 *Newcastle Courier*, 30 June 1876.

27 *Hansard*, 6 June 1873, col. 551.

28 Arch, *Joseph Arch*, chapter 6.

29 Oxfordshire History Centre, CPZ16/14, Letter from John Davenport to Duke of Marlborough Regarding an Analysis of Magistrates in Oxfordshire, 7 June 1873.

30 Skyrme, *The Justices of the Peace,* vol. 2, p. 26.

31 Diana McClatchey, *Oxfordshire Clergy 1777–1869*, Oxford: Clarendon Press, 1960, p. 179.

32 Tomlinson, 'The Decline of the Clerical Magistracy in the Nineteenth-Century English Midlands'.

33 Ibid., Conclusion.

34 Christine Gowing, May 2022.

35 In 1873 there were 114 Oxfordshire magistrates, of which 15 were listed as clerical.

36 Oxfordshire Record Office documents: QFJ volumes 7,8 and 9.

37 *Kelly's Directory for Oxford*, 1925, online, accessed 20 June 2022.

38 *Kelly's Directory for Oxfordshire*, 1924, online. Note: In 1906, the Liberal government abolished the property qualification for county magistrates in the Justices of the Peace Act 'and the squirarchical domination of the magistracy was watered down.' William Cornish, Stephen Banks, Charles Mitchell, Paul Mitchell, Rebecca Probert, *Law and Society in England 1750-1950*, Oxford: Hart Publishing, 2019.

39 Royal Commission on Justices of the Peace, 1946-48 *Report*, London, HMSO, 1948.

Essay 9

1 Beverley McCombs, *The Ascott Martyrs*, Wellington, New Zealand: Writes Hill Press, 2016; Beverley McCombs, *Pratly, Pratley and Prattley Families, Descendants from Oxfordshire, England*, Wellington, New Zealand: Writes Hill Press, 2011.

2 Kate Tiller and Giles Darkes (ed.s), *An Historical Atlas of Oxfordshire, Oxford Record Society,* vol. 67, 2010.

3 Martin Greenwood, *The Promised Land: The Story of Emigration from Oxfordshire and Neighbouring Buckinghamshire, Northamptonshire, and Warwickshire 1815–1914,* Witney: Robert Boyd, 2020.

4 Pauline Ashbridge, *Children of Dissent*, Kershaw Publishing, 2008, pp. 4–5.

5 Look at the case of John Hillard Hillary who came from the

village of Tow Low in the North of England and went to New Zealand in 1879, in J. H. Hillary, *Westland, the Journal of John Hillary, Emigrant to New Zealand,* James, 1995.

6 J. F. C. Harrison, *Early Victorian Britain,* London, Fontana/Collins, 1988, p. 27.

7 New Zealand Passenger Lists, 1870s.

8 Rollo Arnold, *The Farthest Promised Land – English Village, New Zealand Immigration of the 1870s,* Wellington: Victoria University Press, 1981, chapter 6, Oxfordshire and Wychwood Forest, p. 28.

9 Pamela Horn, 'Agricultural Trade Unionism', *Historical Journal,* xv, 1972, 96.

10 G. E. Mingay, *Rural Life in Victorian England,* Stroud: Alan Sutton, 1990, p. 19.

11 M. K. Ashby, *Joseph Ashby of Tysoe, 1859–1919, A Study of English Village Life,* Cambridge: Cambridge University Press, 1961, pp. 88–89.

12 Flora Thompson, *Lark Rise to Candleford,* Oxford: Oxford University Press, 1945, p. 246.

13 H. Rider Haggard, *Rural England,* London: Longmans, Green, and Co., vol. 2, p. 114.

14 See Horn, 'Agricultural Trade Unionism,' 87–102.

15 Arnold, *The Farthest Promised Land,* p. 16.

16 Ibid., p. 28.

17 John Perkins, and the Tackley Local History Group, *Stories From The Past,* July 2020, online.

18 Arnold, *The Farthest Promised Land*, p. 30.

19 Horn, 'Agricultural Trade Unionism,' 97.

20 Ibid., 100-101.

21 Roger Kershaw and Mark Powell, *Family History on the Move: Where your ancestors went and why,* London: Kew, The National Archives, 2006, pp. 120–121.

22 Kevin Brown, *Passages to the World, The Emigrant Experience 1807–1940,* Barnsley: Seaforth, 2013, p. 192.

23 Ibid., p. 156.

24 Barry McKay, *Tackley to Tasmania: Pauper Emigration from an Oxfordshire Village to Australia, and the Wreck of the Cataraqui, 1845,* Tackley Local History Group, 2nd Revised Edition, 1992.

25 Rachel Strachen and the Tackley Local History Group, *The Cataraqui,* online.

26 Tom McKay and Dunvan Waugh, *A Determined Emigrant*, pp. 58–59.

27 Brown, *Passages to the World*, p. 159.

28 Ibid., pp. 161–162.

29 Ibid., pp. 169–170.

30 Ibid., pp. 174–175.

31 Arnold, *The Farthest Promised Land*, p. 28.

32 Tom McKay and Duncan Waugh, *A Determined Emigrant*, Wychwoods Local History Society, no. 11, 1996, pp. 58–59.

33 Pamela Horn, 'Christopher Holloway – Trade Union Leader,' *Oxoniensia*, 33, 1968, 131–133.

34 Quoted in Arnold, *The Farthest Promised Land*, c. 11, p. 4.

35 Ibid., p. 9.

36 Ibid., p. 6.

37 Arnold, *The Farthest Promised Land*, c. 6, 'Oxfordshire and Wychwood Forest', p. 17.

38 Arnold, *The Farthest Promised Land*, chapter 11 'The Transformation of the Immigrant,' pp. 1–16.

39 Ibid., pp. 3-4.

40 Ibid., p. 2.

41 Rollo Arnold, *News from Down Under*, Oxford History Centre, P2/2/N2/5.

42 Wendy Pearse, *Australia Bound: Some Ascott Emigrants*, Wychwoods Local History Society, no. 31, 2016, pp. 16–21.

Essay 10

1 'Rough Music' chapter in E. P. Thompson, *Customs in Common*, London: Penguin, 1991, pp. 467–531; Rosemary A. Jones, 'Women, Community and Collective Action: The 'Caffey Pren' Tradition', in Angela John (ed.), *Our Mothers' Land*, Cardiff: UWP, 1991, pp. 17–41; John Bohsted, *Riots and Community Politics in England and Wales, 1790–1810*, Cambridge, MA: Harvard University Press, 1983; and Beverley McCombs, *The Ascott Martyrs,* Wellington, NZ: Writes Hill Press, 2016, p. 93.

2 Nick Mansfield, *Buildings of the Labour Movement*, Swindon: English Heritage, 2013, pp. 36–39.

3 Three attempts to establish village friendly societies in Ascott failed between 1834 and 1881. It is likely that villagers were

members of the lodge of the large, affiliated society, the Independent Order of Oddfellows founded in neighbouring Shipton in 1877. See Shaun Morley, *Oxfordshire Friendly Societies, 1750–1918*, Oxford: Oxfordshire Record Society, 2011, pp. 37 and 245.

4   There is growing literature on Victorian working-class self-help but a still very good summary is in J. F. C. Harrison, *The Common People, A History from the Norman Conquest to the Present*, London: Fontana, 1984, chapter 9. There were no Methodist chapels in Ascott but villagers may have travelled to neighbouring locations. There was a Baptist chapel in Ascott but that denomination kept out of politics. For the links between Methodism and the NALU see Nigel Scotland, *Methodism and the Revolt of the Field, 1872–96*, Gloucester: Alan Sutton, 1981. His views have been subsequently challenged.

5   Malcolm Bee, 'Co-operation in Oxfordshire, 1860–1913', *Southern History* (1999), 6, 10, 21 and 41. See also Nick Mansfield, 'Paternalistic consumer co-operatives in rural England, 1870–1930', *Rural History*, vol. 23, no. 2, September 2012, 205–211.

6   Mark Curthoys, 'Oxfordshire's Tolpuddle? The Case of the Ascott Martyrs,' *Oxoniensia*, vol. 86, 2021, p. 177, and McCombs, *Ascott Martyrs*, p. 71.

7   Alun Howkins, 'Arch Joseph, (1826-1919)', *Oxford Dictionary of National Biography*, 2004.

8   Nicola Verdon, *Working the Land – A History of the Farmworker in England from 1850 to the Present Day*, London: Palgrave Macmillan, 2017, p.9. Alun Howkins estimates the 1874 membership at around 86,000 with perhaps another 30-40,000 members of regionally based 'Federated' unions. Howkins, Arch, Joseph, *ONDB* and George R. Boyer and Timothy J. Halton; 'Did Joseph Arch rase Agricultural Wages? – Rural Trades Unions and the Labour Market in Nineteenth Century England', *Economic History Review*, 47, (2), May 1994, 310–334.

9   There is evidence of female NALU members in Norfolk – see Alun Howkins, *Reshaping Rural England – A Social History, 1850-1925*, London: HarperCollins, 1991, pp. 189-190.

10 Pamela Horn, 'Christopher Holloway, an Oxfordshire trade union leader,' *Oxoniensa*, vol. 33, 1968, 130-131; John R Millburn and Keith Jarrott, *The Aylesbury Agitator*, Aylesbury: Buckinghamshire

County Council, 1988; and McCombs, *Ascott Martyrs*, pp. 94, 107, 113.

11   Pamela Horn, *Joseph Arch,* Kineton: The Roundwood Press, 1971, pp. 48 and 73.

12   McCombs, *Ascott Martyrs*, pp. 60, 77, 79.

13   Ibid., p. 60 and Curthoys, 'Oxfordshire's Tolpuddle?', p. 177. For Holloway see Pamela Horn, 'Christopher Holloway, an Oxfordshire trade union leader', *Oxoniensa*, vol. 33, 1968, 125–136.

14   Paul Foot, *The Vote*, London: Penguin, 2005, pp. 163–167.

15   Curthoys, 'Oxfordshire's Tolpuddle?,' p.177.

16   Joseph Arch, *The Story of His Life*, London: MacGibbon and Kee, 1966 [1898], p. 143; George Edwards, *From Crowscaring to Westminster*, London: Labour Publishing Company, 1922, pp. 45 and 67.

17   Curthoys, 'Oxfordshire's Tolpuddle?', 177. Christopher Holloway had been elected as a church warden in Wootton between 1877 and 1878, despite fierce opposition, but later he played no part in reformed local government. See Horn, 'Christopher Holloway', pp. 133–134.

18   McCombs, *Ascott Martyrs*, p. 46 and see J. R. Hodgkins, *Over the Hills to Glory*, Banbury, Clifton Books, 1978.

19   For these developments see Nick Mansfield, *English Farmworkers and Local Patriotism, 1900–1930*, Aldershot: Ashgate, 2001, chapter 5, and Curthoys, 'Oxfordshire's Tolpuddle?', 177.

20   Mansfield, *English Farmworkers,* chapter 6 and Clare V. J. Griffiths, *Labour and the Countryside*, Oxford: OUP, 2007.